Schizophrenia
in Late Life

Schizophrenia in Late Life

AGING EFFECTS ON SYMPTOMS AND COURSE OF ILLNESS

PHILIP D. HARVEY

AMERICAN PSYCHOLOGICAL ASSOCIATION
WASHINGTON, DC

Published by
American Psychological Association
750 First Street, NE
Washington, DC 20002
www.apa.org

To order
APA Order Department
P.O. Box 92984
Washington, DC 20090-2984
Tel: (800) 374-2721
Direct: (202) 336-5510
Fax: (202) 336-5502
TDD/TTY: (202) 336-6123
Online: www.apa.org/books/
E-mail: order@apa.org

In the U.K., Europe, Africa, and the Middle East, copies may be ordered from
American Psychological Association
3 Henrietta Street
Covent Garden, London
WC2E 8LU England

Typeset in Goudy by World Composition Services, Inc., Sterling, VA

Printer: United Book Press, Inc., Baltimore, MD
Cover Designer: Berg Design, Albany, NY
Project Manager: Debbie Hardin, Carlsbad, CA

The opinions and statements published are the responsibility of the author, and such opinions and statements do not necessarily represent the policies of the American Psychological Association.

Library of Congress Cataloging-in-Publication Data

Harvey, Philip D., 1956-
    Schizophrenia in late life : aging effects on symptoms and course of illness / Philip D. Harvey.—1st ed.
        p. cm.
    ISBN 1-59147-162-1
    1. Schizophrenia in old age. 2. Older people—Mental health. 3. Geriatric psychiatry. I. Title.

RC514.H347   2005
618.97'6898—dc22   2004010920

British Library Cataloguing-in-Publication Data
A CIP record is available from the British Library.

Printed in the United States of America
First Edition

CONTENTS

Schizophrenia
in Late Life

1

INTRODUCTION:
SCHIZOPHRENIA IN LATE LIFE

Aging has a profound influence on many aspects of functioning in healthy individuals, with notable variation across healthy people in the types and magnitude of aging effects. These influences have only begun to be studied in psychiatric conditions, such as depression and anxiety disorders. Schizophrenia, much like other psychiatric conditions, is a lifelong condition with treatments but no cure. As a lifelong condition, the various features of schizophrenia may interact with aging over the life span. Because schizophrenia is marked by considerable diversity in its clinical presentation even at the time of the first episode, aging also has the potential to increase the variability of the illness as individuals with schizophrenia are differentially affected by aging.

Schizophrenia is the most common severe mental disorder, affecting nearly 1% of the world's population. Although in the past schizophrenia has gone through periods when its definition and boundaries were vague, it is now reliably identified and recognized by trained professionals. Schizophrenia has a variable set of symptoms and considerable variation in onset age, course, and outcome. In fact, diversity and variability, both across individuals and across time within individuals, is the hallmark of schizophrenia, with much research in the disorder aimed at understanding and conceptually reducing the heterogeneity of the disease. Despite advances in the behavioral and pharmacological treatments for the illness, there is still no intervention that is proven to eliminate the symptoms and prevent their reoccurrence. Schizophrenia has a markedly averse impact on those affected, with major impairment in functional capacity, emotional experience and expression, and subjective quality of life. Previous treatments for the illness had substantial adverse effects, with more recent treatments improving on, but not eliminating, these problems. Outcome in the illness is quite variable, with a small proportion of the individuals never experiencing a second episode of illness, a similarly small proportion never demonstrating any recovery from their initial episode of illness, and the remaining three quarters of affected individuals experiencing a course of illness that is episodic and varying in the extent of symptom-free periods and functional capacity.

This book provides information about schizophrenia in late life, comparing the symptoms, treatments, side effects, and other features of older patients with schizophrenia while comparing all of these characteristics to those of younger patients. In many ways the research and clinical attention focused on younger patients with schizophrenia, leading to thousands of publications and millions of dollars of research funding, has never been applied with the same intensity to older patients. This situation is slowly changing, but much like the subtle resistance to studying older healthy individuals, there have been some roadblocks. Among them are the commonly espoused beliefs that older patients with schizophrenia are no different from younger patients and that characteristics of patients at the time of the first episode will necessarily be applicable 50 or more years later. Studies of the development and change of healthy individuals have shown that such assumptions are likely to be wrong, because aging exerts an influence on everyone to a greater or lesser extent. In addition, considerable evidence suggests that at least some people with schizophrenia are more likely to change in their characteristics with aging than others.

This book addresses several issues in the domain of schizophrenia and aging. The central issue is that of age-related changes in the various clinical features of schizophrenia. These features include psychotic symptoms such as delusions and hallucinations, emotional changes, cognitive impairments, and adaptive life skills. Considerable information about all of these domains is available about younger patients with schizophrenia, providing a substantial basis for comparison. We also examine whether the course of schizophrenia changes over time. In younger patients, the signs and symptoms of schizophrenia are variable over time. Some patients have continuous symptoms and others have only sporadic episodes. As many as eight distinct courses of illness have been identified in younger individuals. There is also variability across the different features of the illness, in terms of the consistency of impairment, with cognitive and functional impairments manifesting more consistency over time than psychotic symptoms such as delusions and hallucinations.

It is not clear if this pattern of different courses and differential temporal stability of signs of the illness persists into later life. For instance, do some patients improve in their symptoms and functioning as they age, manifesting fewer signs of the illness and experiencing reductions in the level of care that they require? If so, can any predictors of age-related differences in course be identified, in that patients who are likely to improve in their functioning can be discriminated from those who do not? Does full recovery ever take place? Do the different features of illness have the same patterns of stability over time in older patients as in the typical younger patient previously studied?

Other important issues associated with aging are the treatments offered for schizophrenia and how they might be differentially beneficial and have differential side effect burdens as a function of aging. Although for years the mainstay of treatment of schizophrenia was conventional antipsychotic medications (such as phenothiazines and haloperidol), second-generation medications have been introduced in the past decade with some additional promise in terms of better efficacy and reduced side effects. We review the treatment effects and side effects of the older medications, comparing them to newer medications, and consider whether the best treatments for younger patients are the best choices for aging patients with schizophrenia. Finally, we examine behavioral interventions for schizophrenia. Although psychotherapeutic intervention in schizophrenia has been seen as un-rewarding since the time of Freud, newer developments in remediation, cognitive–behavioral therapy, and skills-training approaches have consider-able promise for the younger patients on whom they have been applied to date. We evaluate whether these interventions have equivalent promise for older patients and explore the reasons why these interventions have not been applied to older patients as thoroughly as they have to younger patients.

Throughout the book, it will be clear that there is much less known about older patients with schizophrenia than about younger ones. Most research on schizophrenia has excluded patients over the age of 55 from study, particularly studies of cognitive functioning and clinical treatment. Only since 1990 has there been any systematic effort to study older patients with schizophrenia. Thus, there has been nearly 100 years of systematic research on younger patients, providing a reasonable basis for comparison with older patients. Although a considerable amount has been learned in the past decade, there are still considerable gaps in knowledge. Where these gaps exist, they will also be highlighted, to help to stimulate research on this important topic. In the rest of this chapter, a brief introduction to the characteristics of schizophrenia is provided, with a focus on understanding of age-related differences in these various domains of the illness.

A BRIEF HISTORY OF THE CONCEPT OF SCHIZOPHRENIA

Schizophrenia has been a concept whose definitional diversity has matched its symptomatic heterogeneity. A brief evaluation of the history of modern conceptions of schizophrenia is very informative for understanding the basis of some of the long-running controversies in the study and treatment of this serious disorder. These controversies have their origin at the end of the 19th century, when the first definitions of schizophrenia were offered.

Dementia Praecox and the Kraepelinian Legacy

Although madness has been recognized since antiquity, clear, syndrome-oriented descriptions similar to current conceptions of schizophrenia appeared for the first time at the end of the 19th century. Emil Kraepelin, professor of psychiatry in Munich, described a condition that he referred to as "Dementia Praecox" (Kraepelin, 1919). He defined this illness as having profound cognitive and functional deficits (i.e., dementia), consistent early-adult age of onset (i.e., praecox), and a course that, if not deteriorating, was stable and generally nonremitting. The core of the illness, in his conception, was the cognitive and functional impairments, resembling those seen in progressive degenerative dementias. This illness was, as he saw it, distinct from affective psychoses in that some of the core features of the illness included impairments in the ability to generate, express, and perceive affects. He also distinguished the characteristics of schizophrenia from paranoia, now referred to as delusional disorder in the current diagnostic manuals, by the absence of generalized intellectual deterioration in the paranoid individual. At the same time, Kraepelin clearly described a variety of paranoid-type symptoms in schizophrenia and defined a paranoid subtype of the illness. Finally, he also distinguished dementia praecox from paraphrenia, a late-onset psychotic condition that is marked by delusions and hallucinations but is distinct from schizophrenia by virtue of the absence of generalized intellectual impairment and distinct from degenerative dementias by virtue of the absence of a progressively deteriorating course. The conception of paraphrenia is still active and is used as a diagnostic entity in some parts of the world.

The unifying feature of Kraepelin's conception of dementia praecox was a focus on the course of the illness. At the time these descriptions were written there was essentially no treatment for the illness. Only one third of the patients ever treated in Kraepelin's day returned home from the massive long-stay institutions that predominated in the treatment of schizo-phrenia at the time (Hegarty, Baldessarini, & Tohen, 1994). As a result of the extended stays that patients experienced, and because of the fact that Kraepelin's lengthy tenure in the same institution allowed him to observe some patients over decades, he was able to develop theories about the course of the illness into later life. His belief was that some proportion of the patients with schizophrenia worsened over time with aging into a more and more impaired state, with greater deterioration in their functioning. The course of schizophrenia into late life was largely ignored until the end of the 20th century, with that research, described in the rest of this book, demonstrating that some of Kraepelin's observations about the late-life course of schizophrenia are again appearing to be validated.

There are several aspects of Kraepelin's descriptions of schizophrenia that are immediately relevant to aging. First, he saw that schizophrenia was an early-onset condition that had many of the features of aging-related cognitive disorders. He saw dementia praecox as more similar to Alzheimer's disease than to manic depressive disorder. Second, he believed that the disorder was persistent over the life span, into old age, and thus believed that there were systematic changes in the illness that occurred as patients grew older. He believed that as patients aged, they became more likely to experience profound cognitive and functional deterioration, with the result being a profoundly deteriorated condition with little contact with the outside world and little interest in this contact. Third, he distinguished psychotic conditions with late-onset from early onset. He believed that paraphrenia was a disorder that had a late-life onset that differed in critical ways from dementia praecox. Paraphrenia was marked by less cognitive impairment and more severe symptoms of paranoia and suspiciousness than dementia praecox. So the contributions of Kraepelin not only included descriptions of schizophrenia in younger individuals and also the first clear focus on aging-related changes as an important topic of study in schizophrenia.

Kraepelin's legacy persists to this day in most of the world, including the United States. In the United States, thinking about schizophrenia was markedly affected for an extended period by the influence of psychoanalysis and by the writings of Eugen and Manfred Bleuler. The writings of the Bleulers (E. Bleuler, 1911; M. Bleuler, 1979) and their long-term descriptive follow-up studies of patients with schizophrenia have elucidated a number of other features of schizophrenia and challenged the conceptions of schizo-phrenia as invariably bleak in its outcome and course over the lifetime.

Eugen and Manfred Bleuler: Schizophrenia and Its Lifetime Course

Eugen Bleuler coined the term *schizophrenia*, and like dementia praecox, the components of the label give clear clues to the concepts that are contained within. Splitting of the self (*schizo-phrene*) was the core of Eugen Bleuler's conception of dementia praecox, and like Kraepelin, Bleuler was also focused on the diversity of schizophrenia. There were a number of divergences between Eugen Bleuler and Kraepelin, however. Bleuler believed that schizophrenia was not necessarily marked by either an early onset or a deteriorating course. Thus, similar to current conceptions in the *DSM*, schizophrenia-like conditions have an onset at any age. Evidence presented later in this book indicates that onset of schizophrenia as currently defined ranges over the entire life span, although the peak incidence of new cases, particularly for males, is early in life. In addition, although relatively poor outcome characterizes many patients with schizophrenia, it is the general consensus that a deteriorating course is largely the exception rather than the rule, particularly in patients followed up for various time periods before the age of 65.

Manfred Bleuler, Eugen's son and a prodigious academic talent in his own right, conducted one of the most impressive follow-up studies of schizophrenia over the life span. Capitalizing on the fact that he lived for an extended period on the grounds of the large psychiatric hospital directed by his father, he followed a large group of patients with schizophrenia over their entire lifetime course of illness. Although his methods were generally impressionistic and his study did not include systematic objective clinical ratings or performance-based measures of cognitive functions or detailed assessments of social, occupational, or adaptive living skills, his research has the benefit of a long-term follow-up of a large sample. Among the conclusions of this study were that there were multiple different outcomes in schizophrenia, ranging from complete recovery to profound dementia and complete disability. As the majority of the study was conducted before the onset of antipsychotic treatments, this study is truly one of the natural courses of illness, unaffected by either the beneficial or adverse effects of antipsychotic treatments. This study, despite concerns about the lack of academic rigor, still stands as a landmark in the field of psychopathology, a lifetime study of a lifetime illness conducted by someone who was intimately familiar with the patients, their parents, and, in some cases, their children. For a full exposure to the breadth of this research, Bleuler's 1978 book, *Long Term Patient and Family Studies*, is an excellent resource.

By the end of the second decade of the 20th century, it was clear that schizophrenia was a lifetime illness and that there were changes in the symptom presentation and course of illness that occurred with aging. Yet for the majority of the 20th century, this was forgotten, and most of the focus shifted to the examination of younger patients. One of the possible reasons for this shift was the fact that for the majority of the 20th century, until the mid 1970s, there was considerable disagreement about the basic symptomatic definitions of the illness. During this period, much of the focus on schizophrenia was diffused by poor definitions, a situation that was altered in 1980 with the introduction of *DSM–III*. Now that schizophrenia can be defined reliably, research on the validity of the concept of schizophrenia has proceeded rapidly.

THE CURRENT DEFINITION OF SCHIZOPHRENIA

Schizophrenia is defined similarly in the two major psychiatric classification systems, the American Psychiatric Association's *Diagnostic and Statistical Manual of Mental Disorders*, 4th edition (*DSM–IV*; 1994) and the *World Health Organization's International Classification of Diseases*, 10th edition (*ICD–10*; 1997). There are several components in these criteria, which are reviewed as they appear in the *DSM–IV*, because that is the most recent and common system in use in the United States. Each of the components of these criteria has the potential to be influenced by aging in individuals with schizophrenia.

Active Illness

To receive a diagnosis of schizophrenia, an individual must be currently experiencing or previously have experienced "an active phase of illness." This active illness is defined by the presence of two of five critical symptoms: delusions, hallucinations, impairments in communication, grossly disturbed behavior, and grossly flattened or inappropriate affect. The differential occurrence of these symptoms may change with aging in schizophrenia, with some arguing that there is a shift in the direction of more negative symptoms and fewer and less severe positive symptoms in older patients. This issue is revisited in detail later because this is important in terms of the diagnosis and treatment of schizophrenia in aging populations.

Duration of Impairment

Signs of impaired behavior must include reduction in functioning beyond some earlier, better level. This impairment must last for at least six months, but it can include periods of maladjustment that precede meeting the full active phase of illness criteria. For instance, an individual who left school, withdrew into his or her room, and remained there for five months would meet criteria for the 6-month duration even if his or her active phase of illness only occurred for the past month. Similarly, an individual with no signs of previous impairment in any domain who had been hallucinating and delusional for 6 months would meet criteria, as long as his or her functioning is impaired. As a result, the active-phase symptoms can last from 1 day to 6 months, as long as other behavioral disturbances of recent origin occur as well. Individuals who meet the active phase criterion with no decline in their functioning, by definition, do not meet *DSM–IV* criteria for schizophrenia. It is unclear, however, how often this happens because individuals with no functional impairment rarely come into contact with mental health professionals. This issue of behavioral impairment is also important in aging, in that individuals with psychotic symptoms with onset late in life (after age 60) may have symptoms of psychosis that are not accompanied by marked reduction in functioning other than that associated with aging itself.

Affective Disorder Exclusion

It is possible to experience delusions and hallucinations, including bizarre delusions and the characteristic hallucinations of schizophrenia, in the context of major depression or bipolar disorder. Thus, if an individual meets full *DSM–IV* criteria for either of these illnesses for the entire period and he or she met the active phase criteria for schizophrenia and any remission of their affective disorder coincides with the remission of their active illness, then he or she does not meet criteria for schizophrenia. Instead, he or she should be diagnosed as affective disorder (either major affective disorder or bipolar disorder, with mood-incongruent psychotic features). If he or she has experienced periods of affective disturbance that both do and do not overlap fully with periods of meeting the active phase of illness criteria described earlier and periods of meeting the active phase criteria for schizophrenia that occur both in conjunction with and in the absence of affective symptoms, then he or she also does not meet criteria for schizophrenia. Finally, if an individual meets criteria for an affective disorder, but only during time periods when he or she also meets the A criteria for schizophrenia and the affective disorder is completely limited to those periods, both diagnoses should be made.

This issue of comorbidity of affective disorder is also an important issue in aging, because there is an increased prevalence of affective disorders in late life. In addition, it has been suggested that some individuals with clear cases of schizophrenia can develop comorbid affective disorders as they age. Discriminating whether an individual with a late-onset psychotic condition has an affective disorder or a schizophrenia-related disorder is an important distinction. It is also important to consider the impact of depression on individuals with a lifelong history of schizophrenia, because the addition of these other symptoms with aging has the potential to increase illness burden and reduce quality of life.

DRUG USE AND GENERAL MEDICAL CONDITIONS

If the symptoms of illness occur exclusively in the context of drug abuse or medical conditions or their treatment, then the diagnosis is excluded. This is a rare exclusion, because there are few drugs that can cause the full syndrome of schizophrenia (including the 6-month duration of impairment). There are also few other illnesses that can produce the active phase of illness and sustain impairment for a 6-month period. It is important to keep in mind that concurrent alcoholism, cannabis abuse, or use of other substances does not preclude the diagnosis of schizophrenia; these additional diagnoses should be applied as well. Likewise, medical conditions that occurred after the onset of schizophrenia in elderly individuals, such as strokes or degenerative dementias such as Alzheimer's disease, do not rule out the diagnosis of schizophrenia: They are additional diagnoses.

However, individuals with Alzheimer's disease routinely experience delusions and hallucinations, as well as cognitive impairments. As evaluated in detail later, some proportion of older individuals who manifest what appears to be late-onset psychosis will be revealed on longitudinal follow-up to meet criteria for a classical neurodegenerative disease. Thus, for many older individuals, the diagnostic process is complicated by the fact that many of the conditions that rule out the diagnosis of schizophrenia are conditions that are of increased prevalence with aging. The issue of the overlap between schizophrenia and neurodegenerative conditions is evaluated in detail later.

Subtypes

Kraepelin believed that the illness was diverse and had a number of subtypes. His classification scheme, with some modifications, has endured to the present day and is contained in the *DSM–IV*. Although there are substantial questions about the validity of these subtypes, particularly in terms of their stability over time and their discriminant validity, they are still present in the diagnostic manual and have historical importance. These subtypes include the paranoid, disorganized ("hebephrenic"), catatonic, and undifferentiated subtypes. Subtype distinctions are quite important in aging as well, in that the prevalence of paranoid ideation is increased with aging, and differentiating whether an individual with a late-life onset of psychosis manifests behavior consistent with paranoid ideation or the paranoid subtype of schizophrenia becomes an important diagnostic challenge.

Course

The *DSM–IV* also classifies the illness based on the course of illness. The classifications include the persistence of the symptoms since the time of the first episode, characterized in terms of the time that has elapsed since the initial symptom presentation as well as the emergence of negative symptoms. Patients whose current state does not meet the full criteria for active phase of illness are characterized in terms of whether they are in full or partial remission and whether they have residual negative symptoms in the absence of other symptoms of the illness.

The issue of whether the current course-based classifications are valid in older individuals is important and is examined in detail. For example, if psychotic symptoms were uniformly reduced in severity as part of the natural course of the illness, the absence of these symptoms might not signify a true remission in the same way as for younger patients. Similarly, if negative symptoms are uniformly increased in older patients, classifications based on negative symptom severity could have different validity than in younger patients, and the threshold for definition would have to be increased.

OTHER IMPORTANT FEATURES OF THE ILLNESS RELEVANT TO AGING

Although schizophrenia has a number of symptoms that are agreed to be part of the diagnostic criteria, there are several additional features of the illness that, although not contributing to the diagnosis, are intrinsic to the condition. These include the prevalence and incidence of schizophrenia, as well as other features that are present in essentially all patients with schizophrenia, such as cognitive impairments, deficits in adaptive life skills, and reduced subjective quality of life. All of these features of the illness are also relevant to aging as well, in that there is evidence that all change with aging in systematic ways; this is explored in detail later.

Prevalence

As described later, schizophrenia is an illness that occurs worldwide. Most evidence indicates that schizophrenia occurs in slightly less than 1% of the population of the world, relatively evenly distributed across countries. The prevalence of schizophrenia is increasing in older individuals as the overall life span increases and more individuals with schizophrenia survive into later life. The changes in the relative prevalence of schizophrenia in older and younger individuals raise important questions about allocation of treatment resources for schizophrenia patients as a group. Because the number of older patients is increasing steadily, increased treatment resources may be required to assist them.

Incidence

The average age of onset of schizophrenia is different across males and females, at approximately 22 for males and 32 for females. There is no evidence that schizophrenia is markedly changing in its incidence over time, as it would if changes in culture, medical care, exposure to toxins, or other environmental factors played a major role in etiology. There is increasing evidence that there are cases of schizophrenia that have an onset quite late in life. These cases appear to be different from earlier onset cases in several critical ways, including gender distribution, lifetime history of functional success, and cognitive functioning. Whether these individuals actually have schizophrenia or a condition that resembles schizophrenia in certain critical domains is an important topic that is considered later.

Mortality

Schizophrenia affects life expectancy in several ways. There is an increased risk of suicide and death in accidents during the first 10 years of the illness, particularly in males, in that approximately 10% of all male patients with schizophrenia die by one of these causes in the first decade of their illness. Following the early stages of the illness, there is less concrete evidence currently available regarding mortality, but there is a common belief that there is a shortened life expectancy in schizophrenic patients. Medical problems associated with schizophrenia and their treatment is an important topic for consideration when thinking about aging in schizophrenia. There is some evidence available that older patients receive substandard medical care, even when compared to younger patients with schizophrenia, and that illness and treatment-related medical conditions may be increasing in older patients with schizophrenia.

Gender Differences

Schizophrenia diagnosed according to *DSM–IV* criteria appears to be somewhat more common in males. There are also gender differences in the severity of a number of the signs and symptoms of the disorder: Male patients with schizophrenia are also reported to have worse adjustment before the onset of the illness, more severe negative symptoms, greater cognitive impairment, and more adjustment deficits than female patients. In contrast, female patients are often reported to have more affective symptoms (e.g., depression in particular) and to have more severe psychotic symptoms, while they appear to have a better overall outcome, possibly because the cognitive impairments and negative symptoms that predict worse functional deficit are less severe in female patients.

However, gender-related differences in the prevalence and incidence of schizophrenia are reversed in older patients, with more patients with late-onset schizophrenia being female and female schizophrenic individuals having a longer life expectancy than males. Other possible changes in classical gender differences that are related to aging are examined later in the book.

Cognitive Deficits

Cognitive impairment is present in most patients with schizophrenia. Studies have indicated that less than one third of the best outcome patients with schizophrenia do not manifest substantial cognitive deficits. These deficits are quite wide ranging and affect nearly all important aspects of cognition, including attention, memory, executive functioning, and verbal and motor skills. Changes with aging occur in these cognitive functions in some patients with schizophrenia. Because these cognitive changes occur against a backdrop of lifelong impairment, they have the potential to lead to increased disability in older patients. Among the important issues in cognitive deficits in schizophrenia are whether cognitive decline is greater than would be expected with aging alone and whether there are groups of patients who have more severe cognitive changes with aging. Finally, the issue of whether these changes can be discriminated from expected age-related increases in degenerative disorders is also important and is addressed later.

Functional Impairments

Independent living is rare in younger patients with schizophrenia, as is employment in the competitive marketplace. Most patients with schizophrenia are dependent on others for their care, and as many as 50% are considered disabled within 6 months of their first psychiatric treatment. This situation leads to an increase in the general societal cost of the illness and makes schizophrenia one of the most disabling of all illnesses—and clearly the most disabling psychiatric disorder.

An important interaction with aging is that some older individuals with schizophrenia are also reported to show additional functional decline as they age. Like cognitive declines, these functional declines occur against a backdrop of lifelong functional impairment, meaning that individuals with a lifetime of disability are showing evidence of even greater impairment. Because patients with schizophrenia often have limited financial resources and family networks over the course of their lifetime, they have few reserves with aging. Thus, aging-related changes in functional abilities, which often strain the coping resources of healthy individuals, may add increased strain to patients with lifelong schizophrenia. A careful exploration of the prevalence and magnitude of functional decline and risk factors for this decline is presented later in the book.

Quality of Life

With substantial cognitive and functional deficits, medication side effects, and persistent and troubling psychotic symptoms, it is not surprising that most younger patients with schizophrenia typically report notably reduced subjective quality of life. Because all of the classical determinants of quality of life in younger patients (e.g., illness variables, treatment side effects, and consequences of disability) are, if anything, increased in severity with aging, there is substantial potential for additional reductions in quality of life that occur with aging. Because quality of life is often poor in aging populations and because consistent correlates of reduced quality of life in healthy population has been studied in detail, an evaluation of the effects of aging and schizophrenia is presented later in the book.

CONCLUSION

All of the symptoms, features, and correlates of schizophrenia have the potential to be affected by aging. After patients with schizophrenia reach older ages, they are exposed to the typical effects of aging, combined with the effects of a lifelong illness that still requires treatment. Differences in symptoms, cognitive impairments, functional status, and quality of life might be expected when comparing older and younger patients because of the lifetime nature of the illness and the fact that the illness itself affects many aspects of functioning that are influenced by aging. The course of illness may change in late life, with some patients possibly manifesting recovery and others either worsening or not improving.

There are many aspects of schizophrenia and aging about which little is known at this time. What is clear is that schizophrenia in late life shares many of the features of schizophrenia in the earlier years, but also has a number of additional features and complications relating to aging and the lifetime history of social and economic disadvantage conferred by the experience of the illness. We examine all of the questions raised and features of illness described in this introductory chapter, reviewing the available data from both comparisons of older and younger patients and longitudinal studies of older patients. We use these data to develop an understanding of how schizophrenia changes over time within individuals. We try to identify predictors of these changes and the treatments, current and future, that need to be applied to schizophrenia as patients age. By the end of this book, the entirety of the current research literature on schizophrenia and aging is reviewed and synthesized into an integrated perspective. Many of the questions posed earlier in this chapter are answered to the extent that data are available, and for the ones where the data are not yet available, it will be clearer as to what new information needs to be collected. Aging is an increasingly important issue, and how patients with a major psychiatric condition such as schizophrenia fare as they age is important to everyone, not just these patients.

2

AGING IN HEALTHY INDIVIDUALS

Among the major features of aging are changes in cognitive functioning and adaptive life skills. These changes vary considerably across different skills domains and also are quite variable across individuals. There are a number of individual differences characteristics that predict the extent to which these changes occur and their consequences for a person who is experiencing changes in his or her skills associated with increased age. This chapter describes these changes and provides some information about how they are relevant to understanding changes in cognition and function with aging in patients with schizophrenia. Keeping in mind that changes in cognitive abilities and self-care skills are normal in healthy individuals will allow for more careful evaluation of the types of abnormalities seen in older patients with schizophrenia. Examination of the factors that lead to extraordinary cognitive and functional changes in healthy individuals will also allow for a more careful examination of whether abnormalities seen in older schizophrenic individuals are a result of schizophrenia or other processes that produce declines in functioning in the population as a whole.

Although this chapter provides what amounts to a brief review of this topic, it is an important and well-researched area. As a result, more comprehensive coverage is provided in several different locations. Excellent books devoted solely to this topic include a classic book by Albert and Moss (1988), which discusses the principles of geriatric neuropsychology, and a volume by Lawton and Salthouse (1998), which provides a wide-ranging array of papers on aging in the healthy population.

THE CONCEPT OF WITHIN-INDIVIDUAL CHANGES

There is considerable variability across individuals in cognitive ability at all ages. This variation in functioning is important to consider when attempting to understand changes in functioning over time. Because of normal age-related declines in performance on certain tests, such as the memory tests and motor speed tests described later in the chapter, older individuals with relatively high levels of functioning may perform more poorly on an absolute (i.e., raw) score basis than average-functioning younger individuals. Thus, the interpretation of performance on cognitive assessments is only meaningful when the results of these assessments are compared to a reference point of previous functioning (Lezak, 1995) and not when compared to some "cut-off score" that denotes impairment. This principle is even more important for individuals who were functioning at the low end of the distribution over the course of their lives. Individuals who were low performers on cognitive assessments when younger, like most patients with schizophrenia, will be found to perform poorly on an absolute score basis when normal, age-related changes in performance occur. Often an individual whose score was quite low when younger will perform below some absolute cut-off for "dementia" or "substantial cognitive impairment" when older, solely on the basis of expected changes with aging (Heaton, Grant, & Matthews, 1991). Yet the magnitude of change that puts them "below the cut-off" could be the same or smaller than that seen in individuals who were higher functioning at baseline whose scores do not cross that barrier.

To avoid attributing pathological significance to normal changes, it is important to consider the full range of performance at both younger and older ages. Conversely, understanding earlier performance is also important to avoid missing marked changes with potential clinical significance in formerly high functioning individuals. It has been shown that without the development of aging-related illnesses such as dementia that rate of age-related change in cognitive functioning is similar in individuals with high and relatively low lifelong intellectual performance (Christensen & Henderson, 1991). However, someone whose performance was at the 99th percentile when 35 and at the 50th percentile at age 75 has actually declined considerably in his or her performance. This decline is potentially even more significant because in tests with a normal distribution of scores, the closer the test performance to the 50th percentile, the larger the absolute change in raw test performance required to have an impact on percentile scores.

CONTENT AREAS OF COGNITION AND FUNCTION

There are multiple domains of cognitive functioning relevant to aging, and a full review of all of them and their profiles of change with aging is far beyond the scope of this single chapter. However, an abbreviated review focusing on the most crucial cognitive functions relevant to the study of schizophrenia is provided.

Intelligence

There are two broad domains of intelligence, referred to as *fluid* and *crystallized*. Crystallized intelligence is the sum total of previous experience and is often referred to as "fund of information" or "knowledge." Fluid intelligence is the ability to solve new problems, develop novel strategies, and to acquire new learning. Intelligence is formally measured with structured intellectual assessments, with the most commonly used one being the Wechsler Adult Intelligence Scale, 3rd edition (WAIS–III; Wechsler, 1998). This test has two major subscales, verbal and performance, which do not specifically map into crystallized and fluid intelligence.

Memory

There are multiple memory domains including immediate or working memory, learning new information, and recalling or recognizing this information after a delay. There are a number of components of the memory system, with the names applied in a somewhat variable manner across studies and investigators.

Verbal Skills

Verbal skills include the ability to understand and produce verbal information. Verbal output can be examined in terms of its semantic content and its syntactic organization.

Motor Skills

Motor skills include the ability to perform unskilled and skilled motor acts, to perform rapidly, and to integrate perceptual and motor skills, such as copying or drawing.

Executive Functioning, Abstraction, and Problem Solving

This content area includes the ability to solve problems and coordinate component cognitive skills. Although this domain includes a large number of different skills, the central feature of these skills is the ability to apply previously learned knowledge and other cognitive skills to solve new problems.

Functional Domains

There are several different aspects of functional skills that also show changes with aging. These include conversational skills, independent living skills, and self-care skills. There are multiple aging-related factors that influence these functional domains, including health status, financial conditions, and changes in cognitive functioning. All of these potential influences on functional status, in addition to normative changes with aging, will be considered.

Intellectual Functioning

Intelligence is a multifactorial construct, with several different domains. In the most general sense, intelligence can be divided into the crystallized and fluid factors described earlier. These two factors have different features and different types of changes with aging. The older an individual is, the more opportunity he or she will have had to increase his or her store of crystallized intelligence. This is particularly true in individuals who have had wide-ranging experiences and have not been disadvantaged, such as by living in a chronic psychiatric hospital. Many of the components of crystallized intelligence are related to the storage and retrieval of information from long-term memory. Crystallized intelligence as assessed by typical IQ tests does not have performance speed demands or time pressure during performance. Thus, any changes in cognitive or motor speed would not be expected to have an impact on performance-based indexes of crystallized intelligence.

Many IQ test measures of fluid intelligence are performed with speed demands, meaning that slowing would result in reductions in performance. Thus, fluid intelligence is likely to be affected by other factors that cause cognitive and motor slowing as well.

NORMATIVE INFORMATION ON CHANGES IN INTELLECTUAL FUNCTIONING WITH AGING

The most straightforward way to examine aging-related changes in intellectual skills with aging is to examine norms from intelligence tests. These norms are based on the performance on the different components of the IQ tests of well-selected reference groups of individuals across the lifespan. Comparison of the raw scores of individuals who are in the 50th percentile provides information about differences in performance associated with aging in individuals who are at the age-group average. In terms of measures of crystallized intelligence, 50th percentile scores for vocabulary and information subtests of the WAIS–III (Wechsler, 1998) are essentially identical at age 20 and age 75. Thus, the population as a whole does not change in its performance on these measures of crystallized intelligence across a 55-year period. Across the distribution of scores, from very high to very low, the lack of change over time is essentially the same. Individuals who are at the 99th percentile at age 20 obtain the same scores as individuals who are the 99th percentile at age 70. Low scores are similarly stable in terms of the relationship of raw scores to percentile scores across the same age range.

Similar results are found when performance on another prototypical index of crystallized intelligence, reading ability, is examined across the life span in normative samples. Word-recognition reading is measured with tests of the ability to read words that are either phonologically irregular, thus prioritizing previous exposure to the words, or increasingly difficult over the course of the test. Performance is indexed by correct pronunciation of the words, with no demands to understand the meaning of the words or to define them. When 50th percentile scores are compared on one of these tests, the Wide Range Achievement Test, 3rd edition (Wilkinson, 1993) across normative samples at ages 18 and 70, there are no differences in the raw scores that are produced. Thus, across an array of tests that examine the lifelong accumulation of information and the ability to retrieve this information, there is no evidence of any changes for the population as a whole in individuals ranging in age from their 20s to their 70s.

In marked contrast, 50th percentile scores on digit symbol coding, a prototypical measure of visual–motor skills and speeded fluid intelligence, change notably across the lifespan. Fiftieth percentile performance at age 20 is 59 to 63 items correctly copied in 120 seconds, whereas for ages 70 to 74, performance at that same percentile would only require 23 to 25 items. Thus, for a measure that has high levels of speed demands, performance at the population median declines by two thirds. An alternative measure of fluid intelligence, block design, shows a slightly less extreme reduction in scores. A 50th percentile score on block design at age 20 is a score of 32, whereas a 50th percentile score at age 70 is a score of 16. Thus, a 50% reduction in normative performance occurs between the ages of 20 and 70 for individuals at the 50th percentile.

The next question to consider is at what age these changes in performance begin to occur and whether they accelerate at some point in the aging process. Digit symbol 50th percentile scores decline by 25% between ages 20 and 64 and then decline by 50% between ages 64 and 74. Thus, fluid intelligence measures with high speed demands have normal declines detectable as early as age 55, but accelerated reduction in performance is detected only after age 65. Block design 50th percentile scores show similar patterns of change from ages 20 to 64 and ages 64 to 75. Thus, across most measures of crystallized intelligence, declines in performance are expected in the general population in shorter periods of time after age 65.

An additional question is whether these declines in performance on indexes of fluid intellectual performance and motor speed are similar at the extreme ends of the distribution. How much do the raw scores differ for individuals who are on the high and low ends of the distributions? Scores at the 99th percentile on digit symbol at age 20 is a raw score of 90, whereas a 99th percentile score at age 70 is a score of 60. Thus, in contrast to the 66% reduction for individuals scoring at the population average, high scores only decline by one third from ages 20 to 70. Individuals scoring at the 5th percentile at age 20 obtain scores of 32 on digit symbol, whereas a 5th percentile score at age 70 is only 8 items. Thus, low scorers at age 20 who were at the same percentile at age 70 would be performing 75% more poorly, revealing an inverse correlation between baseline performance and risk for decline with aging in motor speed that is not seen in crystallized aspects of cognitive functioning (see Christensen & Henderson, 1991, for similar results).

In conclusion, there are marked differences in age-related changes in fluid and crystallized intelligence. Crystallized intelligence does not change with aging to a notable extent. Scores at the top, bottom, and middle of the distribution are similar in 20- and 75-year-old individuals when normative standards for crystallized intelligence are compared. Fluid intelligence changes much more markedly with aging. Depending on the index used, scores at the middle of distribution are reduced by 50% to 66% or more when 20-year-olds are compared to 75-year-olds. Furthermore, individuals scoring lower in the distribution have relatively greater reduction in performance with aging, motor speed in particular, compared to the middle of the distribution. Normative standards for high scorers show relatively less decline than individuals scoring at the middle or the bottom of the distribution. Thus, individuals with poor performance early in life would be expected to decline more in their performance with aging than individuals with average or superior performance. This pattern has important implications for the interpretation of changes in the these ability areas with aging in schizophrenia, where very poor performance is common early in life.

MEMORY FUNCTIONS

The human memory system is complicated and multifaceted. There are many components of this system that are used to perform various memory operations on diverse stimuli, as well as many different ways to conceptualize memory performance. The common conceptual subdivisions of the system focus on both the type of information to be learned and remembered as well as the purpose and duration of storage of the information. Rather than provide detailed references for each of these domains of memory functioning, we recommend detailed texts. Lezak (1995) provides an excellent overview of the neuropsychological perspective on memory, and the classic work by Tulving (1983) describes the normal episodic memory system in detail. Different memory functions vary in the extent to which they change with age, from no changes at all to substantial aging-related change.

TIME-COURSE OF MEMORY: THE PRIMARY–SECONDARY–LONG-TERM MEMORY DISTINCTION

Some information is held in memory for relatively abbreviated periods of time and is then forgotten. A common example is recalling a phone number long enough to dial it or recalling driving directions long enough to execute a couple of simple operations (e.g., turn right at the next light and then look for the third road on the left). This type of memory function is referred to as short-term, primary, or working memory.

The process of learning information that is needed for longer term use is referred to as secondary or episodic memory. Secondary memory encompasses the processes of acquiring new information with exposure, such as in attending a college class or listening to instructions on how to perform the tasks that constitute the core of one's job. Another example is that of learning the names of coworkers or acquaintances after hearing them once or twice. Information that is processed in episodic memory can be either verbal or visual–spatial in nature. The key component of secondary memory is that the information learned is targeted for retrieval, often repeatedly, for adaptive use later. Although it may be useful to forget phone numbers that are dialed only one time, it is an adaptive deficit to be unable to learn information such as the names of your coworkers or the address of your health care professionals.

Among the critical components of the successful process of learning new secondary or episodic memory information is the ability to encode information for storage and later use. Information is more easily encoded if it is somewhat familiar to the individual, but encoding can be hindered if new information is too similar to previously learned information. The process of getting information out of storage so it can be used later is referred to as *retrieval*. This includes both the ability to recall information spontaneously (e.g., "tell me all of the words that I just read you") and the ability to recognize information previously heard and to discriminate it from information that was not previously presented (e.g., "Which 10 of these 20 words did I just read you?"). An additional feature of the retrieval system is its responsiveness to cues. Examples of cued recall could include semantic cues ("Tell me all of the spices in the list of words I just read you"), phonological cues ("The word you are trying to remember rhymes with 'hairs' "), or orthographic cues ("complete this word: Thr _ _ d"). Thus, secondary memory constitutes the highly important functions of encoding new information, remembering it after a delay, and being able to acquire and consolidate new learning.

Once information is thoroughly learned, it becomes part of the individual's long-term knowledge base. For example, information learned early in school, such as vocabulary or how to read, is used repeatedly over the course of the entire life without significant modification other than for updating on the basis of new information. This is what was referred to earlier as reflecting crystallized intelligence. The long-term storage for word meanings is often referred to as *semantic memory*. Semantic memory includes both word meanings and their relationships to other words as well. Knowing both the meanings of *cat* and *dog* and that the two are members of several other hierarchically organized superordinate categories (pets, domestic animals, small animals, mammals, animals, living things) are examples of semantic memory.

There are other memory systems that have importance for changes with aging as well. Procedural memory refers to the ability to learn skills and motor acts that may not have a semantic underpinning. Learning how to sort items on the basis of appearance or to trace patterns are examples of procedural memory. Episodic memory can also refer to memory for sequential environmental and personal events. Remembering what happens over the course of a day and whether or not planned tasks have been completed would be an example of episodic memory, as would recalling that one had run into someone that one knew previously. In a sense, the classical neuropsychological tests of serial multitrial learning are attempts to simulate the naturally occurring environmental processes that are subsumed under the concept of episodic memory. Amnesic conditions are characterized by marked deficits in episodic memory, wherein an individual with an amnesia cannot remember the events that occurred more than a few minutes previously. Patients with amnesic conditions typically have spared procedural memory in the context of this completely impaired episodic memory (Squires & Zola-Morgan, 1996). Such findings, combined with the understanding of the types of lesions that impair procedural and episodic memory, have combined to lead to a better understanding of the brain systems involved in memory.

CHANGES IN MEMORY FUNCTIONING WITH AGING

Long-Term and Semantic Memory

As described earlier, there are modest changes in the aspects of long-term memory referred to as crystallized intelligence with aging. Similarly, there are other aspects of memory that manifest little change with aging. Recognition memory, the ability to discriminate information that was previously presented from information that was not, is performed at essentially similar levels across the entire lifespan. Similarly, the ability to benefit from prompts and cues is also not reduced with aging. Semantic memory also does not change notably over the life span. For example, knowledge of word meanings and relationships between words shows no evidence of change over the life span. Some tasks that are dependent on speeded access to semantic memory, such as measures of verbal fluency (Spreen & Strauss, 1998), appear to be reduced slightly in older individuals. As described later, however, the changes in performance seen may be a result of changes in cognitive speed rather than changes in semantic memory.

Working Memory

Working memory is measured with a huge variety of tasks, largely because working memory is a broad construct and there are a multitude of types of information that can be retained for brief periods of time. Some of these tasks that measure working memory are simple and require only the recall of spatial locations. Such tasks can easily be performed by primates or even rodents (Levy & Goldman-Rakic, 2000). Other working memory tasks require considerably more work and have processing demands that require sorting, adaptive forgetting, and ongoing updating of short-term memory storage (Callicott et al., 2000; Gold, Carpenter, Randolph, Goldberg, & Weinberger, 1997). Age-related changes in working memory tasks are commonly reported, regardless of task complexity (Hartman, Bolton, & Fehnel, 2001). Changes are seen in simple spatial memory tasks, as well as in tasks that have additional processing complexities. For instance, on the WAIS–III subscale of letter–number sequencing, a task requiring the recall and sequencing of letters and numbers, 50th percentile scores for 20-year-olds are 11 and a 50th percentile score for 75-year-olds is 8. Slightly more modest changes in performance are seen for simpler tasks such as memory span for digits. Thus, the ability to hold information in mind and operate on it changes notably with aging in healthy individuals.

Learning and Encoding

One critical memory function is the ability to learn new information with exposure and practice. This learning can take place after a single exposure, such as hearing a story, or across multiple exposures, such as hearing a list of words read to you several times, so that the examined individual can develop a learning curve. Older individuals manifest a reduced ability to learn information, regardless of whether the information is presented one time or several times and regardless of whether the information is verbal or spatial in nature (Mitchell, 1989). For instance, on the WMS, the rate of learning new information is approximately 50% as efficient in 75-years-olds as it is for 20-year-olds, for both single exposures (i.e., paragraph learning) and for multitrial list learning. Similar results are commonly obtained for other aspects of verbal and spatial learning tests. Similar to working memory, encoding and learning are skills that are reduced in individuals as they age.

Delayed Recall

Delayed recall is the ability to retrieve information that was recently learned, without the assistance of prompts or cues. This ability is also reduced with aging, although to a lesser degree than rate of learning (McEvoy & Holley, 1990). In general, the proportion of information that is recalled after a delay is reduced by about 25% from ages 20 to 75, in contrast to reductions of learning rate of close to 50% over this same age range. So, if an individual was able to retain 75% of the information learned at age 25, the same individual would retain about 50% of the information at age 75. Thus, all of the different aspects of secondary/declarative/episodic memory, other than delayed recognition, are found to worsen with normal aging. The implication of these differential changes is that older individuals may be much more competent at recognizing information that they had previously been exposed to than in their ability to spontaneously recall this information. When cognitive impairments in schizophrenia and cognitive changes with aging in schizophrenia are reviewed later, there are some interesting parallels in the domains of aging-related changes and schizophrenia-related impairments in memory functions.

Verbal Skills

Verbal skills consist of the ability to generate and comprehend verbal output. There are many different components of these skills, including the ability to generate appropriate output in response to immediate environmental demands. This ability area is often tested with *confrontation naming*, the ability to name common objects on demand. Another important component of verbal skills is *verbal fluency*. Verbal fluency tests require the production of continuous verbal output in response to various types of demands. For instance, category fluency refers to the ability to respond to the demand to produce words that are elements of various overarching semantic categories, such as animals, fruits, or vegetables. Phonological fluency tests require the subject to produce words that begin with a certain letter or that rhyme with a certain word. There is modest evidence of changes in confrontation naming with aging, with these changes greater for identification of objects than actions (Nicholas, Obler, Albert, & Goodglass, 1985). Verbal fluency changes with aging are also modest compared to changes in episodic memory associated with normal aging (Parkin & Lawrence, 1994). It is also possible that these changes are purely a result of changes in cognitive and psychomotor speed, because fluency tests, almost by definition, provide a limited amount of time to generate the output (Schaie, 1989).

There is also essentially no evidence of reductions in the ability to comprehend others' language with aging. Tests of receptive language skills are performed essentially identically over the life span, with minimal evidence of changes in performance on tests requiring language comprehension up to 80 or more years of age. Thus, this aspect of verbal skills is similar to crystallized intelligence in terms of resistance to change with aging in the healthy population.

Motor Skills

Motor skills include both the ability to perform skilled motor acts, often referred to "fine motor skills" or "manual dexterity," and motor speed. Some assessments of these skills include both dexterity and speed, such as the grooved pegboard test, where an individual is asked to place specially designed pegs into tight-fitting grooves as rapidly as possible.

Tests of motor skills that require copying of complex stimuli with no time pressure reveal no major changes in performance with aging even in the context of worse memory for the competently copied figure over a delay period, when compared to younger individuals (Janowsky & Thomas-Thrapp, 1993). For instance, tests of copying skills are performed at high levels even by individuals over the age of 80, as long as there is no concurrent evidence of visual impairments or motor abnormalities such as tremor in the individual taking the examination.

Major changes in speeded motor skills are detected with aging. As described earlier in the section on aspects of intelligence, tests that require speed, concentration, and copying change markedly with aging. These changes are found even in tests such as trail-making part A, where the only concentration demand is to connect a series of ascending numbers. In normative studies of trail-making part A (reviewed in Spreen & Strauss, 1998), the 50th percentile score for individuals from age 20 to 34 is 26 seconds, whereas the 50th percentile score for 70- to 74-year-olds is 70 seconds. Trail-making part B has more complex tracking demands, requiring alternation between numbers and letters. The effect of aging was essentially the same as for part A, however, in that same normative study the 50th percentile for 70-year-olds was 2.5 times as long as for 20- to 24-year-olds.

Other evidence suggesting that motor speed declines in aging, even without attentional or manual dexterity demands, is found in studies of finger tapping (Spreen & Strauss, 1998). For both male and female healthy individuals, those aged 60 to 69 performed 20% more slowly than individuals from age 20 to 39. These data are also likely to underestimate aging effects, because performance on other speeded tests tends to be considerably reduced after the age of 70. The conclusion from these studies is that motor speed tends to decrease with aging, and manual dexterity without time demands tends to decline much less, in the absence of other contributing factors.

Attentional Skills

Attentional functioning has been studied somewhat less than other cognitive domains in terms of effects of aging. There have been more studies of vigilance and attentional capacity, including dual-task performance, than other aspects of attention. Vigilance performance, the ability to sustain attention and effort in demanding task situations, has been shown to be reduced in elderly individuals (Parasuraman, Nestor, & Greenwood, 1989; Quilter, Giambra, & Benson, 1983). Studies of divided attentional processing, testing the ability to appropriately divide attention between competing task demands, such as dual-task information processing, have also found reduced performance in older individuals. Divided attentional functioning is also a valid index of overall processing resources, in that the ability to perform multiple concurrent tasks requires increases in processing capacity. In several different studies (McDowd, 1986; Wickens, Braune, & Stokes, 1987), although not every one (e.g., Somberg & Salthouse, 1982), it has been shown that older individuals are less able than younger individuals to focus their attention on two competing tasks and to adequately divide their attentional resources according to the task demands. In addition, it also has been reported that older individuals have reduced activation in critical cortical areas than younger individuals. Specifically, activation in the dorsolateral prefrontal cortex, an area implicated in the executive allocation of attentional resources, is reduced in older individuals, and the extent of reduction correlates with performance decrement relative to younger individuals (D'Esposito, Zarahn, & Aguirre, 1999). Thus, information-processing capacity is reduced with aging and is directly correlated with reductions in regionally specific cortical activation. It is not clear whether changes in capacity are caused by changes in the ability to adaptively activate appropriate regions of the anterior frontal cortex or the reverse, but capacity reductions are typically found in older healthy individuals.

Executive Functioning

Long-time stereotypes suggest that aging and wisdom are correlated and that this should be a domain where aging effects are beneficial. Data regarding crystallized intelligence suggest that the ability to access information and experience does not change over the life span and that information increases with increased age. Data regarding performance on tests of executive functioning would address the question of whether the ability to use this information to solve problems is also preserved over the lifetime. Describing executive functions has proved to be difficult, but the essence of these functions appears to be that they involve steps of problem solving in a sequence of planning and execution of adaptive responses. The first step in this process is that individuals must determine what they need or want to do and then develop a global plan. The next step is to identify and organize the steps and elements needed to carry out the intention. Another element of executive functioning is the translation of intention or plan into productive activity. During this stage, there is a continuous process of evaluation of the plan, with shifts following errors in execution. Because executive functioning is thought to involve frontal-lobe functioning, measures that have been proven sensitive to dysfunction of the frontal lobe are often the types of tests that are referred to as tests of executive functioning (see Palmer & Heaton, 2000, for a thorough description of executive functioning). One of the standard measures of executive functioning has been the Wisconsin Card Sorting Test (WCST; Heaton, Chellune, Talley, Kay, & Curtiss, 1993). The WCST is a multidimensional problem-solving test in which individuals are required to identify concepts, respond accordingly, and modify their concepts in response to external feedback. Because the concepts in the test change, the test also requires cognitive flexibility for successful completion. One major barrier to effective performance in executive functioning tests is the inability to adopt a flexible approach to problem solving. Mental inflexibility is difficult to measure and is often assessed through tests of abstraction that emphasize shifts in concept formulation. A study comparing healthy individuals in the 1950s, 1960s, and 1970s found no statistically significant differences between groups on the major indexes of the WCST, suggesting that there is little decline in executive functioning with age, although there were substantial gender and educational differences (Boone, Ghaffarian, Lesser, Hill-Gutierrez, & Berman, 1993). As a result, it appears as though there is more individual-difference variation in executive functioning and more overall variability in performance than in more one-dimensional aspects of cognitive functioning. This may not be surprising, because of the fact that executive functioning tests also require intactness of multiple lower level skills, including perception, attention, memory, and motor skills. As seen earlier, any problem-solving test that has speed demands will also be more likely to show age-associated declines than those that do not require speeded performance.

OTHER FACTORS THAT CAN INFLUENCE COGNITIVE CHANGES WITH AGING

Although many factors can influence test performance, there are several factors that need to be considered when examining aging effects in general. Physical illness is one factor, as are changes in noncognitive domains that can influence performance on multifactorial tests of cognitive functioning. For example, individuals who are physically ill with a variety of common aging-related conditions (e.g., type II diabetes) have some evidence of reduced performance on cognitive tests (Widom & Simonson, 1990), with these effects interacting with the age of the individual to produce greater than expected cognitive deficits. Whether these changes in cognitive functioning are the result of direct illness effects on brain structure or indirect interfering effects on performance are a matter of contention (Draelos et al., 1995). Noncognitive changes associated with illnesses such as arthritis, which may result in impairments in fine motor skills, also require consideration. In addition, normal changes with aging are exaggerated on particularly difficult tests and missed on overly easy ones, as described earlier. This issue is important to consider when comparing healthy older individuals to those with a lifetime history of illness such as schizophrenia that lead to cognitive impairments even in early life. Patients with schizophrenia may appear less impaired than they actually are if the cognitive assessments used to compare them to healthy elders are overly difficult and lead to poor performance on the part of the healthy comparison samples.

A major additional factor that can produce spurious cognitive changes is medications that older individuals receive. A particularly important class of medications is medication with anticholinergic effects. Anticholinergic medications have notable effects on the episodic memory system (Sunderland, Tariot, Cohen, Weingartner, Mueller, & Murphy, 1987) and many different medications have anticholinergic effects (Tune, 2001). The importance of the cholinergic system in memory functions is underscored by the fact that the death of cholinergic neurons in Alzheimer's disease is likely to be the factor that accounts for the substantial memory impairments in those patients with the illness. It has been demonstrated that total anticholinergic load, summed across different medications that have varying levels of anticholinergic effects, predicts the extent of memory impairments seen and the risk for delirium (Tune, 2000). Older individuals with schizophrenia appear even more sensitive to the effects of anticholinergic medication than older healthy individuals, which will be evaluated in detail later.

Other medications can produce cognitive adverse effects. Medications with sedating effects can influence performance on tests of motor speed. These medications have greater effects in older individuals and substantially greater risk for adverse events (Mort & Aparasu, 2002). Because older individuals are more likely to have experienced surgical procedures, the consequences of previous histories of general anesthesia require consideration as well. Although it has been believed previously that cognitive impairment was extremely common in older individuals who have had the experience of general anesthesia, recent studies have not found evidence to support this relationship (Dijkstra, Van Boxtel, Houx, & Jolles, 1998). In contrast, it is clear that coronary artery bypass surgery presents a 30% risk of cognitive decline (Van Dijk et al., 2002). Thus, a careful survey of the full extent of medication usage and history of medical procedures in older individuals is important in considering cognitive changes with normal aging. As a rule, effects of medications and the influence of levels of education are greater in older individuals than in younger ones.

Functional Changes With Aging

As individuals age, their ability to perform several functional skills also changes. From basic self-care skills to complex social functions, reductions in performance with aging occur for the population as a whole. The range of overall functional outcomes varies markedly across individuals, and the variance in functional skills is extremely broad beginning as early as age 70. Some 70-year-old individuals are incapacitated and require extensive assistance from caretakers, whereas others are living independently, working full time, and supporting their relatives with their earnings. There are several different predictors of changes in functional status, with the predictors of independent living, competent self-care, and social functioning all being relatively consistent.

Several different predictors of functional status in late life have been identified, with most having consistent associations with functional status. Most important appears to be cognitive functioning, with impaired individuals more likely to require assistance with activities of daily living (Cahn-Weiner, Malloy, Boyle, Marran, & Salloway, 2000). Also important is physical limitations, in that individuals who are medically ill, particularly on a chronic basis, are more likely to demonstrate difficulties in self-care activities. Although medical illness is correlated with functional deficit, the combination of physical illness and cognitive deficits predicted mortality in a very large-scale Italian study whereas illness alone did not (Landi et al., 2001). Financial factors are also important. Individuals with reduced financial resources are more likely to experience difficulties in living independently (Mathieson, Kronenfeld, & Keith, 2002). Another major predictor of functional status in elderly individuals is the presence of psychiatric impairments. Although the rest of this book focuses on the impairments associated with schizophrenia, depression and related factors are also important. For example, recurrent major depression predicts poor social functioning, particularly if the individuals who are depressed also evaluate their overall health as poor (Lenze et al., 2001). Similar findings have been reported for anxiety symptoms. These findings suggest that concurrent mood disturbance may lead to reduction in functional status when all other factors are considered.

A final issue is that of social support. It has been know for years that older individuals experience functional declines after experiencing the loss of a spouse. This finding is particularly true of males, who are more likely to experience functional decline or even death soon after the death of their spouse. Even at lower levels of intensity, changes in social support are associated with changes in cognitive functioning. Lower levels of social support were found to predict cognitive changes even in individuals who were selected for being particularly high functioning at entry into the longitudinal study (Seeman, Berkman, Charpentier, Blazer, Albert, & Tinetti, 1995). The effects of social support were greater than the effect of age in this population, which comprised individuals with relatively high levels of social and educational success over their lifetimes.

Successful Aging

One of the recent developments in research on cognitive and functional changes with aging has been the study of "successful aging" (Rowe & Kahn, 1998). This research direction, consistent with the notion of positive psychology (Aspinwall & Staudinger, 2002), has chosen to focus on the factors that are associated with particularly good outcomes with aging. These outcomes include independent living until late life, reduced cognitive impairment, and increased quality of life in the face of physical challenges. These are particularly important outcomes, because individuals with more successful aging are happier and less dependent on others until late in their lives. The reason that it is important to focus on this topic in a book on aging in schizophrenia is the marked discrepancy between the lives of individuals who are characterized as being successful in aging and the life experiences, characteristics, and lifestyle choices of individuals with a lifelong history of schizophrenia. There are several individual differences factors that predict highly successful aging. Most of these are easy to understand; individuals with the following characteristics are more likely to age successfully (Albert et al., 1995):

- higher education,
- higher levels of physical activity,
- lower rates of obesity,
- better nutritional preferences,
- greater preference for active intellectual pursuits,
- reduced rates of tobacco use,
- moderate alcohol use.

As noted in the later chapters in this book, older patients with schizophrenia come up short in many of these critical domains. Some of these outcomes are not a result of voluntary choices made by these patients. Reduced educational attainment is associated with schizophrenia, and institutionalized patients do not have as much choice in the domains of diet and exercise. Smoking is a major problem in schizophrenia, and smoking-related illnesses are common causes of death in patients with the illness, as described in the next chapter. Cognitive deficits limit the possibility of patients pursuing some intellectual activities, and many residential settings do not permit any alcohol use, even at appropriate levels. In many ways, schizophrenia is a major source of interference with the factors associated with successful aging. The rest of this book describes the characteristics of patients with schizophrenia in later life, including physical health, cognitive and functional status, and other factors that influence quality of life.

CONCLUSION

Cognitive and functional changes are a normal feature of aging, which can be influenced and either accelerated or attenuated by a number of different individual differences factors. Changes in cognitive functions are more significant in speed of processing and in the rate of learning new information, whereas the ability to access previously learned information is essentially unchanged over the life span. Health, education, and various lifestyle choices influence the extent to which individuals age successfully. Cognitive changes with aging are the most potent predictors of reduction in functional status, including social, independent living, and self-care changes. It is important to consider these changes with aging in the context of changes in cognition and function with aging in patients with schizophrenia.

Normal changes occur, and when changes are found in schizophrenia, they are not likely to be clinically significant unless they are substantially greater than what would be expected with normal aging. Patients with schizophrenia are, unfortunately, likely to have a number of risk factors for worse than normal aging. These factors are the focus of several later chapters in this book.

3

CLINICAL FEATURES AND COURSE OF SCHIZOPHRENIA IN LATE LIFE

Schizophrenia is an illness with a low rate of full recovery. As a result, most individuals with schizophrenia have signs and symptoms of the illness over the course of their lives. The types of symptoms that persist, their severity, the frequency of occurrence, and the length of time between full episodes of the illness are believed to vary widely across patients, although until recently there has been little systematic research on the course and symptoms of schizophrenia later in life. There is some recent evidence to suggest that there are changes in symptom expression with aging, although the extent of these changes is not perfectly clear yet. In addition, it has been previously believed that many patients with schizophrenia experienced a generalized disappearance of their symptoms as they age. Some recent evidence suggests that this is not uniformly the case.

This chapter examines the course of schizophrenia in late life. In so doing, we examine the changes in symptom expression seen in older patients, compared with what we know about the course of schizophrenia in younger populations. We examine the validity of previous ideas regarding changes in the overall presentation of the illness over time, including the theory that aging in schizophrenia shifts toward greater expression of negative symptoms and reduced expression of positive symptoms. We also evaluate the data regarding whether some patients recover fully from the illness in later life, as well as examine some of the characteristics of patients with a chronic course of illness. We examine whether the history of illness before late life predicts the likelihood of change in symptom presentation with aging.

DETERMINING IF THERE ARE CHANGES IN THE SEVERITY OF SYMPTOMS WITH AGING

To address this question preliminarily we focus on the symptoms that are used to define schizophrenia: positive symptoms, negative symptoms, communication disorders, and disturbed behavior. Positive symptoms have been central to the definition of schizophrenia since the time of Kraepelin and Bleuler (see chap. 1, this volume). Compared to other symptoms of the illness, the definition and measurement of positive symptoms has changed little in the past hundred years. Negative symptoms were initially described by both Kraepelin and Bleuler but failed to receive much attention until the past 25 years, at which time they were redefined in a way that has shaped the field's thinking since that point (Strauss, Carpenter, & Bartko, 1974). The *deficit syndrome* was proposed to describe a special subtype of patients with schizophrenia defined by a specific pattern of negative symptoms. (The deficit syndrome is proposed to be a syndrome where the prominent feature is persistent negative symptoms that are primary, not caused by other features of the illness.) To meet criteria for the deficit syndrome, as proposed by Carpenter and colleagues (see Carpenter, Heinrichs, & Wagman, 1988), negative symptoms must meet the requisite condition of being both primary and enduring, in contrast to nondeficit patients whose symptomatic presentation is hypothesized to fluctuate over time. The deficit criteria are based on the assumption that primary enduring negative symptoms will have more significance for subtyping than cross-sectional presentation of a positive and negative dichotomy (Wagman, Heinrichs, & Carpenter, 1987). The long-term temporal stability of the deficit distinction has been established by studies that demonstrated that this classification was stable over time (Fenton & McGlashan, 1994).

Communication disorders, also referred to as formal thought disorder, are common in younger patients with schizophrenia (Andreasen, 1979). These impairments are some of the most striking of those seen in schizophrenia, wherein production of unusual speech is a common feature. Communication abnormalities are diverse in patients with schizophrenia and, like the other symptoms of the illness, there may be several different dimensions of communication disorders in schizophrenia. The symptom burn-out theory also has been applied to communication disorders, where it has been suggested that florid communications are likely to be replaced by reductions in spontaneous verbal output.

The disorders of communication noted in patients with schizophrenia tend to fall into three general types: impairments in the amount of speech, impairments in the level of integration or amount of interconnection of speech, and the production of extremely idiosyncratic language that is never produced by normal individuals (Berenbaum, Oltmanns, & Gottesman, 1985; Harvey, Lenzenweger, Keefe, Pogge, Serper, & Mohs, 1992; Peralta, Cuesta, & deLeon, 1992). These dimensions of communication disorder are not always independent, in that speech can be both overproductive and poorly connected.

The general prevalence of some form of communication disorder in younger patients with schizophrenia ranges from 50% to 90% (Andreasen, 1979; Harvey, 1983). The prevalence of different aspects of communication disturbance varies considerably, with some features being present in as many as 60% of patients and others being much more rare, occurring at a rate of about 10% of patients or fewer (Andreasen, 1979; Andreasen & Grove, 1986; Cuesta & Peralta, 1993; Harvey, Lombardi, et al., 1997a). Factor analytical studies have consistently identified two reliable dimensions of communication disorder in younger patients: verbal productivity and disconnection in speech (Harvey et al., 1992). Some studies have also found evidence of a third factor, comprising rare aspects of communication disorder such as neologisms and word approximations (Peralta et al., 1992). Poverty of speech has proven to be a particularly important aspect of communication disorder in patients with schizophrenia. Patients with poverty of speech early in the course of their illness are more likely to have a more adverse course of illness over time (Andreasen & Grove, 1986). For example, patients with poverty of speech early in the course of their illness are more likely to be found to be psychotic at follow-up, regardless of the follow-up interval, than patients without poverty of speech. Factor analytical studies have found poverty of speech to be related to affective flattening and reduced vocal inflection in speech, suggesting that it may be a part of some underlying dimension that reflects reduction in emotional and language production (Andreasen, Arndt, Allinger, Miller, & Flaum, 1995; Arndt, Allinger, & Andreasen, 1991; Liddle, 1987). Because these aspects of schizophrenia are also related to poor prognosis (Keefe et al., 1987), poverty of speech may be seen as part of a constellation of indicators of risk for poor functional outcome.

PSYCHOTIC SYMPTOMS IN LATE LIFE: A LOOK AT "SYMPTOM BURN-OUT"

For years it has been believed that in later life the severity of psychotic symptoms of schizophrenia is markedly reduced. Symptom burn-out is a conception that suggests that hallucinations and delusions are reduced in severity with age and are replaced with greater negative symptoms, such as reduced affective experience, reduced affective expression, and reduced verbal activity (Bridge, Cannon, & Wyatt, 1978). The data to support this conception have generally been anecdotal, and there was little systematic data collected on this topic.

POSITIVE SYMPTOM SEVERITY ACROSS THE LIFE SPAN IN SCHIZOPHRENIA

There are essentially no long-term studies of the course of psychotic symptoms in schizophrenia that use formal assessments of symptom severity. The primary reason is practicality alone, because it is impossible to plan such a long-term study. Long-term follow-up studies such as those performed by Bleuler (1978) and Ciompi (1980) typically did not perform systematic, structured clinical assessments, focusing instead on more global characterizations of the presence and severity of various symptoms. As a result, some of the data to address the issue of age-related changes come from cross-sectional studies across the life span and short-term longitudinal studies. Although not ideal, they directly address the issue of the prevalence and severity of psychotic symptoms in older patients.

One of the important confounds in these studies is research participant sampling. Older patients who are chronically institutionalized should not be compared to younger ambulatory patients in terms of the severity of their clinical symptoms. A second issue is treatment history, in that older patients often have a history of different treatments than younger patients. Younger patients with a minimal history of treatment may not be comparable to older patients who have extensive histories of various types of somatic therapies. A final issue is that of overall course of illness. Patients with chronic institutional stays would be expected to be quite different from patients who have sporadic psychotic episodes, who themselves are likely to be quite different from patients who have had a minimal history of severe psychotic episodes.

Cross-Sectional Data

In a large-scale (N = 358) study of patients with schizophrenia ranging in age from 25 to 95, all of whom were chronically institutionalized at the time of assessment (Davidson et al., 1995), the severity of positive and negative symptoms was assessed. All were treated with conventional antipsychotic medications, and the same research team assessed all patients with a single set of raters. In this study, there were statistically significant differences in positive symptom severity over the life span, with a linear decrease in the severity of these symptoms from age 25 to age 95. Despite these decreases, the oldest patients in the study (age 75 and up) still had had substantial psychotic symptoms. The average severity of positive symptoms in this age group was consistent with the 40th percentile of the normative group for the rating scale that was used (the Positive and Negative Syndrome Scale [PANSS]; Kay, 1991). Patients from the normative sample had an average age of 40 and were also chronically institutionalized. Thus, on average, patients aged 75 and older had symptoms that were not markedly different from those seen in younger patients with a chronic course of continuous illness and institutional stay. Clearly, these data are not consistent with the idea that psychotic symptoms tend to disappear in older patients with extended institutional stay.

A later cross-sectional study examined older patients with schizophrenia while they were receiving inpatient psychiatric care, either at an acute admission because of a psychotic episode or while they were living in a chronic psychiatric hospital (Harvey et al., 1998). Thus, this study compared institutionalized patients with patients whose life history was marked by sporadic psychotic episodes followed by discharge to the community, followed by stable community tenure. When the severity of positive symptoms was compared across groups, these two samples both had substantial levels of positive symptoms. The severity of these psychotic symptoms did not differ across the two groups, one of whom had experienced a continuous institutional stay of an average of 53 years and the other who had been admitted within the past week.

These data make several points. First, institutionalized patients have psychotic symptoms that are as severe as those seen in patients who had recently been admitted from the community because of a psychotic episode. Thus, these chronic patients have substantial psychotic symptoms on an ongoing basis. Second, acute admissions on the part of older patients are associated with substantial symptom severity, consistent with the 40th percentile of the normative sample for the PANSS. Thus, the severity of psychotic symptoms during an acute episode appears substantial still in later life. These data converge to suggest that, regardless of lifetime functional outcome status, psychotic symptoms are a prominent feature of schizophrenia in later life in patients whose course of illness includes inpatient treatment, whether for an acute admission or an extended chronic stay.

There are limitations to these data, however. A minority of patients with schizophrenia are institutionalized at the present time. Thus, such samples are not necessarily representative of the characteristics of older patients with schizophrenia in general. Also, many patients with schizophrenia do not have numerous exacerbations of their symptoms over their later life, living instead in a state of relative clinical stability in the community. These patients may also provide relevant information to address the issue of general symptom severity over the life span. One recent study examined a group of such patients, largely stable community dwellers whose lifetime course has been marked by relatively few inpatients treatments and never by extended institutionalization in long-stay psychiatric hospitals. In this study, Jeste et al. (2003) compared 290 outpatients with schizophrenia who ranged in age from 40 to 85 to healthy comparison participants of the same age. Although these older patients had a number of impairments relative to the healthy controls, including deficits in life skills, cognitive functioning, and quality of well-being, there was an inverse association of age and the severity of psychotic symptoms. Thus, for patients who have a history of long-standing schizophrenia but who have not had recent severe psychotic episodes, the day-to-day severity of psychotic symptoms appears to be reduced.

Longitudinal Data

When trying to answer the question of whether positive symptoms improve over the years in older patients with schizophrenia, longitudinal data are more relevant than cross-sectional data. In a large-scale study, more than 200 older institutionalized patients with schizophrenia were followed up at a 1-year period (Putnam et al., 1996). There was no evidence of improvement in symptoms over a 1-year follow-up. These results were recently replicated in a 6-year follow-up of more than 400 older patients who were initially recruited while hospitalized (Harvey et al., 2003). Similar results were obtained in an additional large-scale longitudinal study of a slightly younger ambulatory sample (Heaton et al., 2001) followed up over periods up to 6 years. In a smaller study of patients who were referred from care in a chronic psychiatric hospital to nursing home care (Harvey, Parrella, White, Mohs, & Davis, 1999), no differences in symptoms were found over a follow-up period that also averaged 2.5 years. Thus, these data suggest that there is no evidence of substantial improvement in symptoms over follow-up periods ranging from 1 to 6 years in patients ranging in age from the late 40s to the 90s. These data consistently indicate that certain groups of older patients have substantial levels of positive symptoms that are stable over time, but still do not address the issue of the prevalence of these different subtypes of patients in older patients with schizophrenia in general.

NEGATIVE SYMPTOMS IN LATE LIFE: DETERMINING IF THIS IS BURNED-OUT SCHIZOPHRENIA

The symptom burn-out theory posits that when positive symptoms disappear with aging, they are "replaced" by a state in which reductions in cognitive activity, motor activity, and social motivation predominate. Although the evidence presented earlier raises questions regarding the generality of age-related reductions in psychotic symptoms, it is still possible that an increase in prevalence and severity of negative symptoms occurs in older individuals with schizophrenia. After all, normal aging is associated with reductions in verbal output, social activity, and self-care skills (Ashman, Harvey, & Mohs, 1999). There are some data available to address both the issue of changes in negative symptom severity in aging and whether these changes are associated with the illness itself or the processes associated with normal aging.

Cross-Sectional Data on Negative Symptoms in Late Life

The large-scale study of Davidson et al. (1995) found that negative symptom severity was more severe in older patients, showing a linear increase in severity of symptoms in chronic patients from age 25 to 95. These data are consistent with the idea that negative symptoms increase with age. The symptom burn-out model would propose that as negative symptoms increase in severity, they would be replacing positive symptoms, leading to a negative correlation between the severities of these two symptom domains. In that study, however, the severity scores of the two symptom domains were uncorrelated across the entire life span. As a result, the increased severity of negative symptoms was not some type of replacement for positive symptoms, because there is no relationship in the severity of the symptoms. Jeste et al. (2003) reported that the severity of negative symptoms was negatively correlated with age in older patients with schizophrenia who had lived their entire lives in the community. Thus, in this study, both positive and negative symptoms decreased in severity with aging, arguing against the replacement theory. As a result, in patients whose negative symptoms worsened or improved, there was essentially no evidence that there were age-associated replacement of positive symptoms with negative symptoms.

In terms of the issue of whether these changes in negative symptom severity are simply associated with the normal processes of aging, the Harvey et al. (1998) study found that history of lifetime functional outcome status was more strongly associated with negative symptom severity than the age of the patients. Patients with a lifetime history of chronic institutional care had considerably more severe negative symptoms than patients of the same age who had a history of lifetime residence in the community, even when the community-dwelling patients were temporarily hospitalized for a psychotic episode. Thus, it appears that a lifetime history of chronic illness and institutional care is associated with more severe negative symptoms, arguing that systematic changes in negative symptom severity are not a typical consequence of aging in schizophrenia.

Longitudinal Data on Negative Symptoms in Late Life

Several longitudinal follow-up studies of older patients with schizophrenia have suggested that the severity of negative symptoms is either consistent or slightly increasing over short-term follow-up studies. Putnam et al. (1996) reported a slight worsening in negative symptoms at a one-year follow-up period, Heaton et al. (2001) found no worsening in a 2.5- to 6-year follow-up period, and Harvey et al. (2003) found worsening over 6 years only for patients with lower levels of negative symptoms at baseline. Thus, short-term studies do not find evidence of rapid worsening in negative symptoms, as would be expected in a situation in which changes in the environment caused worsening of social and emotional functioning. In fact, even being referred to a nursing home after a lengthy stay in a state psychiatric facility was apparently not associated with worsening of negative symptoms (Harvey, Parrella, et al., 1999), whereas cognitive changes were detected. Some data suggested that older patients discharged from chronic psychiatric hospitals to the community had modest improvements in their negative symptoms (Leff, Thornicroft, Coxhead, & Trieman, 1994). This study would suggest that environmental factors have an impact on the current expression of negative symptoms and that institutionalized patients may show modest improvements if they can be successfully referred to community care but not nursing homes.

An additional important feature of negative symptoms in younger patients is their trait-like nature. Studies of younger patients have indicated that the severity of negative symptoms is quite stable over time (Fenton & McGlashan, 1991; Pogue-Geile & Harrow, 1985) in contrast to positive symptoms, which have a fluctuating course. If negative symptoms were similar in their characteristics in older patients compared with younger patients, then strong temporal stability would be expected.

In the Putnam et al. (1996) study, the correlation across a 1-year follow-up period was substantial for negative symptoms but was essentially zero for positive symptoms. Similar results were found across a 6-year follow-up by Friedman et al. (2001) and Harvey et al. (2003). Thus, even in later life the relative stability characteristics of negative versus positive symptoms appear remarkably similar. Because the same levels of stability of symptoms over time have been reported in both ambulatory and institutionalized patients, the course of negative symptoms does not appear to differ markedly in patients whose levels of symptom severity are quite different. In contrast, the severity of positive symptoms appears similar for chronic and ambulatory patients during a psychotic episode, and the severity of these symptoms is variable over time, even within chronically institutionalized patients.

THE DEFICIT SYNDROME IN OLDER PATIENTS WITH SCHIZOPHRENIA

If the deficit syndrome truly reflects the core of enduring negative symptoms, then it should also be present in late life and have similar correlates as in younger patients. Although this area has not been studied as extensively as other aspects of the illness in late life, there are some data available. The first published data on the deficit syndrome, or enduring negative symptoms, in older schizophrenic patients came from Harris, Jeste, Krull, Montague, and Heaton (1991), who found the deficit syndrome to be present in 37% (total $n = 46$) of their patients. Similarly, Putnam and Harvey (2001) examined a sample of 59 younger (age less than 65) and 174 older (age greater than 64) chronic patients with schizophrenia. They found that 53% of the geriatric patients and 42% of the younger patients met criteria for a modified version of the deficit syndrome. In a younger sample, Carpenter et al. (1988) found the deficit syndrome to be present in 15% of their patients in total ($n = 103$). Thus, older patients in general appear to have a higher prevalence of the deficit syndrome than younger patients.

It is possible that this differential prevalence between younger and older samples is a function of the fact that older patients studied may be more likely to have an established course of illness than younger patients, with some younger patients still having the possibility of recovering from their illness. The deficit syndrome is not simply an alternate definition of chronicity in elderly schizophrenic patients, because only about half of all older institutionalized patients with schizophrenia met criteria for the deficit syndrome. It is also not a simple proxy for severity, because there was no difference in the severity of total positive symptoms at baseline in the patients with and without the deficit syndrome, whereas deficit syndrome patients had evidence of greater negative symptom severity at baseline (Putnam & Harvey, 2001). In terms of correlates of the syndrome, Harris et al. (1991) found that age of onset was earlier in deficit patients and there were also fewer females in the deficit group. Putnam and Harvey (2001) found that the cognitive performance correlates of the deficit syndrome were the same in their older and younger samples as previously reported by Buchanan et al. (1994).

Other than some suggestion that deficit syndrome is more common in older patients, possibly reflecting some sampling bias in the studies completed to date, the deficit syndrome appears to be similar in its presentation in older and younger patients with schizophrenia. Thus, similar to all of the other aspects of symptomatology reviewed up this point, there appears to be consistency across the lifetime in terms of the presentation and correlates of the deficit syndrome in late life.

COMMUNICATION DISORDERS: DISORGANIZED SYMPTOMS IN LATE LIFE

There has been only one published study on communication disorders in older patients with schizophrenia. In that study (Harvey, Lombardi, et al., 1997b), poor outcome patients ranging in age from 18 to 85 were examined with clinical ratings of communication disorders. Similar to the studies of clinical symptoms described earlier, there were age-associated differences in different types of communication disorders. There were reductions in the prevalence and severity of disconnection-related speech disorders and increases in the prevalence and severity of poverty of speech. There were no differences in the rare speech disorders, with the prevalence being low in both groups.

As discussed earlier, there are numerous age-related changes in normal language functioning, with the most prominent one being reductions in verbal productivity. There is some evidence that the reduction in verbal productivity seen in older patients was not a simple effect of aging, in that there were reliable correlates of reduced verbal productivity. Geriatric poor outcome patients who met criteria for moderate poverty of speech had Mini-Mental State Examination (MMSE) scores 10 points lower on average than patients without poverty of speech (Harvey, Lombardi, et al., 1997b). These data indicate that poverty of speech may be related to the types of global cognitive impairment seen in the subset of patients with a deteriorating course of illness and a particularly poor functional outcome (Davidson et al., 1995). No longitudinal data have been produced to indicate that poverty of speech is definitive indicator of poor functional outcome and deterioration over the lifespan, but cross-sectional and short-term longitudinal data have consistently suggested that poverty of speech was related to functional outcome.

DIMENSIONS OF SYMPTOMS IN OLDER PATIENTS WITH SCHIZOPHRENIA

Symptoms of the illness occur with variable prevalence across patients, and there has been considerable interest in the dimensionality of symptoms in schizophrenia. Studies of the factor structure of schizophrenia symptoms in younger patients reveal generally three (Arndt et al., 1991) or five factors (White, Harvey, Lindenmeyer, & Opler, 1997), depending on the breadth of the assessment. When only the symptoms that contribute to the diagnosis of the illness are considered, the factor solutions have been quite consistent at detecting three main dimensions: positive (referred to as "reality distortion" by Liddle, 1987), negative, and disorganized. When a broader assessment is performed, other dimensions typically include affective symptoms and a final factor that is often referred to as activation.

Studies of older patients have revealed essentially the same factor structure as in younger patients. For example, McAdams, Harris, Bailey, Fell, and Jeste (1996) examined the factor structure of commonly used psychiatric rating scales in older patients with schizophrenia with exploratory factor analysis, revealing the typical three-factor solution. White et al. (1997) compared samples of older and younger patients with schizophrenia and found that similar factor structures, comprising five factors, fit the data in older and younger patients. This study used confirmatory factor analysis, which is a more statistically rigorous procedure than exploratory analyses. When the fit of the model was compared across groups, the fit in older and younger patients did not differ significantly. Finally, Sauer, Hornstein, Richter, Mortimer, and Hirsch (1999) used exploratory and confirmatory factor analysis to examine the structure of symptoms in older and younger patients with schizophrenia, with a focus on the correlates of these symptom dimensions. They also found a three-dimensional solution for the factor structure, with disorganized, negative, and paranoid (i.e., positive/reality distortion). When examining the correlates of these symptom dimensions, they found, similar to Liddle's (1987) previous report on samples of younger patients, that the cognitive correlates of negative and disorganized dimensions were different from each, like in previous studies of younger patients. Their conclusion was that not only was the factorial structure of symptoms the same in younger and older patients but that these symptom dimensions had the same cognitive correlates in later life as in younger patients. As a result, the dimensional structure of symptoms of schizophrenia appears to be similar across the age span.

There are several implications of these findings of stable symptom structure over the life span course of the illness. The fact that negative and positive symptoms are separate and discriminable in both older and younger patients suggests that there is not an age-related shift in the structure of symptom presentation. In addition, the correlates of negative and positive symptoms have been demonstrated to be similar in older and younger patients. In younger and older patients, negative symptoms are more severe in patients with poorer lifetime outcome. Negative symptoms are correlated with the severity of cognitive impairments in both younger and older patients

(Addington, 2000; Davidson et al., 1995), whereas positive symptoms are typically found to be uncorrelated with cognitive impairments (Addington, 2000; Davidson et al., 1995). It is also the case that positive symptoms are still more variable in presentation over various follow-up periods than negative symptoms (Harvey et al., 2003; Putnam et al., 1996), again a finding consistent across older and younger patients with the illness. Thus, the dimensional structure of symptoms, both in terms of intercorrelation between symptoms and correlations of these symptom dimensions to other features of the illness, appears to be consistent over the lifespan.

COURSES OF SCHIZOPHRENIA OVER THE LIFETIME

Studies of the prevalence and severity of the different types of symptoms in schizophrenia constitute only one perspective on the effects of aging in schizophrenia on symptom presentation. An alternative perspective is that of examining schizophrenia in terms of its lifetime course. Prospective studies of individuals with schizophrenia over extended periods of time have identified multiple discriminable courses of illness (Ciompi, 1980; Huber, Gross, & Schuttler, 1975; Steinhausen, Meier, & Angst, 1998). These conceptions of the course of illness have focused on several different features of schizophrenia, including the persistence of psychotic symptoms, the emergence or worsening of negative symptoms, and the level of social and self-care deficits.

The different courses of illness previously described can range from full recovery from all symptoms with no residual functional deficit to complete disability and full dependence on others for all their needs. Table 3.1 presents the different courses of illness that have been described previously. As can be seen in the table, psychotic symptoms can occur in patients who vary widely in their functional outcomes, being present in patients who have essentially no disability and lacking in patients who have full disability.

TABLE 3.1
Different Outcomes for Schizophrenia

1. Full recovery
2. Sporadic psychotic episodes with no interepisode impairments
3. Sporadic psychotic episodes with persistent but mild cognitive and negative symptoms
4. Sporadic psychotic episodes with severe functional disability between episodes
5. Frequent psychotic episodes with severe functional disability between episodes
6. No psychotic symptoms but severe functional disability
7. Continuous psychotic symptoms with severe functional disability
8. Continuous psychotic symptoms with complete functional disability

There is considerable evidence that all of these different courses of illness can be identified in some subsets of older patients with schizophrenia.

Full Recovery

Patients with full recovery may be the most difficult to follow into late life. In fact, patients who are fully recovered from schizophrenia are often difficult to follow even early in their lives. This problem is potentially compounded in individuals whose only episode of illness was decades earlier. As a result, this may be an outcome that has been underestimated in some studies. One study that generated a series of reports on full recovery from schizophrenia, however, raises the question as to whether some substantial proportion of patients with schizophrenia may fully recover from their illness late in their lives. This investigation, the Vermont longitudinal study, followed a sample of patients with schizophrenia who had been long-stay residents of a state psychiatric facility (Harding, Brooks, Ashikaga, Strauss, & Breier, 1987a, 1987b). These patients received a specialized skills training intervention before they were discharged from the hospital and were then followed up for at least 10 years and as long as 32 years after their discharge. A surprising number of the patients had evidence of full recovery at follow-up. More than half of the patients were reported to have no evidence of clinical symptoms of schizophrenia, and most were also reported receiving no medication or other treatment. Thus, a large proportion of older patients with schizophrenia who initially had a poor outcome associated with extended institutional stay appeared to recover while not requiring or receiving community-based clinical services.

There are several issues that this study raises. First is that this may be a highly selected group. These patients were treated with a specialized intervention while hospitalized, with most patients with schizophrenia not receiving this level of intensive or specialized treatment. It would be surprising to find many patients who are chronically institutionalized who manifest this level of recovery, possibly because they never receive the type of skills-based intervention that this study's patients received. Second, however, is the issue that there are some other data that indicate that most patients with schizophrenia who have never been institutionalized (or sometimes never even hospitalized at any time) manifest substantially greater impairment across multiple indexes of outcome than the levels of adjustment seen in the Vermont study patients while living in the community. Studies of community-dwelling patients with modest clinical symptoms and minimal lifetime histories of inpatient treatment have reported substantial levels of cognitive and functional impairment (Jeste et al., 2003). As a consequence, the results of this study are clearly outlying in terms of the typical findings regarding outcome in patients with schizophrenia. Yet the results offer promise that some patients with schizophrenia can recover from their illness, even late in their lives and after a history of institutional stay.

Recurrent Psychotic Episodes in Older Patients With Schizophrenia

One of the consequences of deinstitutionalization and medication treatments for patients with schizophrenia has been the development of the "revolving-door" syndrome. Patients appear at a psychiatric emergency room, are evaluated, sometimes briefly admitted for stabilization, and then are discharged after a short stay following partial remission of their psychotic symptoms. Following their discharge, many develop a pattern of noncompliance with treatment, and the patient undergoes the same process again in a few weeks to a few months (Robinson et al., 1999). It is not a surprise to see patients who have a history of as many as 25 abbreviated inpatient treatments. Thus, evidence regarding the occurrence of recurrent psychotic episodes in older patients would indicate that this type of outcome persists into older age.

In one published study (Harvey et al., 1998), a sample of acutely admitted older patients with schizophrenia was examined within one week of their admission to inpatient treatment at an acute psychiatric facility. None of these patients had ever been institutionalized and all were community residents at the time of their admission to inpatient care. All of these patients recovered from their episodes and returned to the community. At the time of their admission these patients were found to have negative symptoms and functional deficits that were markedly less severe than comparison samples of chronically institutionalized patients, who resided either in nursing home care or in a chronic psychiatric facility. However, the severity of their psychotic symptoms at the time of this exacerbation and readmission to inpatient care was equivalent in severity to the chronically ill patients with a history of as much as 50 consecutive years of inpatient treatment. Thus, when patients with a relatively good lifetime clinical outcome, manifesting a course of illness with periods of remission between psychotic episodes and functional adjustment that is adequate to support community residence, experience a psychotic episode, they have substantial severity of positive symptoms. At the same time, even when acutely psychotic, these patients have greater preservation of cognitive and functional skills. Thus, this outcome subtype, episodic psychotic episodes with partial recovery and only minimal interepisode functional impairment, is clearly still found in some older patients with schizophrenia. However, there is a remarkable lack of prospective data on the prevalence of this outcome in older patients, making it impossible to estimate the prevalence of this outcome.

Marked Cognitive and Functional Impairment in Patients Without Prominent Psychotic Symptoms

Some younger patients with schizophrenia spend the majority of their lives without the regular experience of a psychotic episode but are still markedly impaired in social, occupational, and independent living domains. The level of disability, however, in older patients with only modest positive symptoms has been less thoroughly investigated. In one study (Bartels, Mueser, & Miles, 1997a), community-dwelling patients with schizophrenia were compared to samples of patients with affective disorders in terms of functional limitations, clinical symptoms, cognitive deficits, and behavior problems. All of these patients were selected because they were stable community dwellers who were receiving outpatient mental health services. These outpatients with schizophrenia were found to have only modest psychotic symptoms, but were found to have marked cognitive impairments and deficits in adaptive functioning. Relative to patients with affective disorders who were similar in age and duration of illness, schizophrenic patients were found to be more impaired in all of the important functional, cognitive, and behavioral problem domains. Thus, like in younger patients, there is clearly a group of patients who have only modest clinical symptoms but who are very impaired in their functional status. These patients required more assistance from others in self-care and maintenance of residential status than affective disorder patients of the same age, demonstrating that these impairments were not caused by the experience of mental illness or aging alone.

A similar report comes from Jeste et al. (2003), in which patients with modest ongoing psychotic symptoms were found to manifest disability that was considerably greater than samples of healthy controls. Thus, although it is difficult to estimate the frequency of this outcome, it is clear that many community-dwelling older patients fall into this outcome group.

Patients With Complete Lifelong Disability

In 1948, there were 275,000 individuals with chronic schizophrenia living in long-stay psychiatric facilities in the United States (Menninger, 1948), and now there are fewer than 7,500. As the number of patients living in long-stay psychiatric facilities has been reduced enormously, this has not correlated with a realistic improvement in functional outcome. The proportion of patients with schizophrenia who lived independently in 1945 was the same as it was in 1985, indicating the reduction of residents in long-stay psychiatric facilities has not corresponded with an improvement in the outcome of the illness (Hegarty et al., 1994). At this time the typical fully disabled patient with schizophrenia does not live in a chronic psychiatric hospital but in some alternative residence because of the downsizing of psychiatric facilities. Thus, it is important to realize that changes in systems of care can influence estimates of outcome and that older conceptions of the correlation between residential status and functional outcome have reduced validity. "Chronic" no longer means "institutionalized" and "institutionalized" may no longer imply long-term hospital stays.

Several recent studies have focused on the characteristics of older patients who have lived their entire lives in long-term psychiatric care or in an equivalent treatment setting such as nursing homes (Arnold et al., 1995; Davidson et al., 1995). These studies have indicated that these patients have substantial symptoms in multiple domains. Extensive negative, positive, and cognitive symptoms have been reported, as have profound functional deficits. The severity of psychotic symptoms in older patients with major disability has been shown to be similar to that seen in younger patients with a similarly chronic course of illness (Davidson et al., 1995), whereas negative symptoms and cognitive deficits were more severe (Friedman et al., 2001; Gur, Petty, Turetsky, & Gur, 1996). These symptoms have been found to be relatively similar in care systems ranging from public hospitals in several different states in the United States, as well as in the United Kingdom (Harvey, Leff, Trieman, Anderson, & Davidson, 1997) and across nursing care residences in several different states (Bartels, Mueser, & Miles, 1997b).

Again, there are some difficulties in estimating the prevalence of these outcomes. One of the major issues that will require later attention is the estimation of the prevalence of the different major courses of illness in schizophrenia in later life. It is not clear how many patients with schizophrenia manifest each of these courses of illness and whether there are large numbers of older patients who are presently not accounted for and not studied to date. What is clear, however, is that several different studies have suggested systematic differences between patients with a chronic course of illness and those with either sporadic psychotic episodes or patterns of general clinical stability while residing in the community.

DETERMINING IF THE COURSE OF SCHIZOPHRENIA EVER CHANGES IN LATE LIFE

There are major implications associated with the differences in overall outcome associated with the various courses of illness described earlier. Full recovery versus lifetime complete disability are clearly divergent outcomes, but even the difference between lifetime residence in the community, with or without regular exacerbations, and living in a full-care residence have large-scale cost and quality-of-life implications. Although there is no evidence to date suggesting that full recovery from schizophrenia is common in late life (compared with, for instance, apparent recovery from the first episode of illness), there is also no evidence to suggest that there are many cases with abrupt turns for the worse in later life. This is a critical question that needs to be addressed with later research. As mentioned earlier, discharge from long-stay psychiatric care to either community residence or to nursing home care has not been demonstrated to lead to marked changes in the overall course of illness. The extent of influence of these environments on symptoms and the course of illness is explored in more detail later.

CONCLUSION

Schizophrenia is marked by considerable heterogeneity in symptomatology, course, and outcome. This diversity appears to be sustained in late life, and all of the profiles and courses of symptoms seen in younger patients have been detected in older ones as well. Patients with schizophrenia who have been studied to date have considerable symptomatology in late life, and the stability and correlates of those symptoms are the same as those seen earlier in life. Severity of certain symptoms appears to be more affected by the interaction of lifetime outcome status and aging than the stability, factorial structure, or correlates of the symptoms. Patients with lifelong good outcome may improve as they age and chronic patients may worsen in some areas. Despite some support for the idea that positive symptoms may decrease in severity with aging, the major outcome subtypes persist into late life. The majority of older patients who are receiving mental health services, either at an acute admission or outpatient services in the community, have evidence of cognitive and functional impairments, regardless of the severity of their psychotic symptoms. Patients with lifelong disability show no signs of improvement over short-term periods in late life and, as noted in later chapters, some may even experience worsening of their symptoms. Thus, despite the limited data available, there is considerable evidence to suggest that the courses of schizophrenia in later life are consistent with those seen earlier and that the diversity seen in younger patients is, if anything, greater in older patients.

4

COGNITION AND FUNCTION
IN OLDER PATIENTS
WITH SCHIZOPHRENIA

Impairments in cognitive functioning are typical in most patients with schizophrenia, appearing before the time of the first psychotic episode and continuing throughout the lifespan. Cognitive impairments have been detected as early as age 6 in individuals who eventually develop schizophrenia (Crow, Done, & Sackler, 1995) and functional–social impairments nearly as early in life (Done, Crow, Johnstone, & Sacker, 1994). These impairments in cognition appear to be persistent across the lifespan in schizophrenia, without notable improvement or worsening in most patients until later life.

Similar to cognitive deficits, impairments in adaptive life skills are present throughout the lifetime course of schizophrenia as well. Some individuals with schizophrenia manifest severe social deficits from early in their lives (Jones et al., 1993), meaning that severe social withdrawal present at the time of the development of formal signs of the illness may not be a feature that develops at the time of the appearance of psychotic symptoms. Impairments in social, educational, cognitive, occupational, and self-care skills are substantial in a portion of individuals, with this condition referred to as "poor premorbid functioning." Poor premorbid functioning has been known for more than 50 years to predict a more adverse course of illness, with patients experiencing more severe adjustment deficits before the onset of other symptoms being more likely to have persistent symptoms, significant functional deficits, and to experience longer stays in psychiatric inpatient care (Langfelt, 1937). Recent findings have suggested that the primary determinant of functional deficits is cognitive impairment, suggesting an intrinsic relationship between these two domains of deficit in patients with schizophrenia.

This chapter presents current information about cognitive and functional deficits in schizophrenia patients in late life. Some interesting research findings suggest that some schizophrenia patients worsen in their cognitive and functional status as they age. Yet the majority of older patients with schizophrenia appear not to have any changes in their functioning into later life. This chapter will examine these findings, describe the current information regarding risk factors for the decline in the subset of patients whose functioning appears to decline, and evaluate the implications of cognitive and functional changes with aging. We identify possible reasons that the course of cognitive and functional diverges across different patients. To do so, we first briefly examine the characteristics of cognitive and functional deficits in schizophrenia patients in general.

THE CHARACTERISTICS OF COGNITIVE IMPAIRMENTS IN SCHIZOPHRENIA

Despite consistent findings of impairment in a wide range of cognitive functions in schizophrenia, several of these impairments are consistently the most severe. Although performance on tasks measuring old learning or crystallized intelligence, such as reading and vocabulary skills, is often found to be unimpaired or mildly impaired compared to normative standards (Harvey, Moriarty, Friedman, et al., 2000), memory, executive functions, and attentional performance is often found to be markedly impaired (Heaton et al., 1994; Saykin et al., 1991). Even at the time of the first episode, performance on the part of the average patient is consistent with the first percentile of the normal distribution in several of these important skills domains (Bilder et al., 2000; Saykin et al., 1994). Table 4.1 presents a description of the levels of severity of these deficits.

As few as 30% of clinically stable patients have normal cognitive functioning (Palmer et al., 1997) with similar numbers of chronic patients having unimpaired cognitive functioning (Harvey et al., 2002). Most patients with a persistent course of illness have substantial cognitive deficits. These deficits are consistent in severity across changes in clinical state (Harvey, Docherty, Serper, & Rasmussen, 1990) and appear largely stable from the time of the first episode until after middle-age (Rund, 1998). These findings suggest that these deficits are not a consequence of the experience

TABLE 4.1
The Severity of Cognitive Deficits in Schizophrenia

Mild	Moderate	Severe
Perceptual skill	Distractibility	Verbal learning
Recognition memory	Recall memory	Executive functions
Naming	Visuomotor skills	Vigilance
	Working memory	Motor speed
		Verbal fluency

Note. Severity is measured as number of standard deviations (SD) below the mean for normal subjects (mild = 0.5–1 SD; moderate = 1–2 SD; severe = 2–5 SD).

of psychotic symptoms such as hallucinations, a conclusion consistent with the data suggesting that cognitive deficits are often present before other symptoms of the illness are ever experienced (Davidson et al., 1999).

Cognitive deficits are neither caused by nor markedly improved by treatment with typical antipsychotic medications (e.g., Medalia, Gold, & Merriam, 1988), although anticholinergic medications used to reduce the side effects of conventional medications can worsen memory impairments (Spohn & Strauss, 1989). These cognitive impairments are also not a result of motivational deficits because patients demonstrate differential deficits across skills areas that are inconsistent with simply failing to exert adequate effort while being tested (Harvey, Moriarty, Serper, et al., 2000). Finally, cognitive impairments are consistently related to other aspects of the illness, such as negative symptoms (e.g., Addington, Addington, & Maticka-Tynsdale, 1991) and, more important, functional impairments (e.g., Green, 1996). The interrelationship of these features of the illness is described in more detail next.

FUNCTIONAL CHARACTERISTICS OF SCHIZOPHRENIA

Functional limitations are common and severe in patients with schizophrenia. In fact, functional deficits could be argued to be the only symptom of illness that every patient experiences, because meeting the *DSM–IV* criterion B for the diagnosis of schizophrenia means every patient must have a deterioration in his or her functioning that has lasted for at least six months to substantiate the diagnosis of the illness. Patients with schizophrenia do not have to manifest all of the different criterion A symptoms, and it is possible, albeit rare, to receive a schizophrenia diagnosis and never experience delusions or hallucinations.

These functional skills deficits are quite wide ranging and pervasive. Participation in competitive employment occurs in less than one third of patients with the illness, even on a part-time basis (Mueser, Salyers, &

Mueser, 2001), whereas patients with schizophrenia have impairments in social functioning, including few friends, reduced social contact, and infrequent marriage. Independent living is rare, and most patients with schizophrenia begin to receive public assistance within 6 months of their initial diagnosis (Ho, Andreasen, & Flaum, 1997). Finally, patients have self-care deficits ranging from failure to comply with medical therapies and failing to seek medical attention for illness to deficits in skills such as feeding, dressing, and basic hygiene.

DETERMINANTS OF FUNCTIONAL DEFICITS

In the general population and in neuropsychiatric conditions in specific, impaired performance on critical aspects of cognitive functioning is a major determinant of poor global functional outcome (Heaton & Pendleton, 1981). When examining these relationships in schizophrenia, a number of correlational relationships have been identified between specific aspects of functional status (i.e., social, independent living, and employment) and cognitive impairments (Green, 1996; Green, Kern, Braff, & Mintz, 2000). As reviewed in those two comprehensive papers, executive functioning deficits have been shown to be most consistently related to deficits in independent living, whereas attentional deficits are associated with social functioning deficits. Learning and memory deficits appear to be consistently related to impairments in social, independent living, and occupational domains. These deficits also exert a rate-limiting effect on the ability to learn skills in training programs, in that patients with greater attentional deficits have slower rates of learning with practice. So, in younger patients with schizophrenia, one of the major rate-limiters in functional skills acquisition and subsequent performance is cognitive impairment.

What about negative symptoms and their role in outcome? It has been known for years that patients with a chronic course of illness and extended institutional stays are more likely to have severe negative symptoms than higher functioning patients (Keefe et al., 1987). In studies of younger patients that have examined the relationship between negative symptoms and functional deficits, there is a moderate correlation between the severity of negative symptoms and functional impairments (see Green, 1996; Green et al., 2000, for reviews). In studies that have also considered cognitive impairments, the relationship between negative symptoms and functional outcome is reduced or eliminated when the correlation between cognitive deficits and functional status is considered (Velligan et al., 1997). This may be because negative symptoms and cognitive deficits are themselves moderately correlated, as demonstrated in numerous studies involving various definitions of both negative symptoms and cognitive deficits (see Addington, 2000, for an extensive review). Longitudinal studies have suggested that this correlation is not because cognitive impairments are caused by negative symptoms but rather that these are related, but discriminable, traits of patients with schizophrenia (Harvey, Lombardi, Leibman, White, et al., 1996). Thus, it is possible that the correlation between negative symptoms and functional outcome is really a result of the relationship between negative symptoms and cognitive deficits, which leads to a correlation between negative symptoms and functional impairment because of this secondary relationship.

STUDIES OF COGNITION IN OLDER PATIENTS WITH SCHIZOPHRENIA

Research on cognitive functioning in older patients with schizophrenia has focused on a variety of domains of cognition, using methods ranging from global screening measures to comprehensive neuropsychological assessments. The study populations have also varied, examining ambulatory samples of relatively younger outpatients to chronically institutionalized samples of patients living in psychiatric hospitals and nursing homes. Comparison groups have varied as well, from younger and older healthy controls, younger patients with schizophrenia, patients with affective disorders, and patients with Alzheimer's disease. Thus, although there are relatively few studies of cognitive impairment in older patients, there are many reasonable reference points on the severity of impairments from the previous research.

COGNITIVE PERFORMANCE: PROFILE AND SEVERITY OF IMPAIRMENT

In one of the first studies of cognitive impairment in older patients with schizophrenia using contemporary diagnostic criteria, Heaton et al. (1994) reported that older ambulatory patients with schizophrenia had a profile and severity of impairments consistent with the impairments seen in younger patients. Patients had prominent deficits in learning and memory, executive functioning, and attention when compared to healthy comparison participants, even when differences in education and socioeconomic status were considered. Several important additional findings emerged from this study. When older and younger patients were compared, there were no differences in relative impairments in older and younger patients. Patients with schizophrenia, even younger ones, performed more poorly than patients with Alzheimer's disease on most aspects of the cognitive assessment. Thus, although there were no age-associated differences in performance, the level of impairment seen was quite severe in these older ambulatory patients

Studying a large ($N = 358$) group of institutionalized patients ranging in age from 25 to 95, Davidson et al. (1995) reported that there were substantial impairments in cognitive functioning detected in this population. The average Mini-Mental State Examination (MMSE; Folstein, Folstein, & McHugh, 1975) score of patients over the age of 65 was 16, which is in the severely demented range. These findings are consistent with the results of other studies of similarly institutionalized patients in different states and systems of care in the United States (Arnold et al., 1995), in the United Kingdom (Harvey, Leff, et al., 1997), and in Japan (Seno et al., 1998). Also noted in the Davidson et al. (1995) study were consistent age-associated differences in performance on the MMSE with patients between the ages of 85 and 95 receiving an average score of only 9.6, which is lower than the traditional clinical cutoff for severe dementia. This finding is strengthened by the fact that patients with MMSE scores of 0 were excluded from the analysis, indicating that these low scores are not because of patients who refused to cooperate with the assessment.

Studies of specific cognitive abilities in older patients have also yielded findings suggesting, in general, continuity of performance deficits across the life span. For instance, older patients with schizophrenia have greater deficits in rate of learning and delayed recall than in recognition memory (Paulsen, Heaton, Sadek, Perry, & Jeste, 1995), consistent with studies of younger patients. When the frequency of different profiles of impairment was examined in that study, it was found that the most common profile of memory impairment in older patients was a theoretically "subcortical" profile of impairment, consistent with earlier studies of younger patients. This impairment profile consistent with that seen in degenerative conditions selectively affecting subcortical regions such as Huntington's disease, is marked by relatively greater impairment in rate of learning and delayed recall than in recognition memory. Verbal fluency in older patients was also found to be relatively more severe in semantic fluency conditions than in phonological fluency (Harvey et al., 1997b), consistent with the general pattern of impairment in younger patients with schizophrenia (Gourovitch, Goldberg, & Weinberger, 1996).

Also of considerable interest is the profile of generally spared cognitive functions in older patients. In younger patients with schizophrenia, reading ability is so well preserved that it is often used as a proxy for premorbid intellectual functioning (Tracy, McCrory, Josiassen, & Monaco, 1996). In these patients, current intellectual functioning is often found to be as much as 15 points (one standard deviation) lower than premorbid IQ estimated on the basis of reading scores (Weickert et al., 2000). Reading scores appear to be more consistently preserved than vocabulary, suggesting that simple word recognition is more intact than the ability to define information retrieved from semantic memory on demand. Similar findings have been reported for older patients with schizophrenia, even those with a history of chronic institutional care. A sample of older patients with MSME scores consistent with moderate dementia (M = 20.36) and with memory and verbal skills performance more than 1.5 standard deviations below the mean of a sample of healthy older individuals matched to the patients on age and educational attainment had reading scores that were consistent with the level of education that they had completed, in some cases more than 50 years previously (Harvey, Moriarty, Friedman, et al., 2000). This preservation of reading scores in the context of multiple severe cognitive impairments indicates that even in patients with general deterioration, differential profiles of spared and impaired functions persist until late life.

Among the correlates of cognitive functioning in older patients with schizophrenia is their lifetime history of overall outcome. This relationship has been reported in several different studies, comparing ambulatory patients to patients who lived in either chronic psychiatric care or in nursing home care. For example, Evans et al. (1999) found that institutionalized patients performed more poorly on the Dementia Rating Scale (DRS; Mattis, 1973) than ambulatory patients, a finding similar to that reported by Harvey et al. (1998), who used a different cognitive assessment battery. Bartels et al. (1997b) and Auslander et al. (2001) reported that patients residing in nursing home care had more substantial cognitive deficits than ambulatory patients. Kurtz et al. (2001) reported that poorer performance on cognitive tests correlated with measures of functional skills in a sample of older institutionalized patients. So, similar to results reported in younger patients, more substantial cognitive deficits are seen in individuals who have a chronic course of illness and receive high levels of care. Whether these impairments are the cause of this poor lifetime outcome will be evaluated in detail below.

STABILITY OF COGNITIVE IMPAIRMENTS OVER TIME

Several studies have found that scores on both the MMSE and on components of comprehensive neuropsychological assessment batteries are stable at follow-up intervals ranging from one to six years (Harvey et al., 1995; Harvey, Lombardi, Leibman, Parrella, et al., 1996; Heaton et al., 2001). These data indicate that, like in younger patients with schizophrenia, cognitive deficits have a pattern of greater stability over time than positive symptoms of the illness. None of the studies found a pattern of differential stability across performance areas, suggesting that all domains of cognitive functioning are assessed with similar reliability in older patients.

AGE EFFECTS ON PERFORMANCE

In the Heaton et al. (1994) study, ambulatory patients with schizophrenia did not demonstrate any exaggeration of normal age-related differences in performance on any of the tests in a comprehensive neuropsychological battery. Similar results were reported for scores on the DRS, across the age range (Eyler-Zorrilla et al., 2000). Older ambulatory patients with schizophrenia were found to have no greater impairments than younger patients when their scores were compared to the normative performance of healthy controls. In contrast, Fucetola et al. (2000) reported that older patients had selectively greater impairments in executive functioning than younger patients, with no increased age-related differences in other aspects of cognitive functioning. In addition, Granholm, Morris, Asarnow, Chock, and Jeste (2000) reported that older patients had evidence of reductions in their ability to process complex information, as evidenced by increased information processing while performing an attentional task, the span of apprehension test. Thus, even for ambulatory patients, there is some evidence of deterioration in the ability to perform complex and resource-demanding tasks with aging, relative to the changes seen in healthy controls.

When examining institutionalized patients, no age-related differences in performance were found on tests of verbal skills (Harvey, Lombardi, et al., 1997) or on as memory performance (Putnam & Harvey, 1999). However, these two studies of institutionalized patients examined only those with MMSE scores over 18, which was a minority of the potential patients. In contrast, when MMSE scores were compared across the life span, a 3-point per decade difference was detected (Davidson et al., 1995). This difference is considerably greater than the changes expected with normal aging, where community-dwelling older individuals often have MMSE scores above 25 even if they had relatively low levels of lifetime education (Crum, Anthony, Bassett, & Folstein, 1993).

The discrepancies across these studies have not yet been resolved. Studies of older patients selected for having higher levels of global cognitive performance might contribute to the failures to detect age-related changes on neuropsychological tests, because older patients are more likely to be in the group excluded because of lower MMSE scores (Arnold et al., 1995; Davidson et al., 1995). Patients with low MMSE scores would be expected to be the worst performers on difficult neuropsychological tests, and inclusion of more of these patients would have probably resulted in age-related differences in the Harvey, Lombardi, et al. (1997) and Putnam and Harvey (1999) studies.

Another issue is the age of the older patients across the different studies. In the Heaton et al. (1994) study, patients were characterized as older if they were over age 55, and in the Eyler-Zorilla et al. (2000) study, less than a dozen patients were over the age of 65. Normal changes in cognitive functioning with aging gain momentum after the age of 65, meaning that if the changes seen in older schizophrenic patients are an exaggeration of the normal pattern of change with aging, including older patients may be required to identify these changes as well.

WORSENING OF COGNITIVE IMPAIRMENT OVER TIME

The age-related differences in MMSE scores described earlier imply that cognitive functioning must change at some time over the course of the illness in some patients with schizophrenia. Both the discrepancy between reading scores and MMSE scores reported by Harvey et al. (2000) and the premorbid functioning manifested by some chronically institutionalized patients (26 college graduates in the Davidson et al. [1995] sample, 14 with MMSE scores < 10) indicate that these low MMSE scores are not reflective of lifelong intellectual subnormality. Several longitudinal studies of cognitive functioning have been completed, but the results of these studies also have some inconsistencies. In several studies including sample sizes of up 1,300 patients and follow-up periods of up to 6 years (Harvey & Davidson, 2002), cognitive decline has been found in some patients. In the first study, 30% of 160 chronically hospitalized geriatric (age ≥ 65) schizophrenic patients with less severe cognitive impairments at baseline (MMSE scores >17) demonstrated statistically significant cognitive decline over a 30-month period (Harvey, Silverman, et al., 1999). The two predictors of decline included lower education and greater severity of positive symptoms at baseline. The second study (Harvey, Parrella, et al., 1999) also demonstrated cognitive decline over an average of 2.5 years in 57 geriatric schizophrenic patients who entered the study chronically hospitalized but were reassessed after discharge to nursing home care. In the third study a total of 1,301 patients were followed for 60 months, with 199 patients excluded because they developed new onset medical conditions that precluded analysis of their data (Harvey & Davidson, 2002). When these patients were followed over 60 months, 48% of the patients who had baseline MMSE scores over 17 had a decline in their cognitive functioning, with the same profile of predictors identified. When a sample of initially institutionalized schizophrenic patients ranging in age from 25 to 85 were followed for 6 years and compared in proportion and amount of cognitive decline to healthy individuals and patients with Alzheimer's disease (AD; Friedman et al., 2001), it was found that the schizophrenic patients had an age-associated risk of cognitive decline, whereas neither the AD patients nor healthy controls did. The oldest schizophrenic patients (age 75–80 at baseline) dropped by 6 MMSE points in 6 years, whereas schizophrenic patients under the age of 65 did not drop at all. In contrast, patients with AD uniformly dropped by 12 or more points regardless of their age. Thus, younger patients, even those with a history of chronic institutional care, had essentially no risk for cognitive decline over 6 years, whereas older patients had a drop in their functioning that was approximately half that seen in Alzheimer's disease.

In contrast to these findings, a recent larger scale ($N = 142$) longitudinal study of older ambulatory patients with schizophrenia suggested no evidence of cognitive decline (or improvement) over follow-up periods that averaged 60 months (Heaton et al., 2001). In this study a comprehensive neuropsychological assessment was performed, and there was no evidence of change over time in any of the participants. However, only 22 of the 142 patients were over the age of 65 at entry into the study. Thus, the older patients who were found to decline in Harvey and Davidson studies were not well-represented in this study, as they were not in the Eyler-Zorilla study. As a consequence, it is not possible to determine what the basis for the differences in findings was. It is interesting that this same sample of patients was reported to have substantial cognitive deficits at both assessments. Thus, even ambulatory patients whose performance appears stable over time are still notably impaired in their cognitive functioning in their later years. Across these two sets of studies, there were differences in patient samples (chronic versus ambulatory), assessment methods (neuropsychological batteries corrected for demographic factors versus brief screening instruments), and data analytical techniques. Given the modest amount of information available on the course of schizophrenia in late life, it is not possible to determine which of these factors influences the discrepancies between the results. Ongoing research in collaboration between the UCSD group and the Mt. Sinai group is attempting to resolve these differences in findings.

In a study of older chronically institutionalized patients, some of whom were referred to highly desirable community residences, a different pattern of cognitive change was found (Trieman, Wills, & Leff, 1996). Older patients who remained in the chronic care institution deteriorated in their cognitive functioning, whereas patients who were referred to the community did not. Thus, when the results of these two studies are compared, it appears as if community residence may be a correlate of preservation of cognitive status. It is not clear, however, to what extent selection artifacts may be operative in this study, as the process of discharge was not randomized and the patients with greater potential for decline may have had some characteristics, as yet undefined, that led to their being passed over for discharge.

FUNCTIONAL IMPAIRMENTS IN OLDER PATIENTS WITH SCHIZOPHRENIA

Given the evidence presented earlier about cognitive impairments in older patients with schizophrenia, it would be surprising to see that most older patients with schizophrenia did not have major functional deficits. In fact, the characteristics of adaptive deficit are relatively similar in older patients compared to younger patients, with some minor exceptions. First of all, vocational functioning is less of an issue in individuals of retirement age. Second, self-care changes with normal aging, so anticipated changes in this domain must also be considered, as major deficits in self-care often develop in later life in individuals with a lifelong history of self-support and full functional independence. Third, the characteristics of social functioning also change in late life, with social contact reduced in general for many individuals and related to changes in residential status, so these factors must be considered while evaluating abnormal functional status in older patients.

FUNCTIONAL DEFICIT IN LATE-LIFE SCHIZOPHRENIA: METHODS OF ASSESSMENT

Assessment of functional status in schizophrenia has many challenges that are magnified in older patients. In conditions such as Alzheimer's disease, many patients have family members, including spouses and children, who can provide quite accurate reports about their behavior. Given the life history of many older patients with lifelong schizophrenia, this option is quite limited. Informant reports may be inaccurate because many patients with schizophrenia have no relatives with whom they are in contact. Thus, caregivers may be the sole potential informant, and these caregivers may have extremely variable contact with patients. Even in patients who are treated in institutions, informant reports need to be considered carefully. For instance, evening-shift employees would have considerably different contact with patients and might be focused more on behavioral disturbances in the late evening than on self-care activities that may occur during the day shift. Some patients reside in board and care homes where staff responsible for management of the homes may not have any true contact with the patients and may not be able to provide much information about their behavior.

Self-report methods can be used to measure adaptive functions in healthy populations. Many of the questions that are addressed are relatively straightforward (Who cooks the meals? How often do you leave the house? How many friends do you have?) and these questions can be answered without much of a problem. Patients with schizophrenia, because of their reduced awareness of illness, are often quite poor informants and cannot provide much information about symptoms. Similarly, the memory deficits seen in patients in schizophrenia raise a legitimate question about whether older patients can remember correctly what happens on a day-to-day basis. In some domains, however, such as quality of life, self-report is the only reasonable method. For questions about skills, particularly regarding competence in social functions, independent living skills, and self-care, self-report is likely to be markedly limited.

To increase the validity of measurement of functional deficits, performance-based measures have been used in Alzheimer's disease. One of these, the Direct Assessment of Functional Status (DAFS; Loewenstein et al., 1989) was recently evaluated for its utility in patients with schizophrenia (Klapow, Evans, Patterson, Heaton, & Jeste, 1997). This type of performance-based measure has the benefit of eliminating the unreliability associated with self-report or estimation of others' performance by observers who are not trained raters (e.g., clinical staff). In performance-based measures, there are other issues that must be addressed, including content validity and manageability. If analogue skills performance measures do not accurately simulate real-world performance of the skills involved, the increase in reliability will not be marked by a similar increase in validity. If the assessment takes too long or requires complicated props, it may also not be feasible in some clinical settings or in some research studies.

FUNCTIONAL DEFICIT IN LATE-LIFE SCHIZOPHRENIA: SEVERITY OF DEFICITS

Research using each of the different methods described earlier has been conducted to assess older patients with schizophrenia. In addition, information regarding the life history of older patients with schizophrenia suggests major impairments in objective indexes of functional achievement. For instance, in studies of older institutionalized patients, fewer than 10% of patients have ever been married and fewer than 20% have ever been employed (Harvey, Jacobsen, et al., 2000). In one study (Davidson et al., 1995), the modal number of previous admissions was one, and more than 90% of the patients in this large sample had never lived independently. Even in samples of patients living in the community, the rates of marriage and lifetime histories of employment are markedly less than normative expectations. The presence of evidence of reduced functional achievements over the lifetime does not provide much information about the reasons for this underachievement or provide any direct points of intervention. Better understanding of the specific skills limitations of older patients and the correlates of these functional skills that are associated with differences in overall outcome deficits is important for treating older schizophrenia patients.

Functional skills deficits on rating scales that require direct observation, informant report, and interview methods have also been found in both ambulatory and institutionalized patients with schizophrenia. In one study of ambulatory patients with schizophrenia, Bartels et al. (1997a) reported that schizophrenia patients living in community care residences had more functional skills deficits and behavioral disturbances than residents of these same homes who had affective disorders. Deficits in functional skills were relatively greater than the severity of behavioral problems. Harvey, Leff, et al. (1997) compared institutionalized patients in the United States and the United Kingdom on their functional skills deficits. Although impairments compared to normative standards were found in six different skills areas, patients in the United States had greater deficits in social skills while the United Kingdom patients had greater self-care deficits. These differences appeared to be related to environmental differences across the treatment sites in the two countries. United Kingdom patients had no access to television, so they were likely to spend more time talking to staff members and other patients, whereas the United Kingdom patients also received considerably more staff assistance with their self-care. As a result, the U.S. patients received less social attention and less assistance with activities of daily living. Thus, differences in the performance of social and functional skills paralleled environmental factors to which the patients were exposed, leading to the hypothesis that the topography of functional deficits may be related to some environmental factors, even in long-stay psychiatric institutions.

One of the limitations with many functional states rating scales developed for use with younger patients with schizophrenia is that they cover skills domains that are simply unavailable to patients residing in institutional care, such as transportation and cooking performance. In addition, many of the demands of these skills areas change with aging, as many people no longer drive and no longer perform many of their own maintenance activities as they age. As a result, the Mt. Sinai group developed the Social–Adaptive Functioning scale (SAFE; Harvey, Davidson, et al., 1997). This scale covers three different global skills domains, including social functioning, self-care, and disruptive behaviors. All items are designed for patients who are currently living in residential settings, including acute and chronic psychiatric hospitals, nursing homes, group homes, and medical hospitals. In the initial studies using this scale, patients living in chronic institutions were found to be more impaired than acutely admitted patients with a history of community residence in the levels of social and self-care skills deficits but not in the severity of behavioral disturbances. Nursing home patients were also more impaired than the acutely admitted patients in self-care and social functioning and were no more impaired than the patients residing in long-stay psychiatric care (Harvey et al., 1998). Similar results were obtained with different functional status rating scales by Bartels et al. (1997b), who compared community-dwelling patients to nursing home residents. In that study nursing home patients also had more severe deficits in functional domains such as self-care and social skills performance.

One recent development is the use of performance-based measures for assessment of older patients with schizophrenia. As described earlier, Klapow et al. (1997) adapted a performance-based scale developed for Alzheimer's disease, the Direct Assessment of Functional Status (DAFS; Loewenstein et al., 1989). This scale examines financial management, communication skills, menu planning, and other adaptive skills. Older patients with schizophrenia were impaired in each functional skills domain compared to healthy comparison participants. A larger-scale study (Patterson et al., 1997) found that older patients with schizophrenia had more impairment than patients with affective disorders but less functional impairment than patients with AD in social functioning and self-care.

In a more recent development, Patterson and colleagues have created schizophrenia-relevant performance-based assessment measures for self-care and social functioning. In the self-care domain, the UCSD Performance Based Skills Assessment (UPSA; Patterson, Goldman, McKibbin, Hughs, & Jeste, 2001) examines finances, organizational skills, transportation, and other related skills areas. Older outpatients with schizophrenia were found to be impaired in each domain relative to healthy comparison participants in the studies of the development of the scale. The Social Skills Performance Assessment (SSPA; Patterson, Moscona, McKibbin, Davidson, & Jeste, 2001) requires individuals to participate in two role-play interactions that are scored for interest/disinterest, fluency, clarity, focus, affect, grooming, overall conversation, and social appropriateness. Total scores on the SSPA clearly discriminated healthy individuals and patients with schizophrenia. Furthermore, both of these measures had high test–retest reliability, suggesting that scores should be stable over time and useful as outcome measures in treatment studies.

In conclusion, functional deficits are identifiable even in older patients who have lived their whole lives in the community, when they are compared to healthy controls. Within patients with schizophrenia, functional deficits are more severe in patients with a lifetime history of chronic institutional stay. Patients residing in nursing homes are not more functionally impaired than those who live in chronic psychiatric hospitals, leading to the suggestion that functional deficits are not the likely reason for nursing home referral in patients with schizophrenia.

DETERMINANTS OF FUNCTIONAL DEFICITS IN OLDER PATIENTS

As described earlier, cognitive impairments appear to be the major determinant of functional deficits in older patients with schizophrenia. Because research on schizophrenia in late life has largely developed after the time that it became widely known that cognition and function were intrinsically related, most of the research on functional status in older patients has been informed by these findings and has considered the determinants as well as the characteristics of functional limitations.

Studies of performance-based measures of functional deficits in older patients have consistently found that cognitive deficits are more strongly correlated with functional performance than the severity of positive symptoms. Klapow et al. (1997) reported that lower scores on the MMSE predicted impairments in functional skills performance on the DAFS, whereas Patterson et al. (2001) found that performance scores on the Dementia Rating Scale (DRS) predicted functional deficits on the UPSA. In both of these studies negative symptoms were not as strongly correlated as cognitive deficits with the severity of functional impairments. The ambulatory patients in those studies had lower positive and negative symptom severity than that seen in previous studies of institutionalized patients, so reduced symptom severity could be argued to have influenced the results. This concern is obviated by the fact that the severity of positive symptoms was found to be uncorrelated with measures of functional status in severely impaired patients who were either institutionalized or nursing home residents (Harvey et al., 1998), and negative symptoms were found to be less strongly correlated with functional outcome than cognitive deficits across those patients who manifested all of these variations in lifetime-outcome status.

Comparative studies of patients who varied widely in their lifetime functional status have consistently found that patients who have been institutionalized had more severe cognitive and negative symptoms than patients with a history of community residence, with essentially no differences in positive symptoms (Auslander et al., 2001; Harvey et al., 1998). In several studies using different samples of older patients who varied in their levels of lifetime adaptive functioning, cognitive impairments appeared to be consistently related to functional deficits. For instance, Harvey, Sukhodolsky, Parrella, White, and Davidson (1997) found that deficits in verbal skills, episodic memory, and constructional–executive skills in chronically institutionalized patients predicted both self-care and social functions, although they did not predict the severity of deficits in impulse control or other disruptive behaviors. Similar results were obtained by Kurtz et al. (2001), who examined similar samples of chronically institutionalized patients and also found that self-care deficits, but not deficits in impulse control, were predicted by cognitive impairments. The latter were assessed with a similar battery. Harvey et al. (1998) found that cognitive deficits were stronger predictors than negative symptoms of both social and self-care deficits in patients who varied widely in their lifetime functional outcome, with these correlations being similar regardless of lifetime levels of global functional deficit. Similar results were found in a comparative study of chronic patients who received treatment in state hospitals and in VA hospitals (Harvey, Jacobsen, et al., 2000). The VA patients, most likely because of their history of better premorbid functioning and later age of onset, were found to have notably reduced severity of cognitive and functional deficits compared to the state hospital patients. At the same time, the predictors of functional deficits were the same in the two groups. Cognitive deficits were the best predictors of functional deficits, more so than any other aspect of symptomatology, and the magnitude of the correlations was essentially the same.

THE COURSE OF FUNCTIONAL DEFICITS
IN OLDER PATIENTS

As seen from this review of the literature, the older patients with schizophrenia who have the worst functional deficits in cross-sectional studies are those with a lifetime history of chronic institutional care. It is, therefore, possible that these patients have a lifetime history of substantial adaptive deficits that are essentially unchanged over their lifetimes. There are few longitudinal studies of functional skills in older patients, and no studies that included performance-based measures. One study (Harvey, Parrella, et al., 1999) of patients who were referred from chronic institutional care to a nursing home found that there was a deterioration in functional skills, measured by the SAFE scale, over a 2.5 year follow-up period. Patients who deteriorated in the SAFE scale scores also had reductions in their MMSE scores but had no changes in their symptom status. Although these two declines were significantly correlated with each other, the design of this study does not make it possible to determine if changes in MMSE scores preceded declines in adaptive functioning.

Finding that patients who were sent to a nursing home deteriorated in their functional status also raises the question of whether these patients had other factors that were interfering with their functional status, such as changes in their medical status. A recent study (Friedman et al., 2002) examined 124 older patients with schizophrenia over a 48-month follow-up period that included three assessments. In addition to the assessment of functional skills, cognitive deficits, and clinical symptoms, medical status was examined at each assessment. Forty-three different medical conditions and their treatments were evaluated, and baseline and change scores in all of these different domains were examined. Functional status was found to decline over the follow-up period, as did cognitive functioning and health status. In contrast, clinical symptoms were stable over the follow-up period. Changes in medical status were found not to be antecedents of functional or cognitive changes. In contrast, changes in cognitive functioning during the first follow-up period predicted deterioration in adaptive functioning in the subsequent follow-up period. This finding is similar to previous findings in the study of AD, where changes in functional abilities follow from cognitive deterioration. In contrast to the idea that cognitive and functional change is a consequence of increased medical burden and increasing frailty (Cohen & Talavera, 2001), cognitive and functional deficits were found to be antecedents of later increases in medical morbidities. Although this may seem paradoxical and is not likely to be true for the schizophrenia population as a whole (for similar findings, see Auslander et al., 2001, in higher functioning patients), the literature on geriatric medicine has shown clearly that preexisting cognitive limitations lengthen recovery time from a variety of illnesses and injuries experienced in later life (Greene & Ondrich, 1990).

CONCLUSION

The data reviewed in this chapter lead to several conclusions about cognitive and functional status in late-life schizophrenia. First, cognitive and functional deficits have the same general dimensional structure as in younger patients, and the patterns of relationships between these dimensions of the condition are similar. As in younger patients, cognitive deficits predict functional limitations, whereas negative symptoms are less substantial predictors.

There are areas of controversy as well. Most prominently, there are inconsistent findings regarding whether cognitive and functional deficits worsen in late life. Data suggesting decline have mostly involved patients with a chronic course of institutionalization, currently living either in nursing homes or in chronic hospitals. Only patients over the age of 65 have evidence of decline, even in chronic samples. Patients with less evidence of decline are typically younger and have experienced a better lifetime course of illness, with no evidence of chronic institutional stays.

It is clear that these declines are not a result in most cases to obvious alternative factors, such as the presence of degenerative conditions or the increasing medical comorbidities that are often the inevitable consequences of aging. Considerable current research is focusing on this topic, which has major public policy and treatment implications, as addressed in the next few chapters.

5

SCHIZOPHRENIA IN LATE LIFE

There are many features of schizophrenia not included as a formal component of the diagnostic criteria that are substantial parts of the illness. Most of these features are not direct products of the clinical symptoms of psychosis and negative symptoms, which means that they are important features of illness in their own right. These features include awareness of illness, affective symptoms (anxiety and depression not meeting full criteria for a *DSM–IV* [American Psychiatric Association, 1994] diagnosis) and aggressive and belligerent behavior. Schizophrenia also directly affects medical status and life expectancy, which are important public health issues. Finally, differences in the presentation of schizophrenia as a function of gender have been extensively studied in younger patients with schizophrenia, with several studies of older patients recently completed.

This chapter reviews the prevalence and correlates of these other features of schizophrenia, focusing on their characteristics and severity when compared to younger patients. These features of the illness are important from the patients' perspective and may be equal in importance to classical symptoms, cognitive deficits, or functional impairments. Evaluating and treating these aspects of the illness is important to improve the quality of life of older patients with schizophrenia.

DEPRESSION AND ANXIETY SYMPTOMS IN LATER LIFE

Although the presence of severe depressive symptoms in patients with schizophrenia leads to some question about the diagnosis (according to the *DSM–IV* criteria at least), there is no question that depression is both prevalent and prominent in schizophrenia. Despite the centrality of affective blunting in all major conceptions of the illness (e.g., Bleuler, 1911; Kraepelin, 1919), it has been well-understood that depressive symptoms, varying in their severity, occur in many patients

Depression often occurs at the time of the first episode in schizophrenia (Koreen et al., 1993) and is often most severe after partial remission of psychotic symptoms. The phenomenon, called *post-psychotic depression* (Siris, Harmon, & Endicott, 1981), is potentially responsible for much of the mortality in schizophrenia early in the course of illness (Siris, 2001). Longitudinal studies of the life course in schizophrenia have suggested that as many as 40% of patients meet criteria for major depression at any given time (Sands & Harrow, 1999), suggesting that the prevalence of major depression is higher in schizophrenia than in the general population. As a consequence, depression in schizophrenia may be responsible for much of the mortality associated with the condition. Depression is commonly predicted by high levels of awareness of illness (ordinarily considered a good sign) and more severe psychotic symptoms during an episode. It is often seen to be a response to the realization that one is experiencing a serious psychotic illness that has a marked impact on lifetime functional outcome.

Depression increases with aging in the general population, and it might be expected that this would happen in schizophrenia as well. At the same time, if depression early in the course of schizophrenia is a marked risk factor for mortality as a result of suicide, is it possible that the population of late-life patients with schizophrenia would include mostly individuals with a lower risk for depression, possibly as a result of earlier mortality of those who are maximally predisposed?

Research on depressive symptoms in schizophrenia suggests that depression is common in older patients with schizophrenia and that depressive symptoms are not markedly different in presentation from those seen earlier in life. For example, a study by Zisook et al. (1999) involved a highly systematic evaluation of the presence of depression in older ambulatory patients with schizophrenia, performing structured ratings of the severity of depression and examining the correlation between the severity of depression and other features of the illness. It was found that depression scores were higher in schizophrenic patients than in a matched sample of healthy controls and that 20% of female patients with schizophrenia had a Hamilton Depression Rating scale (Hamilton, 1960) score in the clinically depressed range. The best predictor of increased depressive symptoms was more severe psychotic symptoms, with age, negative symptoms, and antipsychotic dosage not correlated with severity of depressive symptoms. These data are consistent with findings regarding postpsychotic depression and suggest that, in older patients as well as younger patients, more severe psychosis is associated with greater risk for the experience of depression. Increased side effects of pharmacological treatment did not predict depression, suggesting that subjective quality of life (as described later) is more responsive to the severity of these side effects than is depression.

Other data on depression in late-life schizophrenia have suggested that this symptom dimension is important and a possible target for intervention. In factor analytical studies of the dimensions of symptoms in institutionalized older patients with schizophrenia, depression and anxiety are commonly found to load on a single dimension that was independent from aggression, negative symptoms, and disorganization (White et al., 1994). Furthermore, these correlations are essentially the same as in younger patients (White, Parrella, et al., 1997) and suggest that the characteristics of depression may be relatively constant over the life span.

One the important feature of depression in late-life schizophrenia is that many of the factors that are associated with decreased subjective quality of life are not associated with depression. For instance, although more severe positive symptoms are reported to be associated with both reduced quality of life and increased depressive symptoms, across several studies depression was not associated with negative symptoms, medication side effects, or more restrictive residential status (e.g., Davidson et al., 1995). Although it might appear that it would be "very depressing" to live in a chronic psychiatric hospital, a nursing home, or a full-care residence, compared with independent living, the data suggest that depression is not a consistent consequence of this lifetime functional outcome.

It is equally possible that the factors that predispose an individual to be chronically institutionalized may also relate to reduced liability to develop depression. As noted, younger patients who develop depression are more cognitively intact and more insightful than those who do not. The research on correlates of chronic institutionalization and high levels of care, reviewed in detail later, clearly suggests that the profile of risk for depression in young patients is inconsistent with the correlates of chronic institutionalization. Thus, development of depression may require intactness of a set of cognitive capabilities where many institutionalized patients with schizophrenia have severe impairments.

Depression in older patients with schizophrenia appears to be common and similar in its characteristics to that seen in younger patients with schizophrenia. Severity of depression appears most strongly determined by the severity of concurrent psychotic symptoms, similar to findings with younger patients. Although younger patients with schizophrenia experience an increased suicide risk associated with their symptoms of depression, there is not yet enough data to reach this conclusion for older patients. Symptoms of depression do not seem to be associated with current residential status, despite the finding that more restrictive residences are associated with reductions in quality of life. It is possible, at least hypothetically, that the selection factors that lead patients to live in more restricted environments actually reduce their risk for development of depression. Major cognitive limitations characterize these patients; possibly they lack the requisite cognitive capacity to fully appreciate their situation and then to develop depressive symptoms in these situations.

AWARENESS OF ILLNESS

This is a feature of schizophrenia that has received much attention in younger patients (Amador, Strauss, Yale, & Gorman, 1991). Described for decades, "insight into illness" or "unawareness of illness" refers to the common finding that many patients with schizophrenia have essentially no awareness that they are having experiences that are uncommon or implausible. Patients appear to act as if hallucinatory experiences are clearly real and that their delusions are factual. Furthermore, they also appear to be unaware of other changes in their behavior and experiences, such as failing to notice major alterations in their affective experience and impairments in their communications skills. As a result, lack of awareness pervades all other aspects of symptoms in schizophrenia.

Numerous studies have examined the prevalence and correlates of this phenomenon. It is quite possible that lack of insight is the most commonly experienced symptom of the illness, rated as present in more than 90% of large samples of patients (World Health Organization, 1972). Most research has suggested that patients who manifest lack of illness also have evidence of cognitive impairments in domains such as executive functioning and memory performance (Young, Davila, & Scher, 1993). Thus, the inability to carefully evaluate experiences for their plausibility and to integrate information from others into opinions and self-evaluations is correlated with impairments in performance on cognitive tests that measure cognitive organization and memory functions.

To date there have been only two formal studies of the prevalence or correlates of insight phenomena in older patients with schizophrenia. In one study (Howard, Castle, Wessely, & Murray, 1993) the authors examined late-onset patients who may have been different in some ways from early onset older patients. This study found no difference in the prevalence of lack of insight in early and late-onset patients. Because lack of insight is common in early adult-onset schizophrenia, these data suggest that this feature does not correlate with onset age. Similarly, other data (Almeida, Levy, Howard, & David, 1996) suggest that lack of insight is common in late-onset patients. Given the continuity of other clinical symptoms into later life, it is not surprising that this phenomenon persists in older patients with young-adult onset. Likewise, as noted before, the types of cognitive deficits that are reported to correlate with lack of insight are clearly persistent into later life. Treatment compliance on the part of older patients is also marginal, consistent with the behavior of younger patients. As a result, when formal studies of the lack of insight phenomenon are completed, it would clearly be expected that older patients would appear similar to younger patients.

AGGRESSIVENESS AND BELLIGERENCE

One of the major points of controversy in the study of schizophrenia is that of the risk of dangerous and aggressive behavior. There have been multiple high-profile aggressive acts performed by individuals with schizophrenia, which often serves to raise public concern about safety of the community and the risk that patients with schizophrenia will become unpredictably violent. Despite occasional episodes of unpredictable violence and the strange and upsetting behavior shown by some patients with schizophrenia, it has proven difficult to estimate the prevalence, severity, and antecedents of aggressive behavior in community-dwelling patients with schizophrenia.

Selective reporting of violent behaviors by patients with schizophrenia may be a factor that influences the impression of the prevalence of aggressive behavior. In addition, if a common precipitant for admission to acute psychiatric care is aggression, dangerousness, or impulsivity, studies of newly admitted patients will find a high prevalence of aggressive behavior (Fux, Weiss, & Elhadad, 1995). A major determinant of aggressive behavior in schizophrenia may be substance abuse (Soyka, 2000; Steinert, Wiebe, & Gebhardt, 1999). As the prevalence of substance abuse has been found to be increasing in schizophrenia, some have argued that aggressive incidents have increased in their prevalence as well (Swanson, Holzer, Ganju, & Jono, 1990). Other potential determinants of aggressive behavior have included neurological impairments (Krakowski & Czobor, 1994) and living in crowded settings in inpatient care (Dietz & Rador, 1982).

One of the important issues in the consideration of violence in schizophrenia is the target of the behavior. It is possible that much of the violence that occurs on the part of patients with schizophrenia is directed at individuals who choose not to report it, such as relatives who are functioning as caregivers. A major reduction in length of acute hospital stay has occurred in schizophrenia in the past two decades. Regardless of the reason, whether it is managed care, cuts in Medicare reimbursement, or improvements in treatment delivery, the average length of stay for acute admissions of individuals with schizophrenia has been reduced markedly since the 1980s. One of the areas in which there has been a marked impact of reduced length of stay is the comprehensiveness of discharge planning. A 7-day admission provides no time for searching for a community residence, and many patients are referred either to relatives or to public shelter facilities.

There has been a substantial increase in the likelihood that the residential plan for a newly discharged patient with schizophrenia will be living with a relative, with as many as 60% of adult patients discharged to the care of their relatives. Thus, these relatives are potentially confronted with the consequences of partially treated delusions or hallucinations that may involve the patient feeling threatened and feeling the need to take action. As a result, violence against relatives is probably quite common and is also likely to be underreported (Estroff, Swanson, Lachicotte, Swartz, & Bolduc, 1998).

A recent study indicated that approximately 25% of acutely admitted younger patients with schizophrenia had an episode of physical aggression in the 3 weeks immediately preceding their admission to inpatient care (Arango, Barba, González-Salvador, & Ordóñez, 1999). In a study of older patients with schizophrenia, it was reported that 27% of both nursing home and state hospital patients had an episode of severe verbal aggression in the past month, and 12% had an episode of severe physical aggression (Bowie et al., 2001). Thus, the prevalence of physical aggression in older patients was only about half of that seen in younger patients. At the same time, the prevalence of verbal aggression was consistent with the rate of physical aggression in younger patients. This shift in the behavioral topography of aggression may be systematic and related to aging. The average age of the nursing home patients studied by Bowie et al. (2001) was 81. Their advanced age may have reduced their ability to engage in physically violent acts, with their aggressive tendencies shifted in the direction of verbal expression of their violent impulses. The rate of verbal aggressive behavior on the part of these nursing home patients with schizophrenia is consistent with the rate of agitated behavior shown by nursing home patients with a diagnosis of Alzheimer's disease (Marin et al., 1997). Thus, these data suggest that it is important to determine how much environmental factors, such as the presence of other aggressive patients providing models for aggression, are responsible for these prevalence figures.

AGGRESSION AND INSTITUTIONALIZATION:
THE DIFFICULT-TO-DISCHARGE PATIENT

Hundreds of thousands of psychiatric patients have been discharged from long-term psychiatric care since the deinstitutionalization movement began in the early 1960s. Yet, there are still a relatively large number of patients, most of them elderly, who are still residents of long-term care. There are some data available that suggest that there are systematic reasons why certain patients remain in long-term psychiatric hospitals while most of the residents of these institutions have long since been sent to live in the community or in nursing homes.

In a large-scale prospective study, White, Parrella, et al. (1997) followed a sample of more than 800 long-stay geriatric psychiatric inpatients, most with diagnoses of schizophrenia, for 4 years during a period when the administration of the institution had received a mandate to markedly reduce their census. All patients had received a comprehensive cognitive, functional, clinical, and medical status evaluation at the outset of the study period, and the characteristics of the patients were related naturalistically to the outcomes of the patients during the follow-up period. Outcomes included remaining in the hospital, being discharged to either a nursing home or to a community residence, or dying before discharge. There were no differences in the severity of positive or negative symptoms across these different outcomes. Patients who were discharged, either to a nursing home or community residence, or those who stayed in the hospital also did not differ overall in their cognitive functioning. Patients who died were more likely to have both more severe cognitive deficits and more severe medical conditions at the time of the initial assessment. Among patients who were discharged, patients with more severe negative symptoms, greater functional limitations, and more cognitive impairments were more likely to be sent to a nursing home. The only factor that discriminated patients who stayed in the hospital from those were discharged, regardless of placement out of the hospital, were the occurrence of more frequent aggressive episodes and higher ratings on a clinical measure of hostility in the patients who stayed behind. As a result, aggression was the factor that led to retention in chronic psychiatric care, not classical symptoms of the illness or cognitive or functional status.

Similar results were obtained in a study that was performed in the United Kingdom. In that study, the Team for Assessment of Psychiatric Services (TAPS) project, older patients with schizophrenia were scheduled for discharge from chronic psychiatric hospitals, and their adjustment was monitored after their referral to community care. Discharges were clinically determined with the goal of discharging all patients from the hospital over a 5-year period. Patients who proved the most difficult to discharge had a similar profile to that seen in the White et al. study. Behavioral problems, specifically unpredictable belligerence, were the major factors that interfered with the patients' discharges (Trieman & Leff, 1996). These difficult-to-discharge patients tended to have more substantial stays in the hospital before the hospital clinical staff was willing to send them to the community; some could not be discharged at all.

Across the life span in schizophrenia, aggressive and dangerous behaviors are major sources of adjustment problems. In fact, aggressiveness appears to be a major factor that predicts risk for acute psychiatric admissions (Fux, Weiss, & Elhadad, 1995), length of acute stay (Greenfield, McNiel, & Binder, 1989), and difficulty in discharge from chronic psychiatric care (Trieman & Leff, 1996; White, Parrella, et al., 1997). Although there are few data on the factors that that predict acute psychiatric admissions in older patients, it is quite likely, given the continuity of other symptoms from younger to older patients with the illness, that this is a major factor predicting inpatient admissions of community-dwelling patients. Aggressiveness is a major determinant of inpatient admissions for patients with dementia (Cohen-Mansfield & Werner, 1998), so there are several lines of evidence suggesting that aggressiveness is the factor that results in inpatient psychiatric admissions for many patients with schizophrenia.

SUBSTANCE ABUSE

For years it was argued that schizophrenic patients were unlikely to have substantial substance abuse problems, because their tendencies toward anhedonia reduced their motivation to abuse mood-altering substances. Recently, it has been acknowledged that substance abuse had reached epidemic proportions in patients with schizophrenia, with as many as 50% of patients abusing at least one substance (Mueser et al., 2000). In contrast, the rate of substance abuse in the American population as a whole is estimated at about 10%, meaning that schizophrenic patients are about five times as likely to be a substance abuser as nonschizophrenic individuals.

Studies of substance abuse in older patients with schizophrenia are lacking at this time. Some of the research on schizophrenia and aging has focused on patients with a lifetime history of chronic psychiatric care and institutional stays, and these patients have had little opportunity over the course of their lifetimes to abuse substances. Because much of the research on older ambulatory patients has focused on nonabusers, it is not possible to reliably determine the prevalence and correlates of substance abuse in these studies. As substance abuse appears to have an increased adverse impact on cognitive functioning of schizophrenic patients who are over the age of 50, the potential of adverse effects of substance abuse in even older patients is quite substantial. This issue will also become more important as the last few long-stay institutionalized patients are referred to the community as well. Many of these patients have had no opportunity to abuse substances, and it is unclear what the results of the sudden emergence of these opportunities, facilitated by discharge from long-stay hospitals, will have.

QUALITY OF LIFE

Quality of life is a critical concept regarding the subjective impression of an individual of how pleasurable and meaningful his or her life is. Under the umbrella of this concept are included such issues as the frequency and quality of social contacts, the subjective meaningfulness of daily activities, the quality of residence, and financial security (Heinrichs, Hanlon, & Carpenter, 1984). One of the major areas of reduced quality of life in schizophrenia is reduction in social contacts. Schizophrenic patients have reduced social networks and are more likely to have much more extensive contact with family members and treatment professionals than with friends. Many more patients with schizophrenia than patients with depression are likely to report that they have either no friends or have no social contact (Graham, Arthur, & Howard, 2002). In addition, reduced awareness of illness, described earlier, has been shown to correlate with inconsistent ratings of subjective quality of life (Doyle et al., 1999).

A variety of different studies of younger patients with schizophrenia has demonstrated consistent reductions in quality of life in social and other functional domains. For instance, in the first systematic studies with contemporary diagnostic criteria, Carpenter and colleagues developed the Heinrichs–Carpenter Quality of Life Scale (QOL; Heinrichs et al., 1984) and examined schizophrenic patients with the scale. Patients with the deficit syndrome had consistently lower scores on the scale, implicating a correlation between persistent negative symptoms and reduced quality of life. These findings are not a result of the differences in overall severity of illness, because some of the studies finding an association between deficit schizophrenia and reduced subjective quality of life found that quality of life differences were greater than differences in positive or disorganized symptoms.

Multiple later studies have identified other predictors of reduced subjective quality of life. Impaired scores on measures of cognitive functions predict reduced subjective quality of life (Brekke, Kohrt, & Green, 2001). Persistent anxiety, depression, and positive symptoms are also associated with reduced subjective quality of life (Huppert, Weiss, Lim, Pratt, & Smith, 2001). Medication side effects are also a principal predictor, because patients who experience more severe extrapyramidal symptoms have lower quality of life, and patients who are treated with medications with fewer side effects have increased subjective quality of life (Revicki, Genduso, Hamilton, Ganoczy, & Beasley, 1999). Finally, residential status is also associated with subjective quality of life. Patients who are discharged to the community from chronic psychiatric hospitals report an improved subjective quality of life (Trieman et al., 1996). Although this could be viewed as a simple consequence of treatment response, studies in which patients were referred to the community after extended institutional stays have found the same results as when patients are referred after much shorter inpatient treatments.

There are several studies that have examined both global and specific aspects of quality of life, as well as the predictors of these scores. Using a scale designed to assess quality of life in medically ill patients, the Quality of Well-Being Scale (QWB; Patterson et al., 1996) examined a sample of older patients with schizophrenia who were living in the community. These patients reported several aspects of reduced quality of life, and their severity scores were consistent with those previously seen in patients who were diagnosed with AIDS. The best correlate of QWB was the severity of psychotic symptoms, which was more strongly associated with QWB scores than ratings of tardive dyskinesia.

In a follow-up study (Patterson et al., 1997), multiple additional measures were collected, including frequency of stressful life events, satisfaction with emotional support, coping responses, positive and negative symptoms, depressive symptoms, social adjustment, and a general quality of well-being (QWB) score. Path analyses indicated that self-reported social adjustment, coping, and emotional support were direct consequences of positive and negative symptoms, as were stressful life events. Furthermore, symptoms of depression fully accounted for the effects of symptoms on self-reported social problems, but not the effects of symptoms on self-reported well-being (SWB). As a consequence, these results suggested that psychiatric symptoms were primary predictors of self-reported well-being and that other behavioral deficits were mediated by depression. In this study, however, there was no comparison across treatments received or differences in residential status and no evaluation of cognitive functioning.

Using a performance-based measure of social functioning, the Social Skills Performance Assessment (SSPA; Patterson, Moscona, et al., 2001), it was found that QWB scores could be predicted from performance scores on the SSPA. SSPA scores were correlated with the severity of negative and cognitive symptoms as well as with directly observed performance on activities of daily living but not with self-reported social functioning. These data indicate that there may be substantial limitations in self-reported social functioning in older schizophrenic patients and that objective indicators of QOL may be important to consider when assessing and treating this population.

Two additional studies (Auslander et al., 2001; Kasckow et al., 2001) examined the effects of current residential status on QWB scores. These two studies each evaluated important subpopulations of older patients with schizophrenia: institutionalized patients, patients residing in full-care community residences, and individuals living on a generally independent basis. In the study comparing institutionalized and community-dwelling patients (Kasckow et al., 2001), substantial differences in SWB scores were found, with institutionalized patients reporting lower QWB. Similar predictors of QWB scores were detected, however, in that severity of positive symptoms predicted QWB scores at both baseline and 6-month follow-up periods. QWB scores were stable over 6 months for the patients who remained hospitalized over this time period, and baseline cognitive and positive symptom scores predicted 6-month follow-up scores. Thus, although reduced QWB scores were found in institutionalized patients, this might be a result their greater level of positive and cognitive symptoms.

When patients living independently were compared with those residing in assisted living (Auslander et al., 2001), relatively similar findings were produced. More severe cognitive and negative symptoms were found in patients residing in assisted living, whereas these same patients had reduced QWB as well. Assisted living patients had additional risk factors for poor outcome, including earlier age at onset, evidence of lifelong social impairments (e.g., reduced rate of marriage and children), and more consistent symptoms of illness over the lifetime. Again, cognitive impairment was found to be the best predictor of reduced QWB.

In a study conducted by a different research group (Cohen & Talavera, 2001), a sample of community-dwelling older patients with schizophrenia was comprehensively examined for their functional status, quality of life (QoL), and for the potential predictors of functional impairments and QoL. Reductions in subjective QoL were greatest in patients with functional impairments, and the best predictors of those functional impairments were abnormal movements, taking anti-Parkinson's medication, and greater negative symptom severity. In addition, medical problems and depression also adversely affected quality of life scores. Although cognitive impairments were not found to correlate with functional adjustment or quality of life, the cognitive assessment performed was different from those used in previous studies of quality of life.

Across all of the studies on quality of life in older patients with schizophrenia, a consistent profile of the determinants of reduced quality of life has been detected. This includes residing in environments associated with higher levels of care, more severe cognitive and negative symptoms, and medication side effects. Although some caution must be used when interpreting the results of studies that relied exclusively on self-reports of older patients, subjective impressions of the patients may well be correlated with their emotional experiences. Depression also appears to be a consistent predictor, although the results of Cohen and Talavera (2001) suggest that depression may be a consequence of functional limitations and that it is a second-order predictor rather than a direct cause of reduced quality of life.

There are still some unresolved issues in quality of life in late-life schizophrenia, the resolution of which might improve the chances of treating reduced quality of life. It is unclear, for example, whether the reduction in quality of life seen in older patients living in chronic institutional care and in full-care community residences is a consequence of the environmental factors in these residences or if it is a consequence of the factors that lead patients to live in these environments. The severe positive and negative symptoms and cognitive deficits that are associated with reduced quality of life also predict residential status. Some studies do suggest that discharge from long-stay psychiatric care is associated with an improvement with quality of life, even if the discharges have nothing to do with current cognitive or symptom status (Trieman & Leff, 1996). Thus, there appears to be a mix of environmental and individual-differences factors that predict reductions in quality of life.

In the interim, it appears that interventions that reduce negative symptoms, depression, medication side effects, and cognitive deficits would be the surest path to improved quality of life in older patients with schizophrenia. Depression and medication side effects are clearly more treatable with current interventions than negative symptoms and cognitive deficits. At the same time, newer treatments, including both pharmacological and behavioral interventions, have the potential to improve these domains of the illness as well. Although discharge from long-term psychiatric care or other reductions in levels of care received may well improve quality of life, the fact that many long-stay patients have aggressive tendencies that make their discharge a potential danger to the community and to themselves may preclude this as a suggested intervention.

MORTALITY AND MORBIDITY

Schizophrenia is associated with reduced life expectancy. Some data have suggested that life expectancy is approximately 20% less than the general population (Hannerz, Borga, & Borritz, 2001), with suicide risk increased 20-fold (Newman & Bland, 1991). As many as 15% of individuals with schizophrenia commit suicide, with the classical risk factors including male gender, early in the course, occurrence of partial recovery, and higher educational status (Baxter & Appleby, 1999). A recent study (Schwartz & Cohen, 2001) found that for female patients, depressive symptoms were a potent predictor of suicidal ideation but not necessarily completed suicide.

Suicide is almost as common in schizophrenia as in major depression and may be slightly more difficult to predict. More patients with schizophrenia are killed in accidents than in the healthy population, and the risk of overall violent death is about 25 times the population average (Osby, Correia, Brandt, Ekbom, & Sparen, 2000). Violent deaths, including homicides and fatal accidents, are much more common in schizophrenia than in the general population (Hiroeh, Appleby, Mortensen, & Dunn, 2001). In that study, the only psychiatric diagnoses associated with greater death rates were substance abusers: drug abusers had a higher rate of suicide and alcohol abusers a higher rate of violent deaths than individuals with schizophrenia. Patients who have recently been discharged from long-stay psychiatric hospitals have a rate of successful suicide that is double that seen in terms of suicide attempts in the hospital (Munk-Jorgenson, 1999). In contrast to the idea that institutional care is uniformly bad, potentially premature discharge is associated with increased mortality from suicide immediately after leaving the hospital.

Other causes of premature death include cardiac and pulmonary problems, as well as diabetes (Brown, Inskip, & Barraclough, 2000). Patients with schizophrenia have several illnesses that are more common than in the general population, with some of these illnesses associated with lifestyle factors (Goldman, 1999). Diabetes is more common in schizophrenia than in the general population and may be exacerbated by certain treatments for the illness (Haupt & Newcomer, 2001). As many as 85% of schizophrenic patients in the United States smoke, and this rate of smoking exceeds the population rate fourfold. Mortality associated with complications of cigarette smoking is a primary cause of death in schizophrenia (Joukamaa et al., 2001). Schizophrenic patients do not develop cigarette habits after the progression of their illness; more than 70% smoke at the time of their first psychotic episode. As a result, most are exposed to a lifetime of smoking at the level of a pack or more per day for many years, and many nonsmoking institutionalized patients have been exposed to second-hand smoke for decades.

One of the potentially complicating factors for evaluating excess mortality in schizophrenia is that of the quality and quantity of health care that patients receive. Schizophrenia is associated with significant financial compromise (Ho, Andreasen, Flaum, Nopoulous, & Miller, 2000) and few individuals with the illness have adequate commercial insurance. As a result, the care that they receive does not include preventative medicine. In addition, they are much more likely to receive care at public hospitals than at teaching hospitals. Some research has indicated that substandard medical care, excluding psychiatric services, is associated with increased mortality. In a large-scale study of quality of medical care (Druss, Bradford, Rosenheck, Radford, & Krumholz, 2001), more than 88,000 Medicare patients were examined for mortality. Several indicators of quality medical care were examined for their administration in patients, including those with a psychiatric illness history, largely schizophrenia. Patients with schizophrenia had a 34% increase in 1-year mortality relative to nonpsychiatric cases. When adjustments were performed for indicators of quality of care, reperfusion, aspirin, beta-blockers, angiotensin-converting enzyme inhibitors, and smoking cessation counseling, the mortality disadvantage for patients with schizophrenia was eliminated. These data suggest that patients with schizophrenia are not offered basic but state of the art medical interventions and the reason for excess mortality may be associated with poor access to what would be considered basic health care for elderly adults. In addition, although some of these factors are associated with increased cost (reperfusion, ACE inhibitors), some of the other medications, such as aspirin, have essentially no acquisition cost, and others (beta blockers) are available as generic medications costing only a few cents per day.

Troubling questions are raised by these findings. Although it is easy—albeit discouraging—to see why certain systems of health care would not want to prescribe expensive treatments to older individuals with a lifetime of psychiatric illness and no way to pay for them (e.g., ACE inhibitors), the failure to use aspirin or to make a referral for smoking-reduction counseling is much harder to explain on a rational basis. It is not difficult to conclude that older patients with schizophrenia are simply not provided basic services, based on our current understanding of the medical and psychological means to reduce mortality in the population in general. These data suggest that the health and well-being of older patients with schizophrenia may not be as highly valued as that of individuals with a lifetime history of no psychiatric illness.

There are a few other studies of mortality in older patients with schizophrenia. Brown et al. (2000) found that much of the excess mortality of older schizophrenic outpatients was associated with the consequences of smoking. In their 13-year follow-up study, they reported that all-cause mortality was about double the healthy population's expected rates, with some of the rates considerably higher than that. Their suggestion was that smoking-cessation treatment had the potential to notably reduce mortality.

In research based on populations who were residents of long-stay institutions, several different findings emerged. Although not directly aimed at mortality, postmortem studies performed by the Mt. Sinai group on long-stay inpatients who died while residing at state psychiatric facilities offer some intriguing perspectives on mortality in older institutionalized patients. In the Mt. Sinai studies, older patients who died at a large extended-stay psychiatric facility received postmortem evaluations of their brains. In the largest of these studies, 100 consecutive postmortem assessments were performed. The average age at death was 76.5 years and the range was from

52 to 101. These patients had low levels of education (about 9 years) and came from low socioeconomic status homes. The average age at death is actually not that different from that expected from a child born in the United States in 2003. As a result, these patients did not die prematurely at all; in fact, on average they outlived their life expectancy. There are probably several reasons for this.

Selection Bias

Patients with schizophrenia who survive early years with increased suicide and risk for other violent deaths may be at low risk for the occurrence of these problems later in their lives. As noted earlier in the discussion of depression, some of the features that lead to chronic institutionalization may reduce risk for suicide. Similarly, patients who smoke for 40 years and do not develop complications may be low on the vulnerability dimension for these problems as well.

Supervision

Institutionalized patients may be more carefully monitored for suicidality than outpatients. The data cited earlier suggesting that suicide happens much more frequently after discharge than during chronic institutionalization supports this argument.

Medical Care

Regardless of the other limitations of institutional care since the 1970s, increased attention has been paid to medical care for chronically hospitalized patients. These patients are clearly more likely to receive annual physicals and thus receive appropriate treatment for their age-related physical illnesses (e.g., hypertension, diabetes) than outpatients with no physicians assigned to manage their care. Relevant to the point discussed earlier, medication compliance for antidiabetic and antihypertensive medications is likely to be much greater for inpatients who are consistently monitored for their medication compliance.

Smoking Restrictions

Although for years chronic state hospital units were filled with a haze of smoke, so were many offices and restaurants. In recent years, there has been an increased focus on restriction of smoking across most environments in the United States, the chronic psychiatric hospital included. Most modern hospitals only allow smoking outside, under restricted conditions and for limited amounts of time. Many older institutionalized patients are no longer allowed to smoke. Thus, despite their lifetime risk of smoking-related problems, those who survive until later life experience reduced risks because of involuntary discontinuation of their smoking.

GENDER DIFFERENCES

Using current diagnostic criteria, the gender ratio in patients with schizophrenia appears to be about 2 to 1 in favor of male gender (Castle & Murray, 1993). Current DSM criteria exclude patients with substantial affective components in their symptoms at the time of their first diagnosis, possibly influencing the relative prevalence of schizophrenia and affective disorders. There have been several studies of gender effects on symptoms in patients with schizophrenia, including two studies of older patients who varied widely in their lifetime functional outcome. The majority of studies suggest that males have an earlier age at first hospitalization (Goldstein, Tsuang, & Faraone, 1989; Hafner et al., 1989; Larsen, McGlashan, Johannessen, & Vibe-Hansen, 1996). Other research has suggested a general shift in onset age between male and female patients, with female patients being much more likely to have a later onset of symptoms regardless of when hospitalization first occurred. In a large-scale population-based prospective study, Castle and Murray (1993) examined the new-onset cases of schizophrenia in a London borough. They found that the average age of onset for males (31.2) was 10 years younger than that of females (41.1). The male–female ratio changed as a function of age of onset, with the ratio at 1.6 to 1 for onset from age 16 to 25 and .2 to 1 for onset age in late life. Age of onset differences may also be related to familial versus nonfamilial status. Albus and Maier (1995) found no difference in age at onset in familial cases of schizophrenia (38 male–male pairs, 29 female–female pairs, and 39 mixed gender pairs), finding an earlier age at onset for males only in nonfamilial cases.

Premorbid social functioning has also been found to be correlated with long-term outcome in males and females. Women tend to show better premorbid social functioning (Childers & Harding, 1990), and the social adjustment of male patients deteriorates at a faster rate after the development of the illness (Larsen et al., 1996). In a 3-year follow-up of first admission schizophrenic patients, females experienced fewer readmissions, shorter lengths of stay after readmission, and had longer tenure in the community without symptom exacerbation (Angermeyer, Goldstein, & Kuehn, 1989). Goldstein (1988) found similar results in a 10-year follow-up study, with women having fewer rehospitalizations and shorter lengths of stay if admitted.

Another critical area in schizophrenia-related gender differences is that of cognitive functioning. One study found that male schizophrenic patients had more impairment on neuropsychological tests of verbal learning and verbal fluency (Hoff, Riordan, O'Donnell, & DeLisi, 1991). Lewine, Haden, Caudle, and Shurett (1997) found an interaction of gender × onset age in neurocognitive impairment. In patients with an early onset, males were more impaired, whereas late-onset females had greater impairment. Thus, patients who had gender-typical age of onset were most cognitively impaired.

In older patients with a lifetime of good functional outcome, these typical gender differences were found (Andia et al., 1995). For instance, female patients had less substantial cognitive deficits and negative symptoms, although they did not differ from male patients in the severity of their psychotic symptoms. When poor outcome patients were studied, there were some discrepancies when the results were compared to the typical gender effects reported. Moriarty et al. (2001) examined 205 geriatric patients with lifelong poor outcome schizophrenia (43% male). These patients were examined for the severity of schizophrenic symptoms, cognitive impairments, and specific deficits in adaptive skills, as well as on demographic differences such as age at first psychiatric admission, premorbid education, and current treatment status. Previously reported gender differences were replicated in these patients with a uniformly poor functional outcome, with male patients having more severe negative symptoms and an earlier age of first psychiatric admission. No differences in cognitive functioning or specific functional deficits were found, however. These findings suggest that negative symptom severity is greater in male patients regardless of functional outcome and that the association of cognitive deficits with gender may only be found in patients with better lifetime functional outcome and no history of long-term institutional care.

An additional systematic study of the effects of gender on aging in schizophrenia was reported by Gur et al. (1996). When they compared younger and older patients with schizophrenia, negative symptoms were reduced across the life span in female patients, and there were tendencies for subtle reductions in symptoms with aging across the two genders. Thus, their findings were similar to those of Moriarty et al. (2001), suggesting that negative symptoms are associated with male gender across the age and overall outcome status of the patients.

The gender-related prevalence of schizophrenia in late life is apparently influenced by differences in survival between the genders. In three studies of entire populations of long-stay patients in three different psychiatric care systems (two in the United States and one in the United Kingdom), there were more female than male patients in residence. The gender ratio ranged from 57% to 70% female, despite the fact that the overall gender ratio for schizophrenia suggests that more males meet diagnostic criteria. This is unlikely to be an artifact of differential retention in the hospital, because difficult-to-discharge patients tend to be male. Thus, it seems likely that gender influences on survival also apply to elderly patients with chronic schizophrenia, as noted in the section on mortality.

CONCLUSION

There are many aspects of schizophrenia that are not part of the diagnostic criteria but are clearly of major importance in the illness. These features appear relatively consistent in their presentation in younger and older patients, in areas in which they have received research attention in older patients. Many of these aspects of the illness have not yet been the focus of a single systematic study.

Perhaps the most important unaddressed issue is that of substance abuse in older patients with schizophrenia. Many older patients with schizophrenia have been referred from treatment environments in which they had no opportunity to abuse substances to various less supervised community residences. These patients would appear to be vulnerable to substance abuse, given the high prevalence in younger patients, but there has been essentially no information collected on this topic in this population. Other aspects of the illness have been described to an extent, but there are still critical gaps in knowledge. For instance, there is no information on the consequences of or effective treatments for depression in older patients. Unawareness of illness has not been studied systematically and it is unknown if the correlates would be the same in older patients as in younger ones. Clearly, the additional features of schizophrenia in late life will be important targets for later research and treatment in the next decades.

6

LATE-ONSET SCHIZOPHRENIA

There are few aspects of schizophrenia in late life more controversial than the existence of late-onset schizophrenia. As one author noted, "Hardly any psychiatric disorder exists that has been described so inconsistently, defined in such an imprecise manner, and about which we have so little sound empirical knowledge as late onset schizophrenia" (Reichler-Rossler, 1999, p. 3). In fact, one of the chapters in that same book was titled, "I Don't Believe in Late-Onset Schizophrenia." The debate began around 100 years ago and is still going on, fueled by changes in the age of onset criteria for schizophrenia across various editions of the DSM and by epidemiological studies suggesting that some individuals meet the full criteria for schizophrenia and have their first symptoms over the age of 45. More confusion is produced by the fact that there are clearly many psychotic disorders that begin in late life, although they do not present with the full syndrome of schizophrenia and because many dementing conditions are associated with symptoms that would meet the A criteria for schizophrenia if they did not occur in conjunction with dementia.

This chapter describes the current thinking about schizophrenia with onset after age 45. The characteristics of patients who meet current DSM criteria for schizophrenia compared with patients of similar age with earlier onset is evaluated in this chapter. The characteristics of schizophrenia with late-life onset are described in terms of epidemiology, symptom severity, cognitive and functional characteristics, and treatment response. The issue of the validity of the concept of late-life schizophrenia is also evaluated in terms of comparison of the critical associated features of schizophrenia across early and late-onset cases. Similar conditions with late-life onset but not meeting criteria for schizophrenia are described and compared to these other two conditions. Finally, special issues in the assessment, study and treatment of this rarer population are examined.

As currently defined in the *DSM–IV* (American Psychiatric Association, 1994), schizophrenia can have onset at any age. As a result, any condition that meets the full criteria for schizophrenia should result in that diagnosis. In contrast, the *DSM–III* (American Psychiatric Association, 1980) required that schizophrenia have an onset age before age 45. The *DSM–IV* definition is in direct contrast to the Kraepelinian tradition (see chap. 1, this volume), in which a condition referred to as "paraphrenia" was diagnosed when there was a late-life onset of psychotic symptoms. Kraepelin (1919) believed that the critical features of paraphrenia were that affective expression and experience was not impaired and that there was no deteriorating course. As a result, the critical features of dementia praecox were lacking, but the presence of Bluelerian (Blueler, 1911) "accessory" symptoms was the central feature. Age of onset was not believed to be exclusively in the elderly population, in that Kraepelin believed that the onset age was later than dementia praecox (30 to 50 years of age or later), and the critical differences were associated with phenomenology associated with differences in onset age.

This concept has retained its life in Europe, where "late paraphrenia" still is a diagnostic concept, although it has been deleted from the latest editions of the official diagnostic manuals. According to current diagnostic systems in the United States, late-onset psychoses that do not meet criteria for schizophrenia should be diagnosed according to their characteristics. For instance, delusional disorder patients cannot have prominent hallucinations or bizarre behavior, thus differentiating them from individuals who meet the full set of criteria for schizophrenia with late onset. If a patient has a known degenerative condition, the diagnosis should be psychosis associated with the degenerative condition. It should also be considered that psychotic symptoms can occur without meeting the criteria for a specific diagnosis. As described later, studies of community samples of elderly individuals find elevations in paranoid ideation and hallucinations compared with estimates of the prevalences of these symptoms in younger individuals.

EPIDEMIOLOGY OF LATE-ONSET SCHIZOPHRENIA

It is difficult to determine, unless treatment records are available or reliable informants are used, the age of onset of symptoms in anyone with schizophrenia. This difficulty arises because of the common unawareness of the illness, which interferes with accurate reporting and also because of other memory impairments that render judgments about the timing of earlier events suspect. Aging compounds this problem of reliability of recall. As a result, the best estimates of the prevalence of newly diagnosed cases of schizophrenia will come from catchment-area studies that examine new admissions for psychotic disorders as a function of age. Although these studies are limited because they, by definition, miss all cases whose severity of illness is so mild that they never require treatment (e.g., elevating the false negative rate), they also have the benefit of a comprehensive diagnostic assessment that reduces the occurrence of false positive cases.

Several community-based studies have examined the prevalence of psychotic symptoms in elderly patients. In one study, Christensen and Blazer (1984) reported an incidence of paranoid delusions of approximately 4% of elderly individuals living in the community, whereas another study reported a prevalence of hallucinations of about 2% to 4% in older male community dwellers (Tien, 1991). It is interesting to note that only half of the participants in the Christensen and Blazer study had ever received mental health attention. Thus, the rate of occurrence of psychotic symptoms in elderly people living in the community is greater than the estimated lifetime prevalence of schizophrenia. As a consequence, caution is required in generating prevalence estimates for schizophrenia in later life, because there is a clear elevation in psychosis with advancing age.

Studies that examined the number of new psychiatric contacts in older patients have generated some interesting and challenging data. In a study examining data from the Camberwell case register, a registry of all cases receiving psychiatric services in an inner-city catchment area in London, Castle and Murray (1993) reported that 28% of patients had their first psychotic episode after age 44 and 12% had onset after age 64. More than half of all psychotic episodes over age 44 met criteria for schizophrenia, whereas approximately one third of those episodes before age 44 met criteria. They found that the average age of onset for males (31.2) was 10 years younger than that for females (41.1) and that the prevalence and associated characteristics of the illness did not differ markedly as a function of the breadth of the schizophrenia criteria that were used. The male–female ratio changed as a function of age of onset, with the ratio at 1.6 to 1 for onset from age 16 to 25 and .2 to 1 for onset age after 76. Patients with late onset were also much less likely to have a family history of schizophrenia, but some increase in familial prevalence of affective disorders was found in these patients. So, in this study, gender was an important predictor of onset age, and family history predicted onset age as well.

In a later study, Castle, Wessely, Howard, and Murray (1997) examined family history of early adult onset schizophrenia in relatives of patients who developed schizophrenia-like psychosis after 60. Starting with the schizophrenic or healthy index cases (probands), the psychiatric status of relatives was examined. This study has the strength of seeking out all relatives for assessment based on the identified status of probands. For relatives of both schizophrenic patients and of healthy controls, the morbid risk was the same. For narrow criteria, the risk for earlier onset schizophrenia was 1.3% for both cases and healthy controls, and for broader criteria, the difference in risk was only 0.1% between relatives of controls and relatives of patients in terms of risk for late-onset psychosis in relatives. The conclusion of these investigators was that late-onset psychotic conditions appeared genetically unrelated to earlier onset schizophrenia.

These findings are in marked contrast to risk rates for familial schizophrenia in individuals with an earlier age of onset. In a comparative review, Castle and Howard (1992) found that risk rates of schizophrenia in the relatives of early adult or adolescent onset schizophrenic index cases ranged from 4.4% to 19.4%, or 5 to 27 times the population base rate of approximately 0.7%. These data suggest that, from the perspective of population genetics, there are clear differences in relative risk rates for familial schizophrenia between earlier and later onset patients with schizophrenia. In addition, the high risk for affective disorders in relatives, reported to be as high as 16.3% in one study (Howard et al., 1997), raises questions about which group of conditions is actually the most common in relatives of individuals with late-onset schizophrenia.

In an earlier review paper, Harris and Jeste (1988) examined all previous studies of late-onset schizophrenia that provided adequate information on demographic characteristics and diagnoses. Their review suggested that approximately 15% of patients with a first episode of schizophrenia were over the age of 60 at the time of first psychiatric contact. In nearly every one of these studies, the proportion of females was greater than that of males in the newly identified late-onset cases. The authors found decreasing prevalence of new cases with age, but that 3%, 7%, and 3% of all cases with schizophrenia had onset from ages 40, 50, and 60 or later, respectively. Clearly, these data indicate that a substantial number of patients with schizophrenia have an onset of schizophrenia later in their lives, raising the issues of the presentation of these patients and what their premorbid functioning was like.

SYMPTOM SEVERITY IN LATE-ONSET PATIENTS

Patients with late-onset schizophrenia are commonly reported to have a symptom profile similar to that described by Kraepelin in his conception of paraphrenia. Hallucinations and delusions are present in most cases, including the presence of bizarre delusions and the "prototypical" hallucinations. Some studies have actually suggested that auditory hallucinations were more common in patients with late-onset schizophrenia than in early onset cases. In contrast, blunted affect, severe formal thought disorder, and grossly disorganized behavior are typically absent. In studies (Almeida, Howard, Levy, & David, 1995; Howard, Almeida, & Levy, 1994) examining the diagnostic distribution of cases with later life psychosis, it has been found that two thirds of the cases in which no "organic" cause could be detected met criteria for schizophrenia and one third for delusional disorder. The older the patient was when assessed, the more likely it was that they would meet criteria for delusional disorder rather than schizophrenia. So, it appears as if patients ranging in age from 45 to 65 or so have a syndrome that appears similar to schizophrenia with predominantly positive symptoms, whereas patients with onset of psychosis after age 65 may be more likely to have exclusively delusional symptoms.

There are several important implications of these findings. Negative symptoms are less severe in late-onset patients, and these symptoms have proven less likely to respond to treatment with antipsychotic medications than positive symptoms. At the same time, hallucinations are the symptom of schizophrenia that is most responsive to these same treatments. In addition, functional deficits, as described later, are more strongly related to negative symptoms and cognitive deficits than to the severity of hallucinations. As a result, the factors that increase vulnerability to severe functional impairment and deterioration in cognitive and functional status over time are less substantial in this population.

GENDER DIFFERENCES IN SYMPTOMS IN LATE-ONSET SCHIZOPHRENIA

As noted, females are more likely to develop schizophrenia with later onset than are males. In addition, family history is less significant as a risk factor for the development of schizophrenia in late-onset patients, implicating environmental or individual-differences factors as vulnerability indicators. When female early and late-onset patients were compared (Lindamer, Lohr, Harris, & Jeste, 1997), there were several notable clinical differences. First, when female late-onset patients are compared to late-onset male patients, they have more severe positive symptoms. When female late-onset patients were compared to female patients with earlier onset ages, the severity of negative symptoms was much less in late-onset female patients. In contrast, male patients did not differ in their negative symptom severity as a function of onset age. These data suggest that there may be effects related to hormonal or other menopausal or perimenopausal factors that are associated with development of late-onset schizophrenia. Although too little research has been conducted to conclusively identify the specific risk factors, the preponderance of female patients with late onset of schizophrenia and the consistent findings of onset age-associated differences in the characteristics of female patients with schizophrenia suggests that this is an important target for later research.

COGNITIVE AND FUNCTIONAL STATUS OF OLDER PATIENTS

There are relatively fewer comparative studies of cognitive functions in early adult onset versus later onset in older patients with schizophrenia. In one comprehensive study, Jeste et al. (1995) found that there were no major differences in either symptom severity or cognitive deficits between patients with late-onset schizophrenia and patients with early onset schizophrenia. Both late- and early onset patients had notable deficits compared to healthy controls, and there were no differences in either profile or severity of the relative deficits compared to the healthy comparison participants. The majority of the late-onset patients in this study were among the group described earlier whose onset age was less than 65 years. Thus, these data suggest that even in patients whose psychotic symptoms develop later, there is similarity to patients with a lifelong history of illness in the domains of cognitive impairment.

In a study of psychotic patients with more diverse diagnoses, including a large number who did not meet the full *DSM–IV* criteria for schizophrenia, Almeida, Howard, Levy, David, Morris, et al. (1995) reported that late-onset psychotic patients had several domains of cognitive functioning in which they were no more impaired than healthy comparison participants. Measures of learning rate and memory span were differentially less impaired than indexes of general cognitive ability and executive functioning. Thus, consistent with studies of younger patients with schizophrenia, more severe cognitive impairments are seen in individuals who meet criteria for schizophrenia than in cases with undifferentiated or affective psychoses.

PREMORBID FUNCTIONING AND OTHER RISK FACTORS IN LATE-ONSET SCHIZOPHRENIA

One of the most consistent findings in late-onset schizophrenia is that premorbid functioning is much less impaired in patients with late-onset schizophrenia than in schizophrenia patients with an earlier age of onset. This reduced impairment includes several different domains, including finding more older-onset patients with premorbid employment, more such patients with marriage or other evidence of intact social functioning, and higher levels of educational attainment. Older onset age is associated with greater intactness of premorbid functioning, with patients having onset over age 65 having the most intact premorbid functioning. For instance, in a comprehensive study (Jeste et al., 1995) comparing patients with later onset schizophrenia (after age 45) to patients with early onset schizophrenia and healthy comparison participants, patients with later age of onset were found to have higher rates of marriage, employment, and to be more likely to have the paranoid subtype of illness. Despite these indicators of better adjustment before the onset of symptoms, symptom severity and cognitive deficits were found to be quite similar in early and late-onset cases. In the context of having higher rates of employment and marriage, late-onset patients were still more likely than healthy controls to have schizoid or paranoid traits during the premorbid period, despite not meeting full criteria for personality disorders. Late-onset patients are also less likely to have children, even if married, than healthy controls (Rabins, Pauker, & Thomas, 1984).

In a study focusing on premorbid personality traits, Pearlson et al. (1989) found that late-onset patients were more likely than younger and older early onset patients to have signs of premorbid schizoid personality traits. These findings are consistent with a number of studies that examined patients who had late-onset psychotic conditions that did not necessarily meet full DSM–III or later criteria for schizophrenia. Social isolation has repeatedly been reported as a correlate of the development of late-onset paranoid symptoms. Although this symptom has often been interpreted as an environmental factor increasing risk for development of paranoid ideation, these findings raise an alternative possibility. It is conceivable that social isolation over the lifetime is a consequence of schizoid personality traits, which lead an individual to prefer isolation and solitary activities, even if they are married, employed, and living independently.

There are some other potential environmental factors that have been reported to correlate with the development of late-onset psychotic symptoms. Changes in sensory functions, both in domains of hearing and vision, have been reported in late-onset psychotic conditions (e.g., Herbert & Jacobson, 1967; Post, 1966). Careful follow-up studies have noted that these sensory impairments may not be specific to late-onset psychosis. Praeger and Jeste (1993) found that psychiatric patients in general, including older patients with major depression, were more likely to have impairments in both hearing and vision than comparison participants without psychiatric conditions.

An additional factor that could not be a result of lifelong personality changes is living alone as a result of being divorced or widowed in later life. In fact, the results of several studies have suggested that there was an increased prevalence of being widowed or divorced in late-onset psychosis cases relative to a healthy comparison sample (Almeida, Howard, Levy, David, Morris, et al., 1995). These data are inconsistent with the idea of lifelong isolation and indicate that current situational factors are more strongly correlated with social isolation than lifelong history. At the same time, it is typical to experience becoming widowed in later life, particularly for females, and although the majority of individuals with late-onset psychotic conditions are female, the absolute rate of development of psychosis after these events is quite rare.

It is possible that, compared to early onset schizophrenia, life events are more likely to precede the development of late-onset psychotic conditions. One of the most commonly applied models is the diathesis–stress model (Zubin & Spring, 1977). The overall framework of this model suggests that there is a necessary but not sufficient predisposing factor for the illness, combined with a similarly necessary but not sufficient stressor that interacts with the diathesis to cause the development of the illness. Such a predisposition could be transmitted genetically or acquired environmentally, although the stressor could be psychological or physiological (Harvey, Walker, & Wielgus, 1986). Predispositions could have measurable psychological or physiological correlates, with the psychological correlates being in the domains of cognitive deficits, personality traits, or behavioral tendencies. Biological correlates of the predisposition could be found in the domains of abnormal brain structure or activity, abnormal patterns of physiological reactivity to environmental stimuli, or genetic markers.

One of the problems with the application of this model to later onset schizophrenia is that it has proven difficult to identify both the predisposition and stressor. Long-term studies of offspring of schizophrenic parents, the group with the easiest to identify predisposition, have failed to identify patterns of environmental experiences that are associated with development of schizophrenia. The most compelling findings in this area (Cannon et al., 2000) suggest that children of schizophrenic parents who experience hypoxia-related obstetrical complications (OCs) have an increased risk of schizophrenic relatives to individuals who have no schizophrenic relatives and have OCs and children of schizophrenic parents born without OCs. In contrast, even rearing by a schizophrenic mother has no impact on risk for schizophrenia in individuals who share genetic predispositions to schizophrenia (Higgins et al., 1997).

The data on the risk factors for late-onset schizophrenia do suggest that a lifelong history of schizoid or paranoid traits combined with environmentally induced social isolation in later life may be related to an increased risk for development of late-onset psychosis. The diathesis appears to be lifelong schizoid tendencies, with the stressor appearing to be isolation-induced by divorce or death of a spouse. Although these data have not been collected prospectively, this is a testable hypothesis that could help to understand some of the inconsistent data collected to date in this area. In fact, if late-onset schizophrenia is the product of schizoid tendencies combined with life stress associated with isolation, intervention possibilities are also quite straightforward.

TREATMENT OF LATE-ONSET SCHIZOPHRENIA

The topic of treatment of older patients with schizophrenia will be addressed later. There are some special issues associated with the treatment of late-onset patients, related to the special characteristics of these patients compared to early onset patients. These characteristics include reduced severity of negative symptoms and cognitive deficits and an increased prevalence of female patients.

Antipsychotic medications are used across psychotic conditions and have proven useful to reduce psychotic symptoms in patients with late-onset schizophrenia and related conditions. Consistent with the idea that late-onset patients manifest a profile of symptoms that is maximally responsive to treatment, studies have suggested that the majority of patients with late-onset schizophrenia are responsive to treatment. Complete remission of symptoms appears to be obtained at levels at least consistent with that seen in younger first-episode patients. For example, Rabins et al. (1984) reported that 57% of patients manifested a full remission of symptoms, and an additional 29% of patients manifested a moderate response to treatment with conventional antipsychotic medications. This rate of response compares favorably to that seen with younger patients treated with conventional medications. A comprehensive first episode study (Robinson et al., 1999) found that 87% of patients met a criterion for treatment response that was consistent with the moderate level of response in the Rabins et al. study. Maintenance of treatment response was actually better in older patients, where the Rabins study found that 29% were symptom free at 2 years and the first-episode patients in the Robinson et al. study had an 80% relapse rate over 5 years (Robinson et al., 1999) and the patients who had one relapse had an 80% or greater risk of having second and third relapses.

In a similar study, Pearlson et al. (1989) reported a 48% full remission rate and a 28% partial response rate following conventional antipsychotic treatment in later onset schizophrenic patients. In this study, premorbid personality factors predicted poor response, with patients with premorbid schizoid personality symptoms responding less efficiently to treatment. An additional predictor of treatment failure was the presence of severe communication disorders, which are typically rare in late-onset psychotic patients.

It appears as if patients with late-onset schizophrenia are more responsive to treatment than patients with pure delusional disorders. Although controlled data are not widely available, there have been a number of reports of poor response to conventional antipsychotic treatment in this population. Patients with delusional disorder respond more poorly to conventional antipsychotic medication (Breitner & Anderson, 1994), with most patients not experiencing marked improvements in their symptoms and many refusing to accept treatment. This poor response is evident at follow-up, where as many as two thirds of patients with delusional disorder have a poor outcome despite treatment (Oojordsmoen, 1988). Even in patients who meet criteria for late-onset schizophrenia, the presence of severe delusions has been reported to be associated with poor treatment response (Rockwell, Krull, Dimsdale, & Jeste, 1994). Thus, the predominance of hallucinations in late-onset schizophrenia may be associated with the excellent treatment response reported in most studies using conventional medications.

One of the major developments in the treatment of psychotic disorders has been the introduction of atypical antipsychotic medications. These medications have reduced incidence of side effects and have additional benefits, such as cognitive enhancement, that are also important in older populations. At this time, the research on the use of these newer medications in late-onset patients is limited to open-label studies rather than the more desirable double-blind studies. The results of these studies have been consistent, however. Patients treated with risperidone, one of the newer antipsychotic medications, were found to manifest a consistent response to risperidone and lower levels of side effects than previous experience with older medications (Jeste et al., 1996). In a later open-label study, risperidone was found to enhance cognition, as evidenced by increases on the Mini-Mental State Examination (MMSE; Folstein et al., 1975) to a greater extent than previous treatment with older medications (Jeste et al., 1998). Even more interesting, in a study of patients with delusional disorder, which is often refractory to treatment with conventional antipsychotic medications, Kiraly, Gibson, Ancill, and Holliday (1998) found that delusional disorder was as responsive to treatment with newer antipsychotics as early onset schizophrenia was in younger patients.

These data suggest that newer antipsychotic medications are a more effective treatment for late-onset schizophrenia than older medications. Although there are a number of these medications and research is lacking on several of them, the bulk of the data indicate that treatment response is greater and side effects reduced with these treatments.

CONCLUSION

Late-onset schizophrenia has several features that may contribute to the controversies regarding this diagnostic entity. The presentation of symptoms is somewhat different, with hallucinations most prominent and negative symptoms generally absent. In addition, the gender ratio of the illness is reduced compared to early onset: the later the age of onset, the greater the female–male ratio. Some data suggest that lifelong schizoid traits and life changes commonly occurring in later life such as the death of a spouse are risk factors for late-onset schizophrenia. Additional research will need to consider whether lifelong schizoid traits lead to increased vulnerability to schizophrenia following stress exposure and whether loss of a spouse in late life is a specific stressor linked to the development of psychosis in predisposed individuals. Cognitive and functional impairments are seen, but some studies find that they are reduced considerably in critical areas compared to early onset cases. Pharmacological treatment has suggested that late-onset patients are more responsive to antipsychotic medications than early onset patients, with newer antipsychotic medications even more effective in inducing remission of symptoms.

The basis for the argument that late-onset schizophrenia is somehow different from early onset cases lies not just in the phenomenological differences. Genetic differences are the most striking difference between early and late-onset cases, with schizophrenia largely absent in relatives of late-onset patients and affective disorder sometimes found to be more common in these relatives than in relatives of healthy comparison participants. Other differences lie in premorbid functioning, where schizoid symptoms are, if anything, more common in late-onset patients before the onset of their illness. Other indicators of social and occupational functioning are much more intact than in earlier onset schizophrenia, again indicating that the early failure to function adequately that is commonly seen in early onset patients is missing in these patients.

There are other issues in late-onset schizophrenia, such as the most appropriate residential treatment modality and the side effects associated with treatment. These issues will be addressed in later chapters. It is hoped that the major differences between early and late-onset schizophrenia, even when patients who meet full criteria for *DSM* schizophrenia are compared to earlier onset patients, will promote additional research and provoke careful thinking about psychiatric nosology and its late-life implications.

7

DEMENTIA AND SCHIZOPHRENIA: SIMILARITIES AND DIFFERENCES

When Emil Kraepelin (1919) first conceptualized schizophrenia, he referred to it as "dementia praecox." Kraepelin chose this term for a reason: He believed that schizophrenia was a condition marked by profound functional deficit, cognitive impairments, a largely unremitting course, and deterioration in most cases. When he chose this term, he was quite familiar with other conditions that are considered dementias; Alois Alzheimer, the doctor who described the disease that bears his name, was a colleague of Kraepelin. Kraepelin had extensive experience with patients who had late-life deterioration in their functioning, and it is not likely that he chose the term "dementia" to describe the disease without substantial thought and a conviction in his accuracy.

In this chapter we examine the similarities and differences in cognitive performance and functional limitations associated with schizophrenia and dementia as it is currently conceptualized. There are many research and clinical questions that must be addressed, including similarities in the course of the conditions, risk factors for the development of dementia in patients with schizophrenia, and the plausibility of differential diagnoses between the two conditions. We also evaluate the neuropathological changes (or lack thereof) found postmortem in older patients with schizophrenia, compared with those seen in patients with Alzheimer's disease and other conditions with distinct profiles of neuropathological changes. At the end of the chapter, we examine the evidence regarding neuropathological changes in schizophrenia and relate the evidence regarding those changes to the course and profile of cognitive impairment in schizophrenia.

DEFINING DEMENTIA

Dementia is a technical term and a broad diagnostic category. The current *DSM–IV* (American Psychiatric Association, 1994) criteria for dementia define it as a condition with impairments in memory and at least one other cognitive function (verbal, perceptual, executive, praxis, or attention); deterioration from a higher, better level of previous functioning; and with the cognitive changes not being a result of a transitory state such as delirium. Thus, individuals with lifelong mental retardation or other conditions that have induced lifelong reductions in their cognitive functioning do not merit the additional diagnosis of dementia unless they deteriorate further in their functioning.

Dementia can be caused by a whole array of different factors influencing the central nervous system, including degenerative conditions such as Alzheimer's disease (AD), head trauma, infection (e.g., HIV, encephalitis), vascular pathology, and substance abuse. Mixed etiologies are also common, with many cases of dementia revealed at postmortem to have multiple etiological features such as the combination of changes associated with AD as well as vascular pathology. Although many conditions that cause dementia are progressive, such as AD and Huntington's disease, there is nothing in the current diagnostic criteria that specifies that a condition must be progressive to result in a dementia diagnosis. For instance, dementia associated with head trauma can result from a single event, despite the fact that most conditions that cause dementia are, in fact, progressive.

Dementia has a different profile of cognitive functioning depending on whether the primary lesion(s) is located in cortical as compared to subcortical regions. As described in detail later, there are different profiles of both memory and verbal impairments seen in dementia associated with cortical or subcortical pathology. There are considerable implications for the neuropathology of late-life schizophrenia depending on whether the pathology of schizophrenia could be conclusively found to be cortical or subcortical. At the present time, research on both of these possibilities has been conducted.

OTHER CONDITIONS SIMILAR TO DEMENTIA

Because a diagnosis of dementia requires that two different domains of cognitive ability areas are impaired, in specific memory and one other substantial deficit in an important ability area, then the presence of a single major deficit does not meet criteria. Thus, the presence of amnesia (memory impairments), apraxia (impairments in cognitive–motoric coordination), aphasia (language deficits), or agnosia (inability to recognize objects) would not alone meet the criteria for dementia. Amnesia and one of these other deficits would meet the criteria, as long as there is evidence of functional impairments.

Delirium is a transitory state that can be caused by fever, drug side effects, or other forms of toxicity. By definition delirium is a condition that is variable in its presentation, occurring episodically during the presence of the risk factors. Dementia is generally viewed as a permanent state, but the current diagnostic criteria does not require that the condition be considered permanent before the diagnosis is made.

Alzheimer's Disease

This disease, first reported by Alzheimer at the outset of this century, is the most common of the dementing conditions. As many as half of all patients with dementia who are over the age of 65 will be found to meet criteria for Alzheimer's disease (AD) at a postmortem assessment (Arriagada, Marzloff, & Hyman, 1992), with the relative proportion of AD compared to other dementias increasing as the age of the patients increase (Rebok & Folstein, 1993). It has an age of onset ranging from the late 30s (rarely) to the end of life, and a prevalence of as much as 6% of the current living population (Terry & Katzman, 1992). These figures are greatly increased in old age, with as much as 50% of the population over the age of 85 meeting criteria for AD (Evans et al., 1989). Most studies note that the course of the illness is around 10 years from the first identifiable symptom, unless the patient does not survive this period (Katzman, 1976). Risk factors for the illness are age, family history of AD, reduced educational attainment, Down's syndrome, head trauma, and female gender (Cummings & Benson, 1983). The neuropathological signature of AD includes amyloid plaques and neuro-fibrillary tangles, localized initially in the medial temporal cortex and hippo-campus and found later in the illness in the more lateral structures of the temporal lobe, parietal cortex, and perisylvian region (Huff, Growdon, Corkin, & Rosen, 1987; Khachaturian, 1985). Plaques are irregularly shaped deposits of amyloid, and tangles are neurofibrillary masses that are irregularly distributed in the same general regions as plaques. The presence of a certain prevalence of these neuropathological stigmata is required for the post-mortem diagnosis of AD according to all current criteria.

The clinical and cognitive hallmark of AD is its progressive course. When measured with a global clinical rating scale, such as the Mini-Mental State Examination (MMSE; Folstein, Folstein, & McHugh, 1975) or the

Alzheimer's Disease Assessment Scale (ADAS; Rosen, Mohs, & Davis, 1984), there is an average deterioration of about 10% per year (Berg, Edwards, Danzinger, & Berg, 1987; Huff et al., 1987; Salmon, Thal, Butters, & Heindel, 1990). Thus, the expected decline in the MMSE is about 3 points per year on the average. This decline is not, however, linear. In the early and later stages of the illness the annual decline is considerably less than in the middle, leading to a curvilinear course (Morris et al., 1993). As a result, the expected annual loss of functioning measured with global scales depends considerably on the severity of illness at the time of first assessment of the patient.

There are multiple aspects of cognitive impairment seen in AD, but the presence and severity of each of the cognitive impairments also depends on the stage of illness. In fact, as the illness progresses, eventually every cognitive function that depends on the intact functions of the cerebral cortex becomes impaired. Some of the cognitive impairments are seen early on in the course of the illness, and others appear later (Welsh, Butters, Hughes, Mohs, & Heyman, 1992). Of these cognitive impairments, some of them become progressively worse over time and in others appear to be stable after their appearance (Morris et al., 1993). The first identifiable sign of cognitive impairment in AD is a profound deficit in episodic memory, either with or without intervening distracting information. This finding is not surprising, because the first subjective sign of the illness is forgetfulness and problems in learning new information. This deficit is substantial in that patients with "mild" AD (MMSE > 23) have been found to learn as little as three words over the course of three exposures to a 10-item serial word list, whereas healthy individuals matched on age and education to these patients learned 8 words (Welsh, Butters, Hughes, Mohs, & Heyman, 1991). In this study, at delayed recall the AD patients recalled fewer than one word (out of 10 possible words) on average, and the healthy comparison participants retained seven out of eight words that they had learned. Deficits in delayed recall did not progress with continued worsening of the illness, and the ability to learn new information with practice appears to worsen steadily with progression of the illness.

Following the impairments in learning and delayed recall memory that appear at the earliest stages of the illness, verbal skills such as confrontation naming and fluency appear to worsen next and progress with a roughly linear course. The next aspect of functioning to deteriorate is praxis and spatial-perceptual operations. These declines appear to be linear as well (Morris et al., 1993; Welsh et al., 1992). Thus, the curvilinear course of AD, as measured by global scales such as the MMSE, may be produced by the scaling properties of the assessment instruments as well as by the actual course of the illness. The "accelerated" pace of cognitive decline in the middle of the illness may be a function of the fact that more of the cognitive functions measured by the instrument are in decline in the middle of the illness than at the very early stages (where only delayed recall and verbal learning are impaired) and in the later stages (where most tests of the cognitive constructs are now manifesting floor effects). It must be noted that there is heterogeneity in the course of cognitive impairment in AD across patients, and these descriptions are based on average statements about large samples of patients.

There are many other aspects of cognitive assessment in AD that merit attention. Executive functioning impairment appears early in the illness. It is possible that deficits in executive functioning are exacerbated, or possibly even caused, by deficits in the cognitive components controlled by executive functions. For instance, a profound deficit in working memory would make adequate performance on an executive functioning test such as the Wisconsin Card Sorting Test (WCST; Heaton et al., 1993) essentially impossible. As in many amnestic conditions, procedural learning (i.e., learning of motor skills) appears to be more intact than declarative learning. In a similar way, implicit memory functions (i.e., memory aided by prompts or cues) appear more intact than explicit memory, although still impaired (Zec, 1993). Recognition memory (i.e., the ability to identify previously presented information) is not spared, in contrast to findings in specific frontal lobe damage (Freedman, 1990) or Parkinson's disease (see later discussion). Finally, a number of studies have suggested that interventions designed to augment memory functioning, including practicing and altering encodability of information, do not benefit patients with AD to the same extent as age-matched controls, patients with affective disorders, or patients with other dementing conditions (Weingartner et al., 1993).

Another important cognitive limitation in AD is that of motor speed and visuomotor performance. Both of these ability areas are impaired quite early in the course of the illness, with some evidence that this is also a progressive deficit (Nebes & Brady, 1992; Nebes & Madden, 1988). The issue of attentional impairment in AD is complex. As a general statement, attentional impairment is a less salient feature of AD than deficits in learning and memory. However, there is still considerable evidence that concentration impairment is present in the illness, especially with continued progression (Kaszniak, Poon, & Riege, 1986). In the area of deficient verbal skills, there is some evidence that letter fluency is less impaired than category fluency until the very late stages of the illness, possibly because of the greater dependence of category fluency on the intactness of the temporal and parietal cortices (Randolph, Braun, Goldberg, & Chase, 1993).

As AD progresses, function is lost to the point that by the time of death, performance on all tests is so poor that all scores are zero (see Zec,

1993, for a comprehensive review). This level of end-state impairment is in contrast to the impairments in the end states of some other cortical and subcortical dementias, where there is preservation of many functions up until the latest stages. Behavioral disturbances in AD, including delusions, hallucinations, agitation, and depression, can also interfere with the assessment of cognitive functions in the illness, and special care must be taken to ensure that low scores are based on cognitive impairments and not behavioral abnormalities (Teri et al., 1992). AD is one of the conditions in which a low baseline level of intellectual functioning is clearly a risk factor for the development of the illness. Several studies have indicated that using an estimate of premorbid functions such as a reading level obtained from the Wide-Range Achievement Test (Wilkinson, 1993) or the National Adult Reading Test (Nelson & O'Connell, 1978) is valid up until the severe stages of Alzheimer's dementia (e.g., O'Carroll, Baikie, & Whittick, 1987). Thus, relative decline can be assessed against a reasonable measure of premorbid functioning.

Schizophrenia and Dementia: Assessing the Overlap

Many patients with schizophrenia have multiple aspects of cognitive impairment. Most patients, even at the time of their first psychotic episode, would be considered to have at least two cognitive impairments, and functional decline is a required component of the diagnostic criteria for dementia and schizophrenia. In studies that have examined the presence of "definite" cognitive impairment in patients with schizophrenia, defined as the presence of at least two aspects of cognitive performance in the impaired range, both good-outcome (Palmer et al., 1997) and poor-outcome patients (Harvey et al., 2002) have a rate of definite cognitive impairments of about 70% or more. Thus, on a purely behavioral level, most patients with schizophrenia meet the *DSM–IV* diagnostic criteria for dementia. Because these impairments are clearly present at the time of the first episode (Bilder et al., 2000; Saykin et al., 1994), many patients with schizophrenia will meet criteria for dementia over the entire course of their illness.

One of the major arguments against the Kraepelinian perspective of dementia praecox has focused on the deteriorating course postulated by Kraepelin. It is clear that some patients are able to live independently over the course of their lives (Hegarty et al., 1994), whereas recent data clearly suggest that some subset of patients with the illness have a deteriorating course. The question regarding dementia praecox in late life, therefore, is not whether patients meet criteria for dementia but whether the dementia that they manifest is an uncomplicated correlate of schizophrenia. We evaluate the overlap with AD first, because it is the most common type of dementia. We address more complicated issues later.

SCHIZOPHRENIA COMPARED TO ALZHEIMER'S DISEASE: PROFILE OF COGNITIVE IMPAIRMENT

As noted earlier, there are a variety of important cognitive impairments seen in Alzheimer's disease. The most prominent at the early stages is delayed recall memory, with deficits in rate of learning also seen. Several studies have been conducted to examine the profile and course of cognitive deficits in AD and schizophrenia. In terms of the profile of cognitive impairments, Heaton et al. (1994) found that patients with schizophrenia underperformed patients with Alzheimer's disease on most aspects of a comprehensive neuropsychological battery. AD patients, in contrast, were more impaired on delayed recall than patients with schizophrenia, regardless of their age. Both younger and older patients with schizophrenia had similar profiles compared to AD patients. One aspect of this study was that the AD patients were not matched to the schizophrenic patients in terms of their global cognitive impairments. Because the profile of impairment in AD changes with progression of the illness (see Welsh et al., 1991), selection of patients with AD at different stages of the illness will result in samples in which the levels of expected cognitive deficits are different.

In a similar study, Davidson et al. (1996) compared patients with schizophrenia and AD to a sample of well-screened healthy individuals. The AD and schizophrenia patients were matched on global cognitive status as indexed by MMSE total scores, age and gender, and were matched to healthy participants on the basis of age, gender, and relative levels of education. When the two samples of patients were compared to healthy controls, the controls performed better on each measure than both of the patient groups. When comparing the patient groups, it was discovered that the schizophrenic patients performed more poorly than the patients with Alzheimer's disease on naming and praxis, and the two groups performed equivalently on rates of verbal learning. Similar to the results of the Heaton et al. (1994) study, patients with Alzheimer's disease performed more poorly than the patients with schizophrenia on delayed recall memory.

CORTICAL VERSUS SUBCORTICAL DEMENTIA PROFILES

Dementing conditions are associated with a certain profile of cognitive impairments. Patients with cortical dementias such as AD manifest impairments in rate of learning, delayed recall, and delayed recognition, as well as in verbal fluency and naming. Subcortical dementias such as Huntington's disease are associated with sparing of recognition memory and object-naming performance, in the context of impairment in rate of learning, delayed recall, and verbal fluency. These profiles of impairment are preserved across the levels of severity of subcortical dementia (Paulsen, Butters, et al., 1995). Consistent with this idea, Paulsen, Heaton, et al. (1995) examined the prevalence of different profiles of memory impairments in patients with schizophrenia, comparing these profiles to those previously established as reflective of cortical versus subcortical dementia. They found that the most common profile in their sample of patients, all of whom had a relatively good lifetime functional outcome, was similar to the profile of subcortical memory impairments (more than 50%), followed by unimpaired profiles, and then, least commonly, cortical profiles. In contrast, when Putnam and Harvey (1999) examined the profile of memory dysfunction in older patients with a lifetime poor functional outcome, they found that the modal profile of impairment was consistent with cortical dementia. They found that recognition memory was as impaired or more than delayed recall, in both verbal and visuospatial stimulus modalities. In this study, the cortical memory profile was the most common profile present in both younger and older patients with chronic schizophrenia, suggesting that this profile did not develop with aging.

In a later study evaluating the validity of the cortical–subcortical classification in schizophrenia, Harvey et al. (2002) examined a large ($N = 239$) sample of geriatric patients with schizophrenia and examined the prevalence of cortical and subcortical deficit profiles. The goal of this study was to evaluate the convergence of profile status based on memory and verbal skills deficits. Patients were classified as having a cortical memory profile if their learning rate, delayed recall, and delayed recognition scores were all impaired compared to healthy controls, and the subcortical profile involved unimpaired (i.e., "spared") recognition memory in the context of impairment in the other two domains. Verbally defined cortical profiles involved impairments in both verbal fluency and naming, with subcortical profiles involving no naming deficits in the context of relatively impaired fluency. In addition, patients could also be classified as unimpaired based on either verbal or memory deficits. Overlap between classification schemes (verbal–memory) was quite poor, ranging from 30% in cortical profiles to 14% in the unimpaired profiles. Fifteen-month stability of classification, based on a reassessment of 147 of the 239 patients from the original sample, ranged from 86% for cortical memory profiles to 50% for subcortical verbal profiles. As a consequence, it appears that, despite the fact that the cortical–subcortical profiles can be readily identified in patients with schizophrenia there is little consistency between impairment profiles across different ability areas.

The profiles generated on the basis of impairments in memory functioning appeared to have the most validity, as evidenced by temporal stability. Additional validation data were published for the use of memory-based impairment profiles at essentially the same time. Using a memory assessment, the California Verbal Learning Test, Turetsky et al. (2002) found support for a cortical–subcortical memory impairment classification in younger patients with schizophrenia based on k-means cluster analysis. One of the strengths of the Turestsky et al. study was the use of corroborating data from neuroimaging and neurophysiological measures, with the patients classified as manifesting a cortical profile evidencing reduced temporal lobe gray matter and hypometabolism, and subcortical patients had enlarged ventricles. This study is particularly important because of its use of multiple biological validating variables. These results suggest that these profiles of impairment are not an artifact of aging, because this was a much younger sample of research participants.

COURSE OF COGNITIVE IMPAIRMENT IN SCHIZOPHRENIA: SIMILAR TO ALZHEIMER'S DISEASE?

As described earlier, cognitive decline in AD is about 10% per year on structured rating scales. Although this decline is not linear on an annual basis, over the course of a decade most patients with AD will progress to the point at which they go from essentially normal performance to scores that are functionally zero. In contrast, poor-outcome older patients with schizophrenia, the ones most likely to show cognitive decline, have age-related differences of about 10% per decade on these structured rating scales (Davidson et al., 1995). So, based on cross-sectional data, it is essentially impossible that the rate of decline in those schizophrenia patients in whom decline is detected could be the same as in AD. Furthermore, even poor-outcome older patients do not decline as a group when followed up at one year with either structured cognitive assessments (Harvey et al., 1995) or neuropsychological batteries sensitive to dementia (Harvey, Lombardi, et al., 1996). In the Friedman et al. (2001) study, which performed a direct comparison study of the rate of cognitive decline in older patients with schizophrenia and AD, considerable differences in course were detected. In schizophrenia, cognitive change over the 6-year follow-up was linearly associated with age, in contrast to AD, where patients ranging in age from 50 to 80 declined at the same annual rate. Even in the oldest schizophrenic patients, aged 80 and up, their rate of annual decline was only one third of the rate of patients with AD, regardless of the age of the AD patients. So it appears that the rate of annual decline of patients with schizophrenia is not consistent with the rate seen in AD. In summary, both the course and profile of cognitive impairments in late-life schizophrenia appear inconsistent with AD.

NEUROPATHOLOGY OF COGNITIVE IMPAIRMENT
IN LATE-LIFE SCHIZOPHRENIA

Despite the fact that the overall course of cognitive impairment in late-life schizophrenia does not appear consistent with AD, it might still be possible that the cognitive decline seen in some patients with schizophrenia was caused by the occurrence of AD in some proportion of schizophrenic patients. This possibility was supported by the report that a substantial proportion of patients with schizophrenia had evidence of classical AD neuropathology at postmortem assessment (Prohovnik, Dwork, Kaufman, & Willson, 1993). Multiple long-term postmortem studies were spurred by this report, all with the goal of determining whether the profound cognitive impairment seen in some older patients was a result of the comorbidity of AD and schizophrenia.

There are several features of these later studies that make them scientifically sound when compared to the initial reports of AD pathology in older patients with schizophrenia. The neuropathology data for the Prohovnik et al. paper were taken from a large-scale brain bank maintained by the New York State Office of Mental Health (OMH). The diagnoses for these cases were based on chart diagnosis, with no possibility for structured confirmation of the diagnoses, and the collection process for the post-mortem specimens themselves was not at all systematic. Because not all cases in OMH facilities received postmortem examinations, the performance of a postmortem assessment might itself be a source of bias. Because this was not a consecutive series of postmortem assessments, it is conceivable that unique features of some of the patients led to their receiving postmortem examinations while other patients did not.

The two large-scale programs of research of postmortem neuropathology in schizophrenia, examining older patients and using "antemortem" assessments, have been in process at the University of Pennsylvania and Mt. Sinai School of Medicine for the past 15 years. These projects have several features in common. Patients are diagnosed during life, eliminating reliance on chart information and chart diagnoses, which are often unreliable in public facilities. Furthermore, patients receive cognitive, clinical, and functional assessments during life, which allows for relating the characteristics of patients to postmortem findings. This is particularly important because older patients with schizophrenia vary widely in their clinical symptoms and cognitive deficits, as well as their course of illness, movement disorders, and treatment status. Without information about this variability in patient characteristics, it would be impossible to study the potential neurobiological substrates of these individual differences and to try to identify factors that might reduce heterogeneity of the disorder.

Three reports from large-scale studies examined the prevalence of AD pathology, as well as other indicators of gross neuropathology, including vascular dementia, Pick's disease, and fronto-temporal dementia. Because the results of all three studies are remarkably similar, the results of the largest one will be described in the most detail (Purohit et al., 1998). In this study, a consecutive series of 100 patients who were diagnosed and assessed during life received postmortem assessments. The average age of the patients at the time of death was over 80, and all 100 patients met clinical criteria for cognitive impairment consistent with dementia. Similar results have been reported in similar postmortem series by the research groups at the University of Pennsylvania (Arnold et al., 1995, 1998), and Columbia University (Dwork et al., 1998).

The prevalence of definite AD pathology in this sample was 10%, consistent with the expected general population prevalence of AD. Similarly, vascular pathology was also in the range of 10%, with an additional 10% of the patients not meeting definite criteria for any form of neuropathology but having a neuropathological diagnosis of questionable pathology—in other words, not a normal brain. All of the remaining brains, despite coming from patients who had evidence of definite cognitive and functional impairment at the time of their death, had no evidence of neuropathology that could account for such gross cognitive and functional impairments. In fact, the prevalence of neuropathological findings consistent with AD was essentially identical to that expected on the basis of base-rate prevalences in the general population, and vascular pathology was actually less than base-rate prevalences.

As a result, 70 out of 100 patients with chronic schizophrenia and substantial cognitive impairments had no evidence of AD or vascular pathology or other potential causes of cognitive impairments. Thus, the severe cognitive impairment seen in late-life schizophrenia is not a result of AD in most cases. This condition appears to be equivalently prevalent in schizophrenia patients with severe cognitive impairment as in the overall population, indicating that schizophrenia appears neither to be a risk nor a protective factor for the occurrence of AD. Vascular pathology appears, if anything, less common in older schizophrenic patients than in the general population, possibly because most of these patients were chronically institutionalized and received consistent medical attention over the course of their lives. As a result, conditions that lead to vascular pathology, such as hypertension and diabetes, are likely to be consistently treated and their morbidity reduced relative to community-dwelling individuals who have to assume responsibility for their own health care.

OTHER POTENTIAL CAUSES OF COGNITIVE IMPAIRMENT

If it is not AD or vascular neuropathology that is causing cognitive impairment in elderly patients with schizophrenia, what is the cause? Several different lines of research have been pursued to date, with variable success.

Neurotransmitter Abnormalities

Several different neurotransmitters are potentially implicated in cognitive decline in older patients with schizophrenia. These include monoamines (dopamine [DA] and norepinephrine [NE]), serotonin, acetylcholine, and glutamate. For instance, Powchik et al. (1998) examined indexes of dopamine, norepinephrine, and serotonin activity at postmortem, finding that patients with schizophrenia had lower levels of these transmitters than healthy controls. These findings are consistent with the findings that drugs that modify activation of these transmitters are effective at reducing some of the symptoms in schizophrenia. More research is required, however, in this area because some assays of the activity of monoamines such as DA and NE may be unstable at postmortem. In a recent, as yet unpublished study, 19 elderly chronic schizophrenic patients (12 of whom were cognitively impaired) were examined at postmortem. All schizophrenic individuals in this study had antemortem evaluations of cognitive functioning within one year of death. Those schizophrenic individuals with cognitive impairment showed marked deficits in cortical serotonergic markers, including both serotonin levels and the metabolite 5-HIAA compared to those without major cognitive impairments. Because serotonergic deficits can be age-related, it is important to note that age was not significantly different in the two groups.

Similar to the serotonin findings, norepinephrine receptor count was significantly reduced in frontal cortex in 12 cognitively impaired schizophrenic individuals compared to 7 schizophrenic individuals with less severe cognitive impairments. There were only trend-level reductions in NE receptors in the temporal cortex. Similar but less pronounced deficits in the major NE metabolite 3-methoxy-4-hydroxy phenylglycol (MHPG) were also found. The data for NE are consistent with the report of Bridge et al. (1985), which described NE deficits in hippocampus and nucleus accumbens correlated with the severity of cognitive impairment close to the time of death. Because noradrenergic deficits can be age-related, it is important to note that age was not significantly different in the two groups.

In contrast, postmortem levels of acetylcholine were also found to be no different in healthy controls and in patients with schizophrenia, with both groups having significantly higher levels of cholinergic indicators than patients with AD. At the same time, the potential importance of this transmitter, despite failure to find reductions overall, is highlighted by the fact that Powchik et al. found that the levels of acetylcholine at postmortem in patients with schizophrenia were correlated with memory deficits identified before death. Consistent with the understanding that memory functions are associated with cholinergic activity, lower levels of acetylcholine and choline acetyl trans ferase (CHAT) were found in patients with poorer memory performance. Thus, although there was no absolute difference in metabolite levels, the possibility exists that imbalances in cholinergic activation underlie cognitive impairments in schizophrenia, a possibility that will be addressed later.

One area of neurotransmission activity in which there were clear differences between healthy controls and older patients with schizophrenia is in the domain of glutamatergic functions. Studies of gene expression at postmortem have found notable differences in receptors from the two major glutamate subtypes: alpha-amino-3 hydioxy 5-methyl 4-isoxazole puodionic acid (AMPA) and n-methyl-d-aspartate (NMDA). Although several studies did not find differences in expression of the receptors for these two subtypes of glutamate in the cortex, they did find differences in the thalamus. There were reductions in expression level consistent with reductions in glutamate receptor activity, as previously identified in schizophrenia (Krystal et al., 2000). In the frontal cortex, however, there were increases in receptor expression. These changes in receptor regulation were compared to those seen in patients with AD, and there were clear patterns of difference. Thus, glutamate-receptor activation is reduced in subcortical regions and increased in the frontal cortex, consistent with cortical–subcortical disconnection seen in studies of other transmitter systems in schizophrenia.

In conclusion, studies of abnormalities in neurotransmission in older patients with schizophrenia have identified consistent correlates of cognitive impairment that are distinct from transmitter changes noted in AD. Several different transmitter systems appear to be abnormal in patients with severe cognitive impairments, but the sample sizes are all small and the studies have all been conducted by the same research groups. This area will clearly be one in which considerable later research is conducted.

Structural Abnormalities in the Central Nervous System

There are several different areas where changes in the structure of the brain may be implicated in cognitive impairments in schizophrenia. These include abnormalities in the hippocampus, thalamus, and temporal lobe, as well as abnormalities in the distribution of white matter in the central nervous system (CNS).

Neuroimaging of the Brain

There is an extensive literature on structural brain imaging in schizophrenia, progressing through all of the different techniques used to visualize the structure of the brain. Beginning with pneumencephalography, low resolution CT scans, and moving through higher and higher resolution magnetic resonance imaging studies, several consistent findings have emerged. Essentially no studies to date have examined older patients with schizophrenia, possibly because of concerns regarding informed consent. As a result, readers interested in this topic should consult one of the many comprehensive reviews of the topic(e.g., Zakaznis & Heinrichs, 1999), which can address methodological details and substantive findings. In brief, enlargement of the cerebral ventricles, increased prominences of the sulci, and reductions in the overall volume of the cortex have been reported. These changes are present in some cases at the time of the first episode and are more common and severe in patients with poorer overall functional outcome.

Relevant to the cognitive and functional decline discussed in the last chapter, some studies of younger patients have reported progressive changes in cortical size over various follow-up studies. Childhood onset (Rapoport et al., 1997), adult first episode (Delisi et al., 1997) and chronic patients (Davis et al., 1998) have all been reported to manifest progressive ventricular enlargement. However, there are clearly subtypes of patients who are most vulnerable to experience decline, with patients with a chronic course of treatment-refractory symptoms and poor functional outcomes more likely to experience cortical changes than those patients who are more treatment-responsible. Because none of these studies included older patients, it is impossible to determine if these progressive cortical changes are associated with the cognitive and functional declines seen in some older patients with a lifetime of poor functional outcome. As of now, this correlation between progressive cortical changes in earlier life and progressive cognitive and functional deterioration in later life is still only possible to interpret on a speculative basis. Clearly, studies of older patients with schizophrenia during the period in which they are most vulnerable to manifest functional decline will be required to address this issue.

Abnormal Cell Distributions

There are several lines of evidence suggesting that there is disorganization in the cellular organization in certain cortical regions in older patients with schizophrenia. It has been hypothesized that reduced neuropil is associated with these abnormalities, which include poor clustering of neurons and abnormal formation of the lamina, as well as reduced neuronal size in the entorhinal cortex (Selemon & Goldman-Rakic, 1998). These impairments are not generic throughout the entire region, being more greatly prevalent in layers 2 and 3. Cellular abnormalities in these regions are not accompanied by evidence of neurodegenerative changes, suggesting that these may be developmentally abnormal features.

Possible White Matter Correlates

Although schizophrenia has been described as a disease of brain connectivity, few studies have examined white matter (i.e., myelin) changes in schizophrenia. Indeed, demyelinating diseases have a well-established association with behavioral disturbances. For example, metachromatic leukodystrophy has been reported to present in early adulthood as a schizophrenic-like psychosis in more than 50% of cases (Hyde, Ziegler, & Weinberger, 1992). In addition, there is a striking similarity between the profile of cognitive impairments in demyelinating diseases such as multiple sclerosis and schizophrenia. For instance, abnormalities in motor speed and episodic memory and problem-solving deficits are seen in both conditions. A number of different observations support the notion of a possible myelin-related abnormality in schizophrenia. Postmortem studies have reported white matter abnormalities such as a selective maldistribution of interstitial neurons in prefrontal white matter in schizophrenia (Akbarian et al., 1996). In addition, DNA microarray analysis of postmortem tissue from the dorsolateral prefrontal cortex of 12 schizophrenic and 12 control individuals demonstrated that five genes, whose expression is enriched in myelin-forming oligodendrocytes, were down-regulated in the schizophrenic individuals (Hakak et al., 2002). Furthermore, using only the myelin-related genes on the microarray to discriminate the controls from the schizophrenic patients resulted in a perfect separation of the groups. These five genes have been implicated in the formation and maintenance of myelin sheaths, which are critical for efficient axonal signal propagation and provide extrinsic trophic signals that affect the development and long-term survival of axons.

Additional support for the involvement of white matter abnormalities in the presentation of schizophrenic symptoms comes from neuroimaging studies. Diffusion tensor imaging, performed with special sequences of MRI, measures the coherence of white matter tracts in the brain and has demonstrated significant alterations in the directionality of white matter tracts in the frontal and temporal cortices of schizophrenic patients (Lim et al., 1999). The technique of magnetization transfer MR imaging (MTI) provides a new contrast mechanism that may be more specific for myelin destruction. In MTI, the exchange of magnetization between the bound protons and free water is represented by the magnetization transfer ratio (MTR), which is considered to be an index of myelin or axonal integrity. Diseases associated with demyelinating processes, such as multiple sclerosis, cause dramatic reductions in magnetization transfer. To date, one MTI study in schizophrenia has been done that has shown significantly different MTR values between schizophrenic patients and controls (Foong et al., 2000). There was about a 2% reduction in the schizophrenic group compared to controls for right and left temporal regions. However, there were no significant differences in frontal or other regional MTR values between schizophrenic patients and controls. This suggests a decrease in myelin in the brains of schizophrenic patients that may be localized to the temporal regions. The authors also suggested that if MTR changes occur in other white matter regions, they are probably subtle. It is therefore possible that subtle changes in axonal and myelin structure in other areas may exist in these schizophrenic patients, but the technique used was not sensitive enough to detect these changes. Whether or not progressive loss of myelin structure may correlate with the progressive changes in cognitive and functional status observed in older schizophrenic patients is a question that should be addressed in future imaging studies.

CONCLUSION

Schizophrenia in late life is often accompanied by cognitive impairments that are reminiscent of dementia. When careful comparisons are made, however, the profile and course of cognitive impairments in schizophrenia appear distinct from both cortical and subcortical dementia. Furthermore, the course of schizophrenia in later life, although marked in some cases by deterioration in cognitive and functional status, is not similar to AD in the rate or extent of annual progression. Postmortem neuropathology suggests that degenerative and vascular pathology is typically absent in these older patients, with the risk for AD and vascular pathology similar to that expected in the general population.

When the causes of these impairments are examined, it seems that schizophrenia may share more with conditions such as multiple sclerosis, in terms of cognitive impairments and neuropathological features, than with conditions such as AD and Huntington's disease. Although there is an extensive literature on neuroimaging in schizophrenia, there are essentially no studies on older patients. Thus, evidence regarding progressive changes in ventricular size reported in younger patients remains only a tantalizing lead for explaining the deterioration seen in older patients. It is easier to say what the relationships between dementia and its neuropathology and schizophrenia are *not* than what they *are*. Future research will have to apply techniques of neuroimaging that have been used extensively in younger patients to older populations to establish a link between changes in the brain and changes in behavior that is not solely dependent on postmortem neuropathological assessments.

8

INSTITUTIONS AND INSTITUTIONAL CARE FOR OLDER PATIENTS WITH SCHIZOPHRENIA

This chapter reviews inpatient treatment modalities for older patients with schizophrenia. Given the changes in mental health service delivery, many of the residents of institutional care are elderly patients with a lifelong history of schizophrenia. Many of these patients have lived in these institutions for decades and have been referred from one institution to another as they aged. Thus, the history of institutional care and the processes of aging in schizophrenia are uniquely related. In this chapter we will examine the characteristics of psychiatric institutions, the treatments that are offered, and the types of patients who receive them. We will also critically evaluate whether long-stay institutional care has any positive features and will present a balanced perspective on changes in mental health care that affect older patients with schizophrenia.

Until the 1960s most patients with schizophrenia received the majority of their care in large psychiatric hospitals. These institutions, many constructed in the early part of the 20th century, were often extremely large and had thousands of beds. During the 1960s, in response to changes in social ideas regarding the treatment of mental illness and facilitated by the effects of older antipsychotic medications on psychotic symptoms, patients began to be discharged from large psychiatric facilities. The goal was to facilitate community care, but the reality of the situation was that there was often no care, no home, and certainly no warm welcome in the community for these former residents of long-stay psychiatric facilities. Since then, alternative institutions have arisen, developed to handle the thousands of patients who were discharged from long-stay psychiatric facilities but who were unable to function in the community. These residences, which include both nursing homes and "locked board and care" homes, provide residential services to older patients with schizophrenia, but the other services received by these patients are likely to be deficient.

THE HISTORY OF INSTITUTIONS

Because of the nature of schizophrenia, with its severe functional limitations and the unusual and sometimes disturbing behavior demonstrated by some patients, the tendency to provide services in sheltered facilities, geographically separated from population centers, has been in effect for centuries. Large psychiatric hospitals have been known to exist for at least the past 300 years. When these hospitals were first operated, it was difficult to tell if they were asylums or prisons. Residents were often shackled and lived in squalid conditions. Diet and sanitation were poor, and patients were often dressed in rags.

Tours were provided to one of these large-scale hospitals, St. Mary's of Bethlem, which is still in operation in London (known now as the Bethlem Royal Hospital). Local residents were guided through the institution to marvel at the behavior of the patients (at that time referred to as "lunatics"). The noise and conditions of the hospital, combined with the contemporary pronunciation of the name of the place, resulted in the coinage of the new word *bedlam*.

Similar hospitals were operated in other countries, including France. Philippe Pinel, who was the superintendent of one of these institutions, the Hôpital de Saltpêtrière in Paris, had a new theory about the treatment of patients with severe mental illness in his hospital. He released them from their chains, advocating "moral treatment" of their problems. The translation of moral treatment is simple: treating them as people with emotional responses. One of the consequences of moral treatment is that many of the patients were actually able to be released from the hospital almost immediately. As noted before, the episodic course of schizophrenia is such that in many cases even severe psychotic episodes can be followed by extended periods of remission. It is quite likely, however, in someone who has partially recovered from a serious period of psychosis, with delusions and hallucinations, the experience of being chained up in a dark and filthy room would interfere with full recovery.

In the United States, there is no evidence that patients were ever chained up. At the same time, until the end of the 19th century, it is also hard to find evidence that they received any services or treatment either. In the United States, the fertile period for the construction of large psychiatric facilities was at the end of the 19th century. In both larger and smaller states, it was common to construct one or more "state hospitals," which served the needs of all of the schizophrenic patients in the entire state. In smaller states with a single hospital, these hospitals were often located in the center of the state, to make transfer of the patients easier and to make it easier for relatives to visit people who were living in the hospital. These hospitals often had farms, workshops, and even a cemetery for the burial of patients whose relatives were not in contact with them or who refused to come to see them.

Although it is difficult to estimate exactly how many patients lived in state psychiatric facilities, because records were not kept in the same way as now, it is estimated that about 275,000 patients lived in chronic psychiatric hospitals in 1948, at the peak of long-stay psychiatric occupancy. Some of the individual hospitals were themselves massive institutions. For instance, one of these hospitals in New York, Pilgrim Psychiatric Center, had as many as 17,500 patients living on the grounds at any one time. In addition, at the edge of the grounds of Pilgrim Psychiatric Center, an additional psychiatric hospital with 7,500 patients was located. Eight miles away to the north an additional hospital, Kings Park Psychiatric Center, housed 6,000 patients, and six miles to the east Central Islip Psychiatric Center housed an additional 5,000 patients. So, within an eight-mile radius, as many as 35,000 patients were housed in long-stay institutional care sponsored by the state of New York, not including the 1,000 veterans who were hospitalized at Northport VA Medical Center 7 miles away.

Although it seems as if this was a massive institutional presence, at approximately the same time, New York also maintained large hospitals with capacities of up to 2,000 patients in each of the five Boroughs of New York City (Queens, Brooklyn, Manhattan, Bronx, and Staten Island). In addition, specialty forensic units were also maintained, at city hospitals and in proximity to Manhattan Psychiatric Center. As a result, the scope of state-provided psychiatric services at the time of the introduction of antipsychotic medications was massive and largely based on an inpatient service model. Other highly populated states had similar patterns of services.

Criticisms of the Asylum Model

During the 1960s, substantial criticism of the large-scale institutional care model began to develop. Critical essays describing the adverse consequences of residing in these facilities on the long-term well-being of patients were published. A community care movement developed and a large-scale plan to provide mental health treatment at community mental health centers was developed. There are several criticisms of large-scale psychiatric hospitals that were advanced, with nearly all of these criticisms having substantial merit at the time.

Patients Become Institutionalized

One of the major criticisms of institutional care is that patients experience a form of social and sensory deprivation that has adverse consequences. These consequences are argued to result in loss of motivation, blunting of emotional responses, and social withdrawal. There is no argument that many institutional settings were deprived and bleak, particularly in years past.

Patients Receive Little Attention

It is argued that patients were largely ignored after their admission to the hospital, receiving little attention and having no plans developed for them. A study performed by Rosenhan (1973) suggested that research confederates simulating mental illness to gain admission to a hospital were undetected for extended periods afterward, even when they never mentioned their complaints again.

Patients Do Not Receive State-of-the-Art Treatments

It is widely believed that treatment advances make their way slowly into the long-stay institutions in which chronic schizophrenic patients received their treatment. As a result, it is argued that these patients, the ones who may be in need of the most aggressive interventions, receive their treatments later than patients in other care modalities.

These criticisms are certainly valid. Since the time of the earlier research, however, the care environment for individuals with serious psychotic disorders such as schizophrenia has changed markedly. At this time, it would be rare for someone who said that he or she heard voices saying "boom," "hollow," and "thud" (the symptoms reported by the simulators in the Rosenhan study) to even be admitted to a psychiatric hospital, and their care would be regularly reviewed with an eye toward immediate discharge in any case. Treatment advances are now actually much more likely to be applied to patients in state psychiatric hospitals than to patients receiving treatment from psychiatrists and psychologists in private practice. Antipsychotic medications were in use at many public psychiatric hospitals in New York in the 1950s, during an era in which the typical treatment offered to patients with schizophrenia in the community was psychoanalysis. At the present time, the proportion of patients receiving the newest medication treatments who are inpatients in New York psychiatric centers is 25% higher than the national average. At the present time, individuals with schizophrenia, particularly older ones, receive extremely well-monitored care in long-stay psychiatric institutions.

THE CURRENT INSTITUTIONAL CARE CLIMATE FOR OLDER PATIENTS WITH SCHIZOPHRENIA

At this time, institutional care is rare for younger patients with schizophrenia. From the high of 275,000 patients 50 years ago, there were fewer than 6,000 patients nationwide in long-stay psychiatric care in 2004. In fact, California has only one remaining nonforensic state psychiatric hospital, in Napa Valley, which has fewer than 300 beds for a state with a population of more than 45 million people. Most states are converting their hospitals to exclusively forensic or geriatric facilities (Bloom, Williams, Land, McFarland, & Reichlin, 1998), so the majority of patients who receive care at long-stay psychiatric facilities are the older patients who are the focus of this book.

Many of the older patients with schizophrenia who leave chronic psychiatric care after extended stays are clearly in no position to live independently. Many have lived their entire adult lives in chronic psychiatric care and have no experience in independent living. Few were ever married or had children, and their advanced age makes it such that few have siblings who would be able to welcome them to reside at their home. As a consequence, most of these patients leave to highly structured residential settings, such as nursing homes or full-care community residences. Both of these modalities of care are described.

LONG-TERM CARE IN THE 1990s

In 1990, I initiated, along with several of my colleagues, including Michael Davidson and Kenneth Davis, a program of research at Pilgrim Psychiatric Center (PPC). This hospital, described earlier, was for years the largest hospital in the world, and it is still clearly the largest nonforensic psychiatric treatment facility in the country. At the time our research program began at PPC, there were more than 3,500 inpatients receiving treatment at the hospital, and 850 individuals over the age of 65 had a diagnosis of schizophrenia. These patients were the focus of an extensive diagnostic and clinical work-up and were also followed longitudinally. This study presents a unique perspective on schizophrenia and aging, because it was a study of the entire population of a large psychiatric facility with the goals from the outset of performing as comprehensive an assessment of schizophrenia and aging as possible.

Of the 850 patients who were residents in 1990, 508 met full DSM–III–R (American Psychiatric Association, 1987) criteria for schizophrenia (Davidson et al., 1995). The typical reason that the other cases' schizophrenia diagnosis was not confirmed was that they had alternative medical conditions that could be responsible for some of the disability seen. Of these remaining 508 patients, the most common number of previous admissions to psychiatric care was one and the average length of current stay was 47 consecutive years. As a result, this was an elderly (mean age = 74) and chronically hospitalized group. Fifty-seven percent were female, likely a result of the differential survival of males and females, because younger admissions for schizophrenia at the same hospital were overwhelmingly male (over 80%). Of these patients, more than 90% were receiving antipsychotic medications, which at the time did not include any patients receiving any of the newer antipsychotic medications. These patients had completed on average 10 years of education, although the oldest patients (86–95) had completed 3 years fewer education than the youngest (65–70). When these patients were compared to samples of ambulatory patients with schizophrenia of the same age who were hospitalized for an acute psychotic episode at the time of their recruitment and assessment (Harvey et al., 1998), institutionalized patients had more severe negative symptoms and cognitive deficits, while having equivalently severe positive symptoms. Furthermore, functional deficits were greater in the institutionalized patients, although in both patient samples cognitive deficits were the best predictor of functional limitations.

There are several conclusions that can be reached from the evaluation of these basic demographic data. First is that many of these long-stay patients had spent the majority of their lives in chronic psychiatric care without a single discharge from the hospital, meaning that this was a highly selected group of patients with a lifetime history of continuous institutional stay. The second major conclusion is that, despite the reduced life expectancy seen in patients with schizophrenia in general, these patients had lived to a relatively old age. When the life expectancies of these patients are calculated, given their year of birth, education, and parental socioeconomic status, they would have been expected to live for 65 years or less. The third conclusion was that this group of patients had no evidence of profound intellectual impairments. In previous years, New York aggressively referred patients at all of its state psychiatric facilities who were suspected of having developmental disability to facilities run by the Office of Mental Retardation and Developmental Disabilities.

The extended life expectancy of this highly selected group was not a result of their being invulnerable to illness. For example, at the first assessment of these patients, they were receiving treatment for an average of 1.8 different physical illnesses (Friedman et al., 2002), with the number of illnesses manifested two years later increasing to an average of 3.0. Many of these older patients had hypertension, diabetes, cardiac problems, and other conditions that were treated with both medications and special diets. Compliance with these diets and medications is ensured in a hospital environment, such that even patients who are generally noncompliant with treatment and other staff instructions are treated with their medications. As a result, medical morbidity because of poor compliance with medical care is markedly reduced in institutionalized individuals.

One of the questions that then arises when examining chronically institutionalized patients is whether specific systems of care have different types of patients in its catchment area. For instance, both the VA and state hospital systems treat long-stay patients, but there is little information available about these patients in terms of their characteristics, both symptomatic and other features of the illness. In one study that addressed this issue (Harvey, Jacobsen, et al., 2000), it was found that state hospital patients over the age of 65 had more severe negative and cognitive symptoms, as well as more substantial cognitive deficits. The two samples of patients did not, however, differ in the severity of their psychotic symptoms. Thus, one of the first clues about the reason for the decades-long retention of patients in long-stay hospitals emerges: It is possible that certain patients manifest symptoms that are so severe, despite state-of-the-art treatment, that it is extremely difficult to discharge them and ensure the joint safety of the patient and the community as a whole.

DISCHARGE OF LONG-STAY PATIENTS

One of the things that occurred during the 1990s was another wave of deinstitutionalization of patients with schizophrenia across all long-stay facilities run by essentially every state. For instance, California closed its largest psychiatric facility, Camarillo Psychiatric Center, in 1996. As a part of this discharge pressure, approximately 50% of the older patients at PPC were discharged during a 2-year period, despite the fact that these patients had remained behind in several previous efforts to reduce the census of the hospital. Full data were available to do a descriptive study on 551 patients, of whom 262 (47.5%) were discharged over a 2-year period. White, Parrella, et al. (1997) examined the characteristics of the patients who were retained and discharged in the first and second year, in a replication design. Over the 2 years, 200 of the 262 patients who were discharged (76%) went to a nursing home, although 16 patients were referred to other psychiatric centers and only 7 (3%) were sent to independent community residences. Of the community care discharges, a single patient was discharged to live by herself and the other six patients were sent to family care homes. Patients who were discharged, regardless of placement, had significantly lower scores on excitement, impulsivity, hostility, and uncooperativeness than the patients who stayed at the long-stay hospital. There were no differences in severity of any clinical symptoms or functional or cognitive deficits between those patients who were retained and those who were discharged. Subsequent analyses of the data indicated that of the patients who were discharged, those who were older and sicker tended to go to nursing homes but that there were no other differences that seemed to determine placement status.

These data are consistent with an archival study of more than 16,000 patients in New York state psychiatric hospitals previously reported by Holohean, Banks, and Maddy (1993). They also found that patients who were institutionalized had high scores on aggressiveness and functional disability but that one third of their patients had only modest symptoms of schizophrenia. These data also highlight the need, described later, to develop treatments that are more specifically effective on aggressive behavior.

Also consistent with these findings are results of the Team for Assessment of Psychiatric Services (TAPS) project. In one of the final papers from this long-term study of deinstitutionalization (Trieman, Hughes, & Leff, 1998), it was reported that the patients who were last to leave long-stay hospitals in the United Kingdom were patients who were aggressive, hostile, and incontinent. These patients were likely to be older male patients with a history of extremely long previous institutional stay. Thus, across countries, the remaining patients in long-stay psychiatric facilities are those patients whose behavior problems are too severe for them to be referred to community residences.

DETERMINING THE BENEFITS, IF ANY, TO DISCHARGE FROM PSYCHIATRIC INSTITUTIONS

It is clear that the reason that governmental entities are motivated to close large hospitals is financial. A question that arises is how well the patients do, across multiple life domains, after discharge. Although the main pressure to discharge patients with schizophrenia is clearly financial, there are substantial data indicating that patients who are referred to the community have an improvement in their quality of life and, in some cases, their symptoms. In a 3- to 5-year follow-up study of discharged patients in Northern Ireland, Donnelley, McGilloway, Mays, Perry, and Lavery (1997) found that 61% had been referred to the community or unstaffed residences. These recently deinstitutionalized patients endorsed several indicators of improvements in subjective quality of life; more than 70% reported that they were happier, healthier, and more independent. It is interesting to note that 13% of the sample had died within this short follow-up period. In a similar study in Australia, Bland and Harrison (1995) found that referral to live with relatives was associated with better outcomes, but also noted that this referral plan was rare for older patients with a longer duration of illness (as discussed earlier). In a follow-up study from the TAPS project, Trieman et al. (1996) reported that older long-stay patients discharged to the community were cognitively and clinically stable, whereas patients who remained in the hospital worsened in both domains. Although this may reflect a selection bias based on clinicians' impression of which patients can be discharged, this result still suggests that a transition to a supported community residence is associated with better functioning than institutional care for older individuals. At the same time, as noted earlier, in large-scale institutions in which there is pressure to discharge patients rapidly, referral to the community is rare and is also likely to be contingent on the age and health of the individual involved.

NURSING HOMES AS THE NEW INSTITUTION

Nursing homes to most people, including most health professionals, are viewed as places in which the last few visits with aging relatives occur before their death. The facts bear out this impression, as a comprehensive study of survival at Washington, DC's largest nursing home (Cohen-Mansfield, Marx, Lipson, & Werner, 1999), found that the average resident lived for 30 months after moving into the home. Despite this relatively short life expectancy for the typical patient, the face of nursing home care is changing, particularly for nursing homes that have a largely poor population whose care is paid for by state entitlements such as Medicaid.

As seen earlier in the White et al. study, large numbers of patients with lifelong schizophrenia are being referred directly from psychiatric inpatient facilities to nursing home care. It has proven difficult to estimate the actual numbers of cases so referred in the country as a whole. As long ago as 1986 it was estimated that as many as 200,000 individuals with lifelong schizophrenia were nursing home residents (Goldman, Feder, & Scanlon, 1986). Based on the results of the White et al. study and other information collected from patients at PPC, it is known that more than 1,400 individuals have been referred from PPC alone to nursing homes in the past decade.

At the same time, the authors of a recent study (Mechanic & McAlpine, 2000) stated their belief that as few as 8,000 individuals with lifelong schizophrenia may be in nursing home care in the entire country. This number is definitely an underestimate, based on several years of New York Office of Mental Health discharge records indicating that many more than 8,000 patients were directly discharged to nursing homes in New York City alone. In addition, our research group has performed clinical assessments on more than 1,500 such patients. The marked discrepancy between these results reflects some of the problems associated with provision of care to older schizophrenic patients in nursing homes.

One reason for this discrepancy is the use of data from the National Nursing Home Survey (National Center for Health Statistics, 1995) to estimate prevalence of older patients with schizophrenia receiving care in nursing homes. These data are not subject to quality control in terms of the diagnoses that are entered. Many older individuals in nursing homes have a diagnosis of dementia, with the prevalence of dementia and depression diagnoses in nursing home residents increasing. As noted previously, many patients with lifelong schizophrenia meet criteria for dementia in late life. Entering a diagnosis of dementia instead of schizophrenia, despite persistent schizophrenic symptoms, would lead to the prevalence of schizophrenia being underestimated. In addition, many patients who had been directly referred from New York state psychiatric centers have diagnoses in their charts that are purely medical. For instance, patients with chronic obstructive pulmonary disease (COPD) and chronic schizophrenia may have their diagnosis of schizophrenia disappear, especially when they are referred for brief treatment at a medical hospital and are then returned to the nursing home. Using reimbursement data coded by diagnosis would miss the schizophrenia diagnosis and tend to underestimate the prevalence of schizophrenia in the nursing home population.

CHARACTERISTICS OF SCHIZOPHRENIC PATIENTS IN NURSING HOME CARE

There have been relatively few studies of the characteristics of schizophrenic patients who are residents of nursing home care. Some of the previous studies have simply used archival records to attempt to characterize the patients, but these studies have considerable limitations. For instance, a study by Sherrell, Anderson, and Buchwalter (1998) examined the charts of 570 nursing home residents who had a history of chronic psychiatric illness. They noted that the charts contained no information on functional status or cognitive deficits, so they rated abstracted chart narratives. They concluded that the majority of the patients had cognitive impairments in the "none to mild" range and that the most common symptom was social withdrawal. This conclusion is particularly interesting because most first-episode patients with schizophrenia in their early 20s meet clinical criteria for dementia on the basis of their typically severe cognitive impairment.

In the 850 charts reviewed at PPC for the Davidson et al. (1995) study, there were no clinical notes regarding cognitive deficits. When formal assessments were performed, the average Mini-Mental State Examination (MMSE; Folstein et al., 1975) score of patients over the age of 75 was 11.9, consistent with severe dementia and profound cognitive deficits (Davidson et al., 1995). These data suggest that reliance on clinicians to spontaneously report cognitive deficits is unlikely to produce results with suitable validity. Clinical assessment has recently been shown to be a poor proxy for cognitive assessment even when clinicians attempt to rate cognitive deficits (Harvey et al., 2001). In that comprehensive study of the relationships between clinical ratings of cognitive deficits and the results of neuropsychological assessments in older patients with schizophrenia, it was found that only 10% of the variance in performance-based test scores was accounted for by clinical ratings. Thus, even in cases in which clinicians use a systematic clinical rating scale to evaluate cognitive deficits, their scores do not correspond with the results of neuropsychological tests.

In studies of the characteristics of long-stay psychiatric patients who were examined while residing in nursing home care after their discharge from chronic psychiatric facilities, several important findings have emerged. In one comprehensive study, Bartels et al. (1997b) compared nursing home residents with chronic psychiatric conditions including schizophrenia to community dwellers with the same diagnoses. Although symptom status was most strongly related to diagnosis (bipolar–schizophrenia) regardless of residential status, nursing home residents, regardless of diagnosis, were more likely to have more severe cognitive and functional deficits, as well as more behavioral problems and indicators of poor premorbid adjustment. The average MMSE score of the nursing home residents was in the severely demented range. A similar study (Harvey et al., 1998) also found that nursing home residence was associated with more severe negative and cognitive deficits, as well as greater functional impairments, and nursing home residents had less severe positive symptoms than community dwellers and chronically institutionalized patients.

TREATMENTS RECEIVED

There has been a long-time controversy about the quality of care received by psychiatric patients in nursing homes. Because staff in nursing homes are not necessarily trained to manage psychiatric patients and because many nursing homes do not have access to mental health consultation services, patients in these homes run the risk of receiving lower quality treatment. In fact, one study (Burns et al., 1993) suggested that aggressive behavior was likely to be managed by general practitioners rather than through mental health consultation, despite the prevalence of aggression in institutionalized patients with schizophrenia. In addition, the older the patient, the less likely that mental health services were offered. Older patients and those patients with more impairment in their activities of daily living (ADLs) were less likely to receive mental health consults at nursing homes than higher functioning patients (Shea, Streit, & Smyer, 1994). Perhaps this outcome reflects a lack of understanding about the substantial impact that schizophrenia and related conditions have on ADLs. As noted earlier, any intervention that reduces cognitive impairments is likely to result in improvement in the performance of functional skills.

Staff training and competence is widely variable across nursing homes. Research aimed at understanding staffing patterns and its relationship with outcome in nursing homes has produced several findings of potential interest. For instance, Timko, Nguyen, Williford, and Moos (1993) reported that the staff in public sector nursing homes were treating patients with greater disability and had less formal training than staff working in VA nursing homes. As a result, patients in those public sector nursing homes that accept the large proportion of older schizophrenic patients are least likely to have access to specialty mental health care.

There has been a long-time controversy regarding the use of antipsychotic medications to treat nursing home residents. In fact, enough concerns had been raised about this issue that Congress took action. The Omnibus Budget Reconciliation Act of 1987 (OBRA-87) led to the development of disposition categories for the discharge of patients with chronic mental illness to nursing homes and provided standards for the use of antipsychotic medications. These guidelines provided maximum doses and specified certain schedules of treatment for patients receiving these medications.

There has been considerable controversy about these regulations. Llorente et al. (1998) reported that the majority of individuals residing in nursing homes who were receiving antipsychotic medications were receiving dosages within guidelines. The exception were patients with schizophrenia, who were found to be much more likely to receive doses of medication that were too high according to the standards. In contrast, in our own research, we (Bowie et al., 2001) found that nursing home patients (N = 114) were five times more likely than patients receiving care at a state or VA long-term psychiatric center to be receiving no antipsychotic medications at all. The nursing home patients in this study had the same severity of psychosis as the state hospital patients, however, despite the fact that they were much more likely to have had their treatment with antipsychotic medications discontinued after their referral to the nursing home. In addition, these nursing home patients were twice as likely to be receiving conventional antipsychotic medications as patients at a chronic psychiatric center.

These data raise some questions regarding the impact of short-term financial motivation in treatment decisions. It is superficially less expensive to provide no medication at all to patients than to provide treatments. The acquisition cost of older medications is markedly less than that of newer medications, providing a financial incentive to use older treatments. In situations in which insurance providers do not provide additional supplements for the greater costs of the newer medications, nursing home operators may choose to use older medications, despite their liabilities, in schizophrenic patients. In addition, it is extremely rare that any mental health services other than medications are ever provided to nursing home residents. Mental health services such as psychotherapy are often reimbursed at extremely low rates for public insurance, making it unlikely that mental health providers would be motivated to see these patients as independent practitioners. These low reimbursement rates make it unlikely that nursing home operators would be motivated to include these services as part of the daily reimbursed bed rate.

DETERMINING IF THERE ARE ADVERSE EFFECTS OF LIVING IN A NURSING HOME FOR OLDER SCHIZOPHRENIC PATIENTS

As noted earlier, referral of patients from the institution to live in a supportive residence or with a willing family member is associated with improved adjustment. Yet this is far from the typical referral, as seen from the results of the White, Parrella, et al. (1997) study, in which only one of more than 800 patients received this discharge plan. The issue arises as to whether, in the current climate of care, referral to a nursing home has adverse consequences relative to remaining behind in a long-stay psychiatric facility.

There are several ways to address this question, focusing on symptoms, cognitive and functional status, as well as medical comorbidity and mortality. In one study addressing this issue (Harvey, Parrella, et al., 1999), 57 patients who were referred from a chronic psychiatric hospital to nursing home care were followed up from 18 months to five years later (mean follow-up duration of 30 months). These patients had evidence of considerable cognitive and functional decline over the follow-up period. These deteriorations were not a result of changes in positive or negative symptoms, which were found to be stable over time. So, in contrast to the results of studies that found that patients referred from chronic psychiatric care to community residences had stable to improving clinical status, these patients had notable deterioration in their functioning within the 2.5 years after referral from a chronic psychiatric hospital to a nursing home.

This study is, of course, limited by the fact that patients who were identified for referral to a nursing home might have been selected in some way for potential to deteriorate. In a randomized clinical trial (Linn et al., 1985) a large sample of VA patients with either schizophrenia or dementia were randomized to either stay in a long-stay psychiatric hospital, be transferred to a different psychiatric center, be referred to a VA nursing care unit, or be sent to a community nursing facility. Six- and 12-month follow-up revealed that across both diagnoses, patients who were referred to the community nursing home were doing more poorly in terms of self-care, behavioral deterioration, mental confusion, depression, and satisfaction with their care. The group transferred to another long-stay hospital ward was found to be doing better than the patients referred to nursing home care. There was a substantial cost benefit for referral to community nursing, which may be offset by the deterioration in functioning seen soon after referral. These differences were also not a result of differences in medication treatment, which was consistent across the follow-up period. So, across randomized and nonrandomized studies, referral to nursing home care is associated with deterioration in functioning. Because the state hospital patients were initially much lower functioning than the VA patients in the Linn et al. study, these findings suggest that deterioration in functioning after nursing home referral occurs across patients with a wide range of baseline functional status.

In addition to reductions in functional status, there is the additional question of whether there are even more serious consequences of nursing home referral. There are no systematic studies of mortality rates in patients with schizophrenia after referral to nursing home care. In data analyzed from the National Nursing Home Survey (Castle & Shea, 1997), there was no differential effect overall for mortality of nursing home residents who received mental health treatment from specialists or general practitioners. However, for patients with schizophrenia, as well as those with other psychotic conditions, there was a statistically significant reduction in mortality if specialists provided their mental health treatment. Because the causes of mortality in older patients with schizophrenia are different than in younger patients, there is clearly an effect on mortality that is not a result of reduction in suicide or accidents. It is entirely possible that the involvement of mental health professionals in treatment of older patients with schizophrenia is associated with better management of side effects, particularly tardive dyskinesia, than that which occurs with general medical interventions for mental health treatment. The unfortunate fact is that the majority of older patients with schizophrenia in nursing homes never receive consultation from a mental health professional, indicating that they are generally in the group in which excess mortality may be detected.

MAKING A JUDGMENT ABOUT INSTITUTIONAL CARE

Several different studies from the TAPS project suggest that older patients with schizophrenia who are discharged from long-stay psychiatric hospitals and referred to supportive and fully staffed community residences experience improvements in their functioning and in their quality of life. Equivalently substantial data demonstrate that referral to a nursing home leads to deterioration in functioning relative to that seen in long-stay psychiatric facilities. A closer look at the types of services provided in the community in the TAPS project suggests that this level of service is not likely to be provided any time soon to public-sector mental health patients in the United States.

At the outset of the TAPS project, high-quality, relatively modern large homes were purchased and used to house the patients who were referred from the hospital. The anticipated revenue to be realized by the British government from the sale of the valuable property on which the long-stay public hospital was located covered the cost of these homes. These homes were then staffed with trained mental health workers who were already experienced at the inpatient behavioral management of patients with schizophrenia. These homes held between 8 to 16 formerly hospitalized residents, each of whom were living in excellent conditions with good supervision, the potential for social interaction, and good diet and nutrition. Compared with typical residences for community-dwelling psychiatric patients in the United States, these homes were luxurious and were staffed with extremely competent individuals.

It is likely that a similar experiment would happen in the United States. In California, the state closed its largest psychiatric facility, Camarillo State Hospital, in 1996. Patients at that facility were sent to a large number of other treatment modalities, including locked board and care. Such a community residence is operated as a board and care home, in which the patients are not allowed to enter and leave the residence according to their own wishes. These homes, like nursing homes, typically do not have on-site mental health services and, in contrast to nursing homes, often do not have on-site medical consultation. Although some board and care homes have regular contact with consultant psychiatrists (Fleishman, 1997), this is not a licensing requirement. No data are available on the outcome of patients who receive treatment in such facilities in terms of relative adjustment compared to life in the long-stay psychiatric hospital or the nursing home. What appears likely, however, is that there is little resemblance between one of the community homes in London studied in the TAPS project and the current model of locked board and care that has been applied to a large number of older patients with schizophrenia who have been discharged from long-stay inpatient care.

All of the available data indicate that nursing homes appear to be a poor residential choice for patients with chronic schizophrenia. In these homes patients appear to have a shorter life span and greater risk for functional and cognitive decline than in chronic psychiatric institutions. These data have arisen from randomized clinical trials and from naturalistic studies, indicating that selection biases cannot be the reason for the findings. As a result, despite attempts to regulate nursing homes and avoid referrals of patients with schizophrenia there, these homes are still in common use as a referral source and appear to have adverse effects on their residents.

DETERMINING IF THERE ARE PATIENTS WHO CAN NEVER BE MANAGED IN THE COMMUNITY

The data collected to date suggest that there is a small minority of patients who cannot survive outside a full-care psychiatric institution. These are patients with severe behavioral problems who put the public, fellow residents, staff members, and themselves at risk wherever they are. The constant supervision as well as high levels of medical care provided at the contemporary long-stay hospital appears to be the only safe treatment option for these patients. It is not clear what the prevalence of this type of substantial behavioral problems are in the community, but there are some patients who clearly require this level of care.

CONCLUSION

The huge psychiatric institutions of the twentieth century are a thing of the past. Many of the patients who had extended stays there were discharged to the community, and the research data indicate that, depending on the type of residence to which they were sent, most of these patients have experienced an improved quality of life. This reduction of the size of these institutions has been the product of several different pressures, some positive and some definitely not. Nursing home care has emerged as a common residential option for older patients with schizophrenia, but nearly all of the data collected indicate that patients who were doing poorly before referral do even more poorly after their discharge to nursing homes. These adverse effects include cognitive and functional decline as well as increased mortality. Reasons for these declines are likely to be poor treatment choices, including excessive medication doses, the use of older medications, failure to treat patients with antipsychotics because of their cost, and staff with little or no experience or motivation in the area of treating older psychiatric patients. Long-stay psychiatric hospitals provide medical and psychiatric services to older patients that are consistent with or better than current community standards, suggesting that patients who reside there are not receiving inappropriate or excessive treatment. There is little reason to believe that most patients with schizophrenia cannot be managed in a minimally restrictive treatment setting. After all of the changes that have occurred, the long-stay psychiatric hospital is changed. It still exists, and it serves a highly select group of patients who are currently impossible to treat in any other location.

9

PREVIOUS TREATMENTS FOR SCHIZOPHRENIA: EFFICACY AND ADVERSE EFFECTS

Treatment of schizophrenia has been a challenge since the earliest definition of the illness. At this time, treatments for schizophrenia are often characterized as evidence-based. Older treatments for schizophrenia were also considered evidence-based by their proponents, but the quality of the evidence was quite variable. This chapter presents the history of treatment of schizophrenia from 1890 to 1990. This epoch was selected because of the multiple treatments offered to patients with schizophrenia, which are now known primarily because of their adverse events, in contrast to newer treatments that are described later. Understanding these older treatments is important for the study of older patients with schizophrenia, because the persistence of many of the adverse effects of these treatments continues to affect a large proportion of these older schizophrenia patients. As a consequence, developing understanding of older treatments, their persistent effects, and the rationale behind these treatments is still important, both to evaluate the current state of these patients and to understand their life histories. This chapter describes the treatments and hospital conditions affecting older patients with schizophrenia, with a focus on persistent consequences of those treatments. It is important to review these interventions briefly to obtain a historical perspective on the hospitals to which patients who are currently in their late 70s and older were admitted at the outset of their illness. This review focuses on treatments with the potential for lasting side effects, which rules out many of the more benign treatments such as hydrotherapy.

HISTORICAL CONTEXT

It is difficult to imagine the conditions in a long-stay psychiatric hospital from the late 1890s to the 1950s. Hundreds to thousands of patients lived in large wards in large buildings. Many of these patients were actively hallucinating, delusional, and explosively violent. Incoherent screaming was common, while other patients were assuming bizarre postures, grimacing, and gesturing. Others were completely silent, sitting expressionless for days. Some of these patients, characterized as manifesting the catatonic subtype, were so unresponsive to the environment that even major events failed to capture their attention.

Similarly primitive was the understanding of the causes of the illness. Theorists as far back as Kraepelin (see chap. 1, this volume) advanced the belief that schizophrenia was a brain disease affecting the frontal lobes, and various biological theories of the origin of psychotic behavior were advanced in these early days of neuropsychiatry. These theories ranged from dental infection, to malformed intestines, to oxygen deficiency. In the absence of any detailed knowledge of brain function and neurotransmission, many of these theories were not even aimed at brain function as we understand it today, focusing on peripheral abnormalities that are now known not to produce biological changes that even cross the blood–brain barrier and enter the central nervous system. Treatments ranged from twirling a patient in a chair until he or she because dizzy and vomited—piloted by one of the champions of humane treatment, Benjamin Rush—to operations that extracted teeth, adrenal glands, and parts of the brain.

Some of the intervention applied in the late 1890s and early 1900s have completely died out, and the patients who were exposed to those interventions are no longer alive. Many surviving older patients with schizophrenia have been exposed to a whole array of other interventions, and the consequences of these treatments are still affecting some of them today. These interventions included such benign interventions as soaking in tubs and being wrapped in wet sheets. Also included were a variety of different procedures designed to induce convulsions, including inductions of fever, infusions of metrazol, insulin (to cause an insulin coma), electro-convulsive therapy, as well as frontal lobotomy, high doses of barbiturates, and conventional antipsychotics. Although the current generation of younger patients will not be exposed to most of these interventions, new developments in treatment may also make current treatment "advances" seem as primitive or barbaric in a few decades as well.

INOCULATION THERAPIES

Patients with schizophrenia were injected with a wide array of substances, including horse blood and blood from individuals who had just experienced a seizure. These therapies were based on the idea that blood-borne cells would stimulate appropriate regions of the brain. Needless to say, there is little contemporary evidence that would support such an intervention.

CONVULSIVE THERAPIES

Based on the now-discredited clinical observation that patients who had experienced seizures had a partial remission of their symptoms, several different interventions were administered that included the induction of convulsions. It was also believed that seizure disorders and schizophrenia did not co-occur in the same patients, leading to the conclusion that convulsions (or their correlates) must be beneficial for symptoms of schizophrenia. Several different methods for inducing convulsions were implemented. Naturally occurring convulsions from fever, endogenous seizure disorders, and from glucose infusion leading to insulin shock were the originally occurring models for this intervention.

Insulin Coma Therapy

Insulin coma therapy intervention involved reduction of glucose levels until the seizure threshold was reached. Similar to the convulsions that occasionally occur spontaneously in insulin shock, this procedure led to a sustained seizure that was reversed through the administration of glucose. Variants of this procedure were often administered dozens of times to patients with schizophrenia. Some data from follow-up studies of older patients treated with this procedure have suggested that insulin coma therapy is not associated with detectable cognitive changes approximately 35 years following the final treatment (Davidson et al., 1995). These data are likely to be biased, however, because they were based on a study of patients who were chronically institutionalized, which might be associated with greater cognitive impairment on the part of the patients who never received this insulin coma treatment. This treatment intervention was used in many

American hospitals until the 1950s, meaning that a number of surviving patients have received this treatment.

Electro-Convulsive Therapy

Electro-convulsive therapy (ECT), previously referred to with the less-sanitized name "Electro-shock," is the only somatic treatment of those described to this point that is still in use. This technique was developed in the late 1930s in Italy and was widely used in the United States starting in the 1940s. In the initial applications of this technique, a current was passed through the head from electrodes located on the skull over each of the cerebral hemispheres and a convulsion was induced. During the early applications of this procedure it was common to see that the intense convulsion produced fractures. After the introduction of curare to induce muscular paralysis, the rate of fractures declined.

ECT treatment was widely used to treat patients with schizophrenia, although the research literature throughout its use has indicated that it, like other convulsive procedures, produced a greater benefit in patients with affective disorders. This treatment was widely used and was often repeated multiple times. For instance, in a sample of 308 older patients with schizophrenia from Pilgrim Psychiatric Center (PPC) examined by Davidson et al. (1995), 72 of these patients had been treated with ECT. The median number of ECT treatments administered to these patients was 24, but some patients received more than 150 sessions of ECT. Again, no immediately obvious effects of ECT were detected when patients who had and had not experienced the procedure were compared to each other, but this is a particularly low-functioning sample.

Patients with schizophrenia still are treated with ECT. Most commonly ECT is used in cases in which patients are refractory to treatment with all different pharmacological interventions and also have significant behavioral problems. As recently as 2001, a large-scale study originating in Thailand (Chanpattana & Somchai Chakrabhand, 2001) reported that 54% of 293 patients with "treatment-refractory" schizophrenia had benefited from the addition of ECT treatments to conventional antipsychotic medications. At the same time, these patients did not improve in their negative symptoms, and some actually worsened, suggesting that their overall outcome is likely to be completely unaffected by this treatment. ECT has remained a completely controversial topic, despite marked improvements in the use of the procedure (Fink, 2001). These improvements include the use of unilateral ECT and lower electrical doses, leading to markedly reduced memory deficits after the procedure (Lisanby, Maddox, Prudic, Devanand, & Sackeim, 2000). At the same time, there is no other mainstream treatment in psychiatry that is banned in a large state, as was ECT in California. It is clear from the research on ECT and depression that relapses are common after treatment and that maintenance treatments are required. There are clearly not enough data in schizophrenia to determine if maintenance ECT is beneficial, and there are essentially no data suggesting that ECT improves overall outcome, even in patients whose treatment-refractory psychotic symptoms are improved.

LOBOTOMY

Although scattered attempts to enter the brain and perform neurosurgery to treat schizophrenia occurred throughout the 19th and early 20th centuries, frontal lobotomy was aggressively adopted as a treatment strategy in the middle of the 20th century. This strategy was adopted on the basis of procedures initially developed and popularized by Moniz (1964) a Portuguese neurologist who won the Nobel prize for the implementation of this technique in humans. Although the theoretical justification for this procedure was scanty and quite internally inconsistent, the procedure was widely adopted.

Although various techniques to perform prefrontal lobotomies (or leucotomies, the more precise term) were developed, the principal outcome of this procedure was placement of a large lesion in the white matter of the anterior frontal cortex. This lesion was generally placed anterior to the dorsolateral region and extending inward toward the ventricles, severing the connecting tracts to subcortical regions such as the thalamus and the limbic system. Several different instruments were developed to perform the procedure, from an ice pick to the leucotome, a sharpened scalpel on a 9-inch handle, but the incisions were generally placed in the same location on the skull regardless of the procedure used to make that incision.

Postmortem examination of the brains of individuals who experienced a frontal leucotomy found widely variable lesions across patients treated with this procedure (Pakkenberg, 1989). It should not be surprising to see this finding, because the two versions of the leucotomy procedure, as described earlier, would produce vastly different lesions even if applied consistently. Because many surgeons performed the procedure differently from each other and even varied the procedure from patient to patient, the variation in the lesions would be expected to be great.

Determining the Rationale for Leucotomy

There are a wide range of consequences of frontal lobe lesions. As far back as the middle of the 19th century, it was known that personality changes, including increases in irritability, changes in motivation, and tendencies toward inappropriate behavior, were common in patients with damage to the frontal lobes. In addition, changes in the ability to solve problems and persist in application of appropriate effort have also been noted. Cognitive deficits were noted in monkeys who had lesions in the frontal lobe (Jacobsen, 1935), with the primary impairments being in working memory.

One of the major indications for leucotomy was not schizophrenia but rather disruptive behavior. In fact, hallucinations were never viewed by the proponents as a treatable symptom for leucotomy. A major consequence of certain frontal lobe lesions is the induction of a profoundly apathetic state. Thus, in an individual who was anxious, self-destructive, or uncooperative, induction of apathy would have the consequence of reducing the expression of these traits. Many patients who experienced a leucotomy were reported to experience periods of functional deficits that followed their leucotomy. For instance, it was commonly reported that patients experienced periods of incontinence and complete dependence on others. At the same time, many patients did experience reductions in their disruptive behavior. Thus, patients who were treated with leucotomy experienced a number of symptoms of frontal lobe damage, some of which were viewed more positively by clinicians who were managing these patients than others.

Consequences of Leucotomy

Leucotomy was never viewed as a benign procedure by the entire field. One of the principal complaints was mortality. Estimates of the number of patients who died while receiving a leucotomy procedure varied from 3% to 6%. Given that other treatments for the illness had similar mortalities but no efficacy either, these figures were generally accepted as a reasonable risk by proponents and a travesty by opponents. (Note that the risk of potentially fatal aganulocytosis with clozapine treatment is about 3% as well.)

Given the primacy of the frontal lobe in problem solving and other executive functions, it would be expected that some focus on cognitive changes would have appeared during the period when these procedures were being performed. Although many studies were conducted during this time period, most of the studies used assessments of intellectual functioning, finding no evidence of postsurgical decline. One of the major problems with this approach is that tests of intellectual functioning have been shown to be generally insensitive to frontal lobe damage (Stuss & Benson, 1986). Even in cases in which there are clear personality and behavioral changes, there are often modest cognitive changes from baseline.

There have been several structured studies to examine the consequences of leucotomy in patients with schizophrenia. For instance, the National Institute of Mental Health (NIMH) sponsored a study of patients who had experienced a leucotomy (Mirsky & Orzack, 1977), and several other studies were performed in the decades following the termination of leucotomy as a treatment for schizophrenia. Most comprehensive of these was the Northampton VA hospital series. This study is unique in several ways. The investigators in the study were among the world's foremost authorities on the functions of the frontal lobe. Patients were examined with neuroimaging procedures to discriminate the variance associated with the size of the frontal lobe lesion associated with the leucotomy. In addition, they were examined with a thoroughly comprehensive set of assessment that were sensitive to effects of frontal lobe lesions as well as to general aspects of intellectual functioning.

In the Northampton study there was a paucity of findings regarding the correlates of leucotomy. Patients who did and did not experience a leucotomy generally were indistinguishable, and the size of the lesion and its location had essentially no relationship with cognitive impairments in the surgically operated group. The one finding that could have been related with leucotomy was an increased tendency to demonstrate proactive interference on a memory test. Interference effects are reported in patients with frontal lobe damage, so this finding could be attributed to the consequences of the leucotomy (Stuss & Benson, 1986). On the other hand, a single deficit detected in patients whose brains are notable for massive surgical lesions leads to the conclusion that there are not massive changes in cognitive functioning associated with the use of leucotomy in patients with schizophrenia.

Some studies have found more substantial deficits in patients with leucotomy. For instance, Mirsky and Orzack (1977) reported that schizophrenic patients treated with leucotomy made more perseverative errors on the Wisconsin Card Sorting Test (WCST; Heaton et al., 1993) than comparison samples. Teuber, Corkin, and Twitchell (1977) failed to confirm this finding. Deficits in the WCST would be expected in patients with lesions in the orbital frontal cortex, because lesions in this region induce perseveration (Stuss & Benson, 1986). Confounding this effect is the fact that patients with schizophrenia in general demonstrate increased perseveration.

One of the intriguing findings associated with studies of leucotomy is that patients who experienced a "recovery" after their treatment were found to differ in their cognitive functions from those who were still institutionalized. For example, Benson et al. (1981) reported that patients who experienced a leucotomy and had a "good" level of recovery (community residence, minimal persistent symptoms) had intellectual performance scores that were higher than the comparison sample of schizophrenic patients who did not receive a leucotomy. It is possible that the patients with higher levels of

intellectual functioning and better outcome recovered despite the leucotomy, with the procedure itself not affecting outcome or, conceivably, on
cognitive functioning.

Does this mean that leucotomy had no effects on cognitive functioning
in patients with schizophrenia? It is likely that the reason that detection
of adverse cognitive effects of leucotomy has proven difficult is the low-
baseline problem. Patients with schizophrenia have surprisingly low scores
on measures of frontal lobe functioning, and worsening may be difficult to
detect. An additional problem is selection bias. In most studies the comparison group is patients of the same age with a diagnosis of schizophrenia,
many of whom were not as behaviorally disturbed. It may be that the patients
who were selected for the procedure were impaired in their functioning at
the outset.

Long-Term Effects of Leucotomy in Elderly Patients
With Schizophrenia

Approximately 20% (51 patients) out of a total sample of 308 elderly
patients (Davidson et al., 1995) had been exposed to the leucotomy procedure, and their clinical symptoms, global scores on cognitive measures, and
rates of side effects were compared to patients who did not experience
this procedure. Although there were no differences in Mini-Mental State
Examination (MMSE; Folstein et al., 1975) scores or in positive symptoms,
there was a surprising finding of a statistically significant reduction in the
severity of negative symptoms in the patients who experienced a leucotomy.

In a study of the cognitive functioning of a subset of these patients
who had been treated with a leucotomy, we (Harvey, Mohs, & Davidson,
1993) set out to comprehensively evaluate the potentially interactive effects
of aging and the previous experience of a leucotomy in older patients with
schizophrenia. We identified 24 patients who had received a leucotomy
who met several inclusion criteria: overall clinical dementia rating (CDR)
of 2.0 (moderate) or less, leucotomy operative report in the chart, and all
chart information regarding education and diagnostic status present. The
24 cases that met all of these criteria were contrasted to two comparison
groups. One group was a sample of 48 patients with no history of leucotomy.
These patients were matched 2 to 1 to the leucotomy group on the basis
of age, gender, premorbid educational status, and year of admission to the
psychiatric hospital. Thus these two groups were equated on variables that
could potentially confound the results of the cognitive assessment.

Another, smaller sample controlled for an additional critical factor:
the indication for leucotomy. Over the course of reading all of the charts
of patients who had a diagnosis of schizophrenia (more than 800), we
identified a small group of patients who had the "certificate of approval"

for a leucotomy but never received it, because of either administrative errors or withdrawal of consent by the relatives whose approval had been solicited. Because these patients had been approved for the procedure, they shared whatever behavioral indications for being exposed to leucotomy were operative at the hospital during the leucotomy era.

These three samples of patients were compared on cognitive tests that have been reported to be sensitive to frontal lobe functioning in both human and animal studies. These included the WCST, tests of spatial-delayed memory and spatial-delayed alternation, and the difference of delayed recall and delayed recognition memory. In addition, the individuals were tested on measures of verbal fluency, a cognitive test sensitive to lesions of the posterior frontal cortex, relatively far from the site of the leucotomy lesion, as well as tests of verbal learning and tactile sensitivity. As a result, this was a battery of tests putatively sensitive to functions of frontal and nonfrontal brain regions. Additional assessments were performed, including clinical symptom ratings and ratings of self-care deficits with a structured rating scale.

When the three patient groups were compared, there were three differences between the groups. The largest difference was in self-care, with the patients who experienced leucotomy most impaired. In the cognitive domains, there was an increased frequency of perseverative errors on the WCST and a relative deficit in recall as compared to recognition memory in the leucotomy groups. There were no differences on nonfrontal tasks such as memory or perceptual sensitivity and no differences in intelligence as estimated by the Raven's (1976) Progressive Matrices. When patients who were approved for the procedure but did not experience it were compared to the other groups, there were no statistically significant differences. However, the group who was approved for the leucotomy performed closest to the leucotomy group on all of the frontal lobe measures collected.

These data tentatively suggest that preexisting deficits in tasks of frontal lobe functioning may identify the patients who were likely to receive a leucotomy and also suggest modest worsening in these same cognitive functions after the leucotomy. The biggest impairments seem to be in the domain of self-care, the modal adverse outcome reported in the multiple impressionistic follow-up studies of leucotomy reviewed by Valenstein (1986).

An additional study that we performed again highlights the backdrop of impairment in tests that are sensitive to frontal lobe functions. Research in both animals and humans has focused on the role of the frontal cortex in working memory. These studies have indicated that different frontal lobe regions may be responsible for different aspects of working memory. Spatial-delayed response (i.e., simple delayed working memory) has been known for the past 20 years to activate the dorsolateral prefrontal cortex (Kojima & Goldman-Rakic, 1982), whereas simple object alternation tests (i.e., respond to the opposite of your last response) are responsive to focal lesions in the orbital cortex (Freedman, 1990). Delayed-alteration tasks (i.e., respond to the opposite of your last correct response) are apparently dependent on both the orbital and dorsolateral regions of the prefrontal cortex (see Seidman et al., 1995, for a comprehensive review). When patients with schizophrenia are tested, the typical impairments are greater for object alternation and delayed alternation than for simple delayed response. In fact, Seidman et al. (1995) found that patients with schizophrenia were essentially normal in their simple delayed-response performance, whereas they were considerably impaired in object alternation and delayed alternation.

Because the bilateral leucotomy procedure preferentially destroys tissue in the orbital frontal cortex, anterior to the dorsolateral prefrontal cortex, it would be expected that this procedure would lead to preferential impairments in object alternation and delayed alternation, while sparing delayed-response performance. Blum and Harvey (1997) examined 24 older schizophrenic patients, 12 with and 12 without a leucotomy, as well as 12 healthy comparison individuals. All participants were selected for similarity in age and gender, and the schizophrenic patients were matched for premorbid education. All schizophrenic patients were selected from the community and were not institutionalized at the time of assessment. Participants were examined with the three working memory tests just described. There was no specific or general effect of leucotomy in that all schizophrenic patients performed worst on object alternation, followed by delayed alternation, followed by delayed response. In effect, the findings of Seidman et al. (1995) were completely replicated, and the patients who had experienced a leucotomy failed to perform any worse than patients who had not been exposed to this procedure. Again, these data indicate that dysfunction of the frontal cortex provides such a strong signal in schizophrenia that even highly validated neuropsychological measures cannot detect a sign of deterioration associated with leucotomy.

CONVENTIONAL PHARMACOLOGICAL TREATMENT OF SCHIZOPHRENIA IN LATER LIFE

Pharmacological treatment of schizophrenia has been the primary intervention offered to patients with this illness for the past 45 years. Few older patients with schizophrenia have never received pharmacological treatments, and many have been treated with antipsychotic medications for their entire history of illness. Although like most areas of research in schizophrenia in late life there is less research and fewer data than for younger patients, but there is substantial information on the effects and consequences of antipsychotic treatment in older patients with schizophrenia. The current population of older patients with schizophrenia contains many of the patients who received antipsychotic treatment in America when it was first introduced. As a result, these older patients are the ones whose treatment helped to develop our current understanding of how antipsychotic medications work and their clinical benefits.

Conventional Antipsychotic Medications

The discovery of the antipsychotic effects of chlorpromazine was a medical landmark of a magnitude comparable to the discovery of penicillin. Psychotic symptoms, in schizophrenia and other conditions, are remarkably responsive to treatment with these medications, to an extent comparable to the effectiveness of most successful treatments in other domains of medicine. After the introduction these medications in the 1950s, there was an exodus of patients from long-stay psychiatric treatment. Although the follow-up care provided to them ranged from absent to inconsistent, the fact that many of these patients experienced a remission of their psychotic symptoms for the first time in years was a truly remarkable thing. Enhancing the miraculous appearance of these symptom improvements was the fact that there had been essentially no previous treatments with any efficacy at all. As a result, within 15 years of the introduction of these treatments, the population of long-stay psychiatric hospitals was reduced by two thirds (Wyatt, 1991).

Psychotic symptom reduction, in response to treatment with conventional antipsychotic medications, has been reported to be as high as 90% at the time of the first psychotic episode (Robinson et al., 1999). Rates of response to these treatments decrease across successive psychotic episodes, to the extent that the rate of treatment nonresponsiveness to conventional medications can approach 30% in patients with an established course of illness (Kane, Honigfeld, Singer, & Meltzer, 1988; Lieberman, 1999). Studies of spontaneous remission of psychotic symptoms conducted before the introduction of these medications suggested that about 30% of patients with schizophrenia manifest some improvement in their symptoms without treatment (Huber et al., 1975). Thus, the relative response rate, correcting for patients who would remit without treatment, is about 60% at the time of the first episode. The odds that a psychotic patient with schizophrenia will experience moderate or greater reduction in his or her symptoms with conventional antipsychotic treatment are quite high. In fact, the rate of relapse in the first-episode patients reported on by Robinson et al. (1999) who had close to a 90% successful response over their first year of treatment was 82%, with 78% of those patients who recovered from their first relapse having a second relapse within the same 5-year period (Robinson et al.,

1999). Supporting the benefit of maintaining antipsychotic treatment was the finding that the best predictor of relapse was stopping antipsychotic medication, which increased the risk for relapse approximately five-fold.

Strengths of Conventional Medication Treatment

There are several beneficial aspects of treatment with conventional antipsychotic medications. Patients who receive treatment with medication shortly after the initial episodes of psychotic symptoms tend to have a better overall lifetime outcome (Wyatt, 1991). Although there are some failures to find that the "duration of untreated psychosis" (DUP) predicts later overall outcome (Ho et al., 2000), these failures were often from studies whose patients had duration of untreated illness that could be measured in months. Studies that compared patients who were untreated for years, such as patients studied at the time of introduction of these medications and patients from environments in which the introduction of these medications were delayed, and contrasted their outcome to that of patients who received treatment within a few months of the development of their psychotic symptoms have found more consistent results (Quinn, Moran, Lane, Kinsella, & Waddington, 2000).

Characteristics of Older Antipsychotic Medications

Older antipsychotic medications share a common characteristic: They block the dopamine D_2 receptor. No medication to date that fails to occupy this receptor has ever proven to be an effective antipsychotic medication. Dopamine receptor blockade is only associated with antipsychotic effects within a certain narrow range of occupancy, as determined by research involving Positron emission tomography (PET) scan technology. Most typically, blockade of approximately 70% of the D_2 receptors is associated with antipsychotic effects, and extrapyramidal side effects occur with greater frequency when receptor blockade reaches 80% (Farde et al., 1992). Thus, there is a narrow range of receptor occupancy that is associated with treatment efficacy without major side effects. Conventional medications vary widely in their potency in terms of dopamine-binding. Low-potency medications, such as chlorpromazine (the original antipsychotic known as Thorazine), are only 2% as potent in their antipsychotic effects as high-potency medications such as haloperidol or fluphenazine.

It is important for the reader to understand that when older medications were introduced in the 1950s, there was no idea about why they worked. The theories of dopamine activation as a model for the cause of schizophrenia developed following the results of the treatment of patients with these medications. The dopamine-blockading effects of antipsychotic medications were not discovered until the 1960s, and the first comprehensive theory of dopamine as a cause of schizophrenia was not published until 1972. Dopamine-receptor subtypes were discovered in the 1980s, and the regional distributions of these receptor subtypes were elucidated with laboratory studies and then examined in humans with PET scan methodology in that same general time frame.

Dosing for conventional antipsychotics escalated wildly in the 1960s through the 1980s. This escalation was based on the fact that although antipsychotic medication treatments were effective at reducing psychotic symptoms for many patients, there was a substantial proportion of patients whose symptoms were not responsive to these treatments. One of the strategies used to address this problem was increased medication doses. When haloperidol was first introduced, it was available in 0.5 and 1.0 mg dosages. By the late 1980s, standard clinical treatment protocols (e.g., Davidson et al., 1991; Robinson et al., 1999) at academic centers used starting haloperidol dosages of 20 mg per day for both first-episode and chronic patients, with these dosages escalating to 40 mg per day if patients failed to respond immediately. The concept of neuroleptic mega-dose therapy or "rapid neuroleptization" was also advanced, with patients treated at times with up to 10 mg of haloperidol per hour, up to 120 mg per day (see Quitkin, Rifkin, Kaplan, & Klein, 1975, for a systematic study showing that this procedure was ineffective). Thus, older patients with schizophrenia are likely to have been treated with extensive doses of conventional antipsychotic medications.

Studies of receptor binding on the dopamine receptor have indicated that 2 mg to 4 mg per day of haloperidol offers optimal to slightly greater than optimal receptor binding on the D_2 receptor (Kapur & Remington, 2001). Doses 20 to 30 times that high appear excessive. At the same time, these are the doses of conventional medications that many older patients with schizophrenia have received. It is important to evaluate recent treatment studies to determine how current standards for treatments with newer antipsychotic medications compare to earlier efforts.

Studies examining state hospital patients, including older patients with schizophrenia, indicated that the most substantial predictors of receiving a high dosage of medication were a continuous course of unremitting illness and aggressive behaviors (Krakowski, Kunz, Czobor, & Volavka, 1993). Clinicians who increase the dose of older antipsychotic medications may be attempting to increase side effects such as sedation. For instance, low-potency antipsychotic medications have more substantial sedating effects than high-potency medications such as haloperidol. In a naturalistic study of the use of high- versus low-potency conventional medications in older patients, Sommer et al. (1998) found that clinicians gave relatively higher doses of high-potency medications than low-potency medications. Because high-potency medications are less sedating, clinicians apparently increased the dose in this sample of treatment-refractory aggressive patients to achieve an effect that is not provided by the medications. Those authors suggested that a better pharmacological strategy would have been to add on medications that are sedating but do not carry risk of the substantial side effects described later in the chapter.

Current Dosing Standards

Several recent studies have attempted to determine the current treatment standards for older patients receiving treatment with older antipsychotic medications. Guidelines have been suggested for the treatment of older patients, recommending a maximum of 500 mg of chlorpromazine or the equivalent per day. A survey of older patients indicated that the typical dose received by patients was within this range (Sommer et al., 1998), despite the variation across high- and low-potency medications described earlier. Thus, it appears that current dosing standards for older patients are being adhered to. Despite regulations aimed at correcting this problem, patients in nursing homes are more likely to receive inappropriate doses of these medications or not to receive antipsychotics at all.

Liabilities of Conventional Medication Treatments

Several major liabilities of treatment with older medications have emerged over time. Both long-term (e.g., tardive dyskinesia [TD]) and short-term (e.g., extrapyramidal symptoms [EPS]) side effects are quite common in patients treated with these medications. Some of these side effects are nearly irreversible and can cause long-term morbidity and mortality on their own. As many as 60% of patients with schizophrenia who receive treatment over a lifetime with conventional antipsychotic medications will develop TD, and the initial incidence of this treatment in older patients is close to 15% per year (Jeste et al., 1999). Negative symptoms (e.g., flat affect) are much less improved with conventional antipsychotic treatments, compared to the efficacy of these medications on positive symptoms. Finally, a substantial minority of these patients develops a pattern of nonresponse to treatment over time (Lieberman, 1999).

Cognitive Change With Conventional Antipsychotic Treatments

As noted earlier, the best predictor of functional skill level in schizophrenia is cognitive functioning, with negative symptoms also found to be important. The severity of psychotic symptoms appears to be much less strongly associated with overall functional outcome. Positive symptoms are reduced much more than negative symptoms by treatment with conventional antipsychotic medications. This is also true of the relative effect of conventional medications on cognition compared to positive symptoms. A possible reason for the lack of improvement in outcome associated with conventional antipsychotic treatments (Hegarty et al., 1994) is related to these profiles of differential efficacy for such older medications. One of the most consistent findings in the research literature in schizophrenia is that conventional antipsychotic medications have remarkably limited effects, beneficial or adverse, on cognitive functions in schizophrenia (Medalia et al., 1988; Spohn & Strauss, 1989).

There are a number of methodological problems in studies of the cognitive effects of older medications. Many studies did not use random assignment, and others allowed the use of adjunctive medications that might have confused the results (Blyler & Gold, 2000). Finally, almost none of the studies controlled for practice effects through the use of alternate forms of tests that were used in repeated-measures designs. Yet the majority of these methodological problems would have favored finding a positive effect of conventional medications relative to the comparator conditions. Despite a significant bias in favor of positive findings, they are remarkably absent from the literature. Several studies (e.g., Bedard, Scherer, Delorimier, Stip, & Lalonde, 1996; Bedard et al., 2000) have demonstrated that treatment with conventional antipsychotic medications is associated with impairments in procedural learning, when compared with no treatment or treatment with newer antipsychotic medications. In addition, studies examining rate of learning of more complex skills, such as the continuous performance test (CPT), have yielded similar results. Finally, patients with schizophrenia who are tested repeatedly while treated with conventional antipsychotic medications do not show the level of practice-related improvements shown by healthy individuals tested with the same tests (Harvey, Moriarty, Serper, Schnur, & Lieber, 2000). As a consequence, one of the possible impairments induced by treatments with conventional medications may be subtle and impossible to detect at a single assessment but may be critically important for functional outcome.

Extrapyramidal Side Effects

Parkinson's disease is an illness in which dopamine neurons in the nigro-strial dopamine tract, connecting the substantia nigra to the corpus striatum, begin to die. The deaths of these neurons set off a cascade of biochemical processes, leading to an imbalance of the cholinergic and dopaminergic neurotransmitter systems. A principal consequence of this imbalance is the development of motor symptoms, including rhythmic movements of resting musculature. These tremors, noted by Parkinson in his essay,

"The Shaking Palsy," start in the upper extremities and face and can, with progression of illness, involve the shoulders and upper truncal regions. These symptoms, referred to initially as extrapyramidal symptoms (EPS) because of their involvement with the pyramidal motor tract, provided one of the first clues about the mechanisms of action of antipsychotic medications.

Treatments for Parkinson's disease include treatment with supplemental dopaminergic agents and suppression of cholinergic activation with medications that blockade cholinergic receptors, referred to as anticholinergic medications. Because it has been discovered that patients with Parkinson's disease who were treated with dopaminergic agents such as l-dopa often developed psychotic symptoms, it quickly became clear that reduction of EPS in schizophrenic patients was most safely managed with anticholinergic medications. These medications became widely administered in patients with schizophrenia.

Several drawbacks of anticholinergic medications are apparent. The cholinergic system is critical for episodic memory. As a result, administration of anticholinergic medications, particularly in high doses, causes substantial impairments in episodic memory performance. In patients with schizophrenia, episodic memory deficits are often the most substantial area of cognitive deficit. Studies have indicated that use of anticholinergic medications, used in as many as 50% of patients receiving older antipsychotic medications, had a direct and adverse effect on memory performance (Spohn & Strauss, 1989; Strauss, Reynolds, Jayaram, & Tune, 1990). Serum levels of anticholinergic medications also predicted performance impairments, suggesting a dose-dependent effect on episodic memory functioning.

EPS is clearly a problem in older patients with schizophrenia. Older individuals are more susceptible to EPS at similar doses of antipsychotic medications. It has been reported that as many as 70% of older patients with schizophrenia receiving older antipsychotic medications experience clinically significant EPS (Byne et al., 2000). The severity of EPS is also associated with the severity of cognitive impairment. In a comprehensive neuropsychological study of older patients with schizophrenia (Palmer, Heaton, & Jeste, 1999), there was a significant relationship between reduced rates of learning, impaired motor skills, and the presence and severity of EPS. The troubling possibility that some major functional changes in the brain are associated with liability to EPS in older patients with schizophrenia should raise significant concern about treatment of patients with schizophrenia with older antipsychotic medications.

In addition to being more sensitive to conventional antipsychotic medications and more likely to develop EPS, older individuals are also more susceptible to the effects of anticholinergic medications. For instance, in a study of older institutionalized patients with schizophrenia (Davidson et al.,

1995), MMSE scores were 8 points lower in patients receiving treatment with conventional antipsychotic medications plus anticholinergic medications than in patients receiving antipsychotics but no anticholinergics. An 8-point difference in an impaired population such as this actually reflects approximately 50% worse performance associated with treatment with anticholinergics. Patients treated with anticholinergics were uniformly receiving what would be considered a very low dose, 2 mg per day of benztropine, suggesting that even low doses of these medications have substantial adverse effects in this population.

In another study of older outpatients (Heinik, 1998), MMSE scores, as well as scores on a comprehensive neuropsychological assessment battery, were lower in patients treated with anticholinergic medications. Although patients receiving any dose of the anticholinergic medications were more impaired than patients receiving none, there was an additional dose–response curve. Patients receiving 10 mg per day of trihexyphenidyl were found to be more impaired on the neuropsychological battery and MMSE than patients receiving 5 mg per day of the medication. Thus, even at low doses of anticholinergic medications, both ambulatory and institutionalized older patients with schizophrenia have been found to experience substantial adverse effects of these medications.

These data clearly suggest that doses of conventional antipsychotic medications that require the use of adjunctive anticholinergic medications may result, indirectly, in cognitive impairments in critical domains. Furthermore, the presence of EPS itself is associated with reductions in cognitive performance. Clearly any attempt to safely use reduced medication doses with older patients has the potential of considerable gain for the patients. One study attempted to examine the safety of antipsychotic medication dose reduction in older patients (Harris, Heaton, Schaltz, Bailey, & Patterson, 1997). Twenty-seven patients with schizophrenia had their dosage tapered in structured increments to determine their lowest effective dosage. These patients were compared with patients similar in age, gender, and education who were currently off antipsychotic medications or maintained on stable doses of antipsychotic medications over an 11-month follow-up study. Patients in the taper group had their medication reduced by approximately 40% over the follow-up period; 30% of the patients in the taper group experienced some increase in psychopathology, although no patient required hospitalization. Extrapyramidal symptoms continued to improve over time in the taper group. There were some complex changes in the cognitive performance of the taper group, with motor speed improving and memory scores worsening. Because of the small sample size, more research needs to be performed in this area, but it seems that for ambulatory patients, there is little risk of substantial worsening with a dose reduction that is adequate to reduce EPS. It is not clear if these results would hold up in institutionalized patients or in patients who had more substantial baseline levels of psychopathology.

Tardive Dyskinesia

If there is any result of conventional antipsychotic treatment for schizophrenia that may be reasonably compared with frontal lobotomy, it is tardive dyskinesia (TD). TD is a neurological side effect that occurs spontaneously in schizophrenia and is markedly increased in prevalence in patients treated with conventional antipsychotic medications. This condition is marked by torsional movements of the musculature of the face, truncal regions, and extremities. The lifetime prevalence of TD among people with schizophrenia who are treated with conventional antipsychotic medications approaches 60%, and after its appearance it is irreversible, although the expression of the symptom can be masked. For instance, antipsychotic dose reduction often reveals TD, whereas, as noted earlier, antipsychotic dose reduction reduces EPS. Thus, the relationship between TD, EPS, and conventional antipsychotic medication dosages is roughly reciprocal.

TD was first reported clinically within five years after the introduction of antipsychotic medications. As currently understood, duration, dose, and age at first antipsychotic exposure are all risk factors for development of TD (Jeste et al., 1998). Patients with illnesses other than schizophrenia are more likely to develop TD with equivalent antipsychotic dosing. The widespread use of conventional antipsychotic medications in the 1970s for the treatment of conditions other than schizophrenia, combined with poor diagnostic criteria for schizophrenia itself, led to the exposure of many individuals without schizophrenia to conventional antipsychotic medications.

Although the TD syndrome was described in Kraepelin and around 10% of patients with schizophrenia developed TD before antipsychotic medications were ever introduced, this syndrome is a devastating condition. Patients with TD have more severe cognitive impairments than patients who have never developed this condition (Karson, Bracha, Powell, & Adams, 1990). Cognitive impairment may be more than a risk factor for the development of TD, however. Prospective studies of the development of TD have indicated that at the time of development of TD, there is a notable change in cognitive performance, particularly episodic memory (Waddington, 1995). Furthermore, oral–facial TD, which is the most disfiguring variant, is also the subtype most strongly associated with decline in cognitive functioning (Waddington & Youssef, 1996).

Studies of the prevalence of TD in older patients have revealed several things about TD and aging in schizophrenia. In a study of chronically institutionalized patients with an average duration of regular (albeit not continuous) antipsychotic treatment of about 40 years (Byne et al., 1998), the prevalence of TD was found to be just over 60%. Similar results have been found in other surveys of slightly younger samples. These data would indicate that there may be an asymptote in the risk for the development of the condition at some point. Relevant to this point, in our sample of more than 800 patients with schizophrenia, we found a new incidence of only 16 cases over a 5-year follow-up. Closer review of those cases also suggested that 12 of them might have had medication changes that revealed a previously masked case of TD. Thus, the "real" new incidence of TD in older patients with lengthy and continuous antipsychotic treatment is less than 0.5% over 5 years, or about 1 in every 1,000 cases per year.

These lifetime prevalence figures mask a more substantial problem, despite how high they seem on their own. When the lifetime prevalence figures are examined, they are based on cases with a largely young adult onset of antipsychotic treatment and years and years of treatment before the initiation of follow-up. In patients who begin to receive antipsychotic medications for the first time after the age of 60, there is a huge difference in the risk rate for TD. In a study examining newly incident TD in older patients, Jeste, Lacro, Palmer, et al. (1999) reported that 60% of a substantial sample of patients with schizophrenia or other psychotic conditions whose antipsychotic treatment was initiated or resumed after a substantial interruption developed TD within 3 years. Thus, the lifetime cumulative prevalence for 75-year-old institutionalized patients with schizophrenia was equaled on a new-case incidence basis within three years when conventional antipsychotic treatment was initiated in later life. In a similar but shorter study, substantial new incidence of TD (corrected cumulative annual incidence of 29%) was detected within nine months of initiation of antipsychotic treatment in a group of patients with mixed psychotic conditions (Jeste, Lacro, Bailey, et al., 1999). In addition, patients who are middle-aged and older appear to have an increased risk of development of TD with continued conventional antipsychotic treatment. For example, Calagiuri, Lacro, Rockwell, McAdams, and Jeste (1997) followed a large sample of outpatients with schizophrenia over a 3-year period while they received "treatment as usual" with conventional antipsychotic medications. These patients had a high risk rate of the development of newly incident severe TD, with the risk rate at 2.5% after one year, 12.1% after 2 years, and 22.9% after 3 years. The best predictor of risk for TD was antipsychotic dosage, with patients treated with higher doses at higher risk for development of TD.

It has been believed that there were ways to "prevent" the occurrence of TD, such as using the lowest possible dose of antipsychotic medication. However, in the Jeste, Lacro, Bailey, et al. (1999) study cited, the medication dosage of haloperidol that was used was 1 mg per day, which is a modest dose by any standards. These data indicate that use of conventional antipsychotic medication carries with it a massive risk of the development of TD in older patients. As described in the next chapter, this is a risk that can be completely avoided.

CONCLUSION

Conventional antipsychotic medications have been used for 45 years to treat the psychotic symptoms of schizophrenia. These medications reduce the severity of psychotic symptoms to a moderate or greater extent in 90% of first-episode patients with schizophrenia. Failure to respond to treatment develops over time in some patients, but even in patients with extended histories of conventional treatment, more than 70% still receive benefit. Despite the fact that the psychotic symptoms of the illness are substantially reduced, these medications do not provide wide-ranging cognitive enhancement, and it can be argued that they have limited benefit in terms of improvement of functional outcome. As a result, there were not substantially more patients living in the community and experiencing stable remissions of their symptoms 30 years after these treatments were introduced than when patients were treated with lobotomies.

The most substantial liability of these medications is in the side-effect domains. EPS is caused by these medications, and the medications used to treat EPS exacerbate the memory deficits of patients with schizophrenia. TD occurs in more than 60% of patients with a lifetime of conventional antipsychotic treatment. When older patients are exposed to these medications, however, their risk for development of TD can be as high as 29% per year, and the 60% risk level is reached after three years. TD is associated with increased mortality and morbidity and with disfiguring changes in appearance and cognitive decline.

10

RECENT DEVELOPMENTS IN PHARMACOLOGICAL TREATMENTS

One of the major developments in the treatment of schizophrenia in general, with special implications for the treatment of schizophrenia in late life, is that of novel antipsychotic medications. This chapter describes the promise of the newer medications and some of the controversies regarding their use and evaluates their benefits for treating older patients with schizophrenia.

These medications, introduced in the United States starting in 1989, have a number of features that render them considerably different from older medications. There are a wide variety of newer antipsychotic medications currently available in the United States and worldwide. These medications have been available for a variety of time periods, with clozapine reintroduced in the United States in 1989, risperidone brought to market in 1994, and olanzapine, quetiapine, and ziprasidone introduced since 1996. There are several other newer antipsychotic medications that will be brought to the market in the next two to three years as well. All of these medications have a number of similarities and differences, with all of these medications sharing the features of being serotonin–dopamine antagonists (SDA). The feature that they share with conventional antipsychotic medications is that they block the dopamine d_2 receptor and the serotonin 5-HT2_A receptor subtype. Medications that block serotonin receptor subtypes without dopamine d_2 antagonism have proven ineffective as antipsychotics.

Despite their common characteristics, these medications vary widely in several critical parameters. There is considerable variation in the extent to which they block other neurotransmitter receptors, including histamine, acetylcholine, norepinephrine, and other variants of the dopamine and serotonin receptors. In addition, the time course with which they block the dopamine receptors varies widely, with risperidone exerting the longest lasting blockade and clozapine and quetiapine the shortest. Similarities between these medications in cognitive-enhancing effects, therefore, are likely to be a result of the combination of serotonin and dopamine blockade, and differences, if any, are likely to be a result of other aspects of neurotransmitter antagonism.

A considerable amount of attention has been paid to the beneficial effects of these medications, in both younger and older patients with schizophrenia. These benefits, to be reviewed later, include both improvements in efficacy, cognitive enhancement, and reduced side effect profiles. Although there is more evidence regarding some of these issues available for younger patients, the applicability of these findings to older patients is probably considerable.

The first of these medications was clozapine, a medication that been in use in Europe for more than 20 years. Its use was initially discontinued in the United States because of the potentially lethal side effect of agranulocytosis. The interest in the reintroduction of this medication, despite this side effect that occurs in about 3% of patients exposed to the drug, was its effect on the clinical symptoms of patients who failed to manifest a beneficial response to treatment with conventional antipsychotic medications. In a landmark study, Kane et al. (1998) demonstrated that approximately 25% of patients who manifest essentially no clinical response to treatment with conventional antipsychotic medications manifested a beneficial response to clozapine. These results have been replicated multiple times, with the typical estimate being that about a quarter or a third of patients whose clinical symptoms have essentially no response to traditional treatments have a marked clinical response to clozapine.

There are additional benefits to clozapine treatment. Clozapine produces essentially no extrapyramidal symptoms (EPS) and has no risk for the development of tardive dyskensia (TD). Recently clozapine was shown to be superior to treatment with olanzapine for reducing suicide and suicidal behavior (Meltzer et al., 2003). There are additional side effects from clozapine, including increased salivation and weight gain. At the same time, these side effects do result in permanent neurological changes, such as are seen with the development of TD.

Since the introduction of clozapine, a number of additional newer medications have also been investigated. These medications have been shown to have a profile of clinical benefit that is better than that seen with conventional medications, including increased efficacy on positive and negative symptoms in acute treatment studies (Marder & Meibach, 1994), improved prevention of relapses (Csernansky, Mahmoud, & Brenner, 2002), and beneficial profiles of side effects (Simpson & Lindenmayer, 1997). For all of the newer medications, EPS is reduced relative to conventional treatments, and for those medications for which systematic studies have been performed, risk for the development of TD appears to be markedly reduced to nonexistent even for older patients.

COGNITIVE ENHANCEMENT WITH NEWER ANTIPSYCHOTICS

The studies on cognitive enhancement in schizophrenia reflect one of the newest developments in the study of cognition in schizophrenia, with all of these studies published since 1993. These studies used a wide range of tests, with some using only a few neurocognitive measures and others conducting a more comprehensive neuropsychological assessment. The number of different neurocognitive tests included in each of the double-blind and open-label studies ranged from 1 to more than 25.

Six of the seven randomized, double-blind studies reported significant neurocognitive improvement on at least one measure following treatment with atypical antipsychotic medication compared to conventional antipsychotics (Harvey & Keefe, 2001). Seven of the nine open-label studies demonstrated improvement following treatment with atypical antipsychotics. Overall, 14 of 16 studies demonstrated improvement in some aspects of cognitive functioning compared to treatment with conventional antipsychotic medication. A meta-analysis of the studies published up to July 1998 found that, overall, the effects of these medications relative to conventional treatment was statistically significant (Keefe, Perkins, Silva, & Lieberman, 1999). A review of the literature of all of the studies completed up until 2001 suggested that effect sizes of the cognitive improvements were in the moderate range, for many of the different cognitive measures (Harvey & Keefe, 2001). Studies have examined cognitive improvement following treatment with risperidone, clozapine, aripiprazole, olanzapine, quetiapine, and ziprasidone. Each of these medications, other than aripiprazole (the medication that was most recently introduced to the market) has been used in a study that found improvement on at least one domain of cognitive functioning relative to treatment with conventional medications. Thus, the improvement seen with these medications is not associated with clinical change relative to no treatment or relative to never being treated, but rather is a benefit relative to previous treatments for the illness.

Because this is the early stage of this research, there are several questions that are not yet answered. First, does the cognitive change found in these studies lead to functional changes? None of the previous studies had the appropriate combination of large enough sample size, long enough study duration, and selection of appropriate functional outcome measures to address this question. The one study that addresses this issue directly (Buchanan et al., 1994) reported that changes in memory functioning, either improvement or worsening, was associated with concurrent changes in scores on the Heinrich–Carpenter Quality of Life Scale (Heinrichs, Hanlon, & Carpenter, 1984). This was a 1-year study, but the last 44 weeks were open-label in nature, which could have influenced the results of the functional-skills measures. Later studies will have to examine the direct influence of these medications on functional-skills measures.

Second, are the results of these studies influenced by the research methods used? Many studies of clozapine have used open-label research designs. One reason for this is that clozapine treatment requires weekly to biweekly blood drawings, which are difficult to justify in a research design in which patients may be randomized to a pharmacological condition that does not require such procedures. As a result, research participants may not be willing to participate in such studies. The one study in which there was a blinding procedure found that clozapine's cognitive enhancing effects were inferior to both risperidone and olanzapine and essentially no better than conventional antipsychotic treatment (Bilder et al., 2002).

SPECIFIC STUDIES OF OLDER PATIENTS

Relative to the number of studies on younger patients, there are relatively limited data on the clinical and cognitive effects of newer antipsychotic medications, as well as on the side-effect profiles. Most of the previous studies were open in nature, and many have had small and particularly heterogenous subject samples.

In one large-scale study, Davidson et al. (2000) presented the results of a 1-year open treatment study in which older patients were switched to treatment with the newer antipsychotic medication risperidone. These patients manifested clinical improvements in both positive and negative symptoms. When these patients who were switched to risperidone were compared to a demographically similar large sample of patients receiving treatment with conventional antipsychotic medications over the same one-year time period, the clinical changes seen were significantly greater in the risperidone-treated patients relative to the comparison sample. These findings indicated that within the parameters of an open study, risperidone treatment was more beneficial in patients with chronic schizophrenia than remaining on conventional treatments. In addition, the severity of extrapyramidal side effects was reduced after the switch to risperidone treatment.

In a large-scale double-blind study, older patients who were initially treated with conventional antipsychotic medications were switched to treatment with either risperidone or olanzapine (Jeste, Barak, Madhusoodanan, Grossman, & Gharabawi, 2003). These patients were treated for 8 weeks and examined for changes in clinical symptoms, movement disorders, and cognitive functioning. The results indicated that patients treated with either of these two medications improved in positive and negative symptoms of schizophrenia and had reductions in their levels of EPS over the course of the study. In addition, no patients developed new-onset cases of TD during the trial. Thus, despite an average of more than 35 years of treatment with older antipsychotic medications, these patients manifested a good clinical response to treatment with either of the two most widely used antipsychotic medications. This study is particularly important because the results suggest that even patients with extremely long duration of previous treatments with conventional antipsychotic medications can still experience a substantial clinical benefit after a transition to newer medications.

Several different studies of the influence of newer medications on cognitive functioning have been reported. The majority of these studies were open-label studies, with no attempt to have the raters unaware of the clinical status of the patients (e.g., Jeste et al., 1998). In these open studies the results were quite consistent. Patients who were examined at baseline and switched to treatment with risperidone were found to improve in global cognitive functioning, as well as in specific aspects of cognitive performance such as verbal skills and episodic memory (Berman et al., 1996). Despite the consistency of these results, the reasons for the improvements cannot be conclusively demonstrated to be unrelated to the research methods used.

When the influence of risperidone and olanzapine on cognitive functioning was examined in a double-blind study (Harvey, Napolitano, Mao, & Gharabawi, 2003), both medications were associated with improvement over eight weeks of double-blind treatment, relative to treatments at baseline, which were largely conventional antipsychotics. These improvements were largest in episodic memory, a critical outcome-related aspect of cognitive functioning, but were also noted in executive functioning and motor skills. Because this study was too short to address the issue of functional changes, it is still not clear whether these cognitive changes would have the desired result of improving functional outcome.

Future studies will be required to determine if the improvement in cognitive functioning with newer antipsychotic treatments is as consistent across medications in older patients as it preliminarily appears to be with younger patients. In addition, it will need to be determined if the apparent effects of improved cognition are not simply the result of dose-reduction phenomena. Many patients who are switched from older to newer medications were receiving high doses of these older medications. Antipsychotic dose reduction has been reported in some studies (Seidman, Pepple, & Faraone, 1993) to influence some aspects of cognitive functioning. As noted by Harvey and Keefe (2001), many patients were receiving particularly high doses before their switch, and in some studies in which a parallel comparison was performed between older and newer medication, the dosage of the newer medications was much lower than comparative dosage of the older conventional treatments. It has been argued that all of the beneficial cognitive effects of newer medications are a result of the effects of dose reduction of conventional antipsychotic medications (Carpenter & Gold, 2002). The best way to test for this effect would be studies that are longer, to determine if the influence of the switch to newer medications is purely transitory. In the one extended study of treatment with newer versus older medications, Purdon et al. (2000) reported that the effects of newer antipsychotic medications increased over a 1-year period. Although the small sample size of this study may limit the inferences, the dosing of the older comparator medication, haloperidol, was quite low by contemporary standards. In contrast, a study by Green and colleagues (2002) found no differences in cognitive change between patients treated with low doses of haloperidol and the newer antipsychotic risperidone. Whether these results apply to older patients with schizophrenia is yet to be determined.

SIDE EFFECTS WITH NEWER MEDICATIONS

Studies with younger patients have conclusively shown that newer medications can be effective in dose ranges in which classical side effects are much lower than with conventional medications. EPS, for instance, is absent in some newer medications (e.g., clozapine) and present at greatly reduced prevalence and severity for the other newer medications. This is particularly important because older patients with schizophrenia are known to be vulnerable to EPS at much higher rates than younger patients. Other related side effects, such as dystonic reactions, are also reduced in prevalence with newer antipsychotic medications compared to older medications. As a result, the use of anticholinergic medications to prevent side effects, as is commonly used with conventional antipsychotic medications, can largely be avoided in older patients treated with newer medications. As described in the last chapter of this volume, these medications are associated with notable impairments in episodic memory, with these impairments increased in older patients.

The Jeste et al. (2003) study described earlier found that treatments with newer medications reduced EPS relative to previous treatment. Similar results were shown in the Davidson et al. (2000) study. These data clearly indicate a better safety profile for newer medications compared to conventional treatments. Perhaps the most striking difference between older and newer medications in the elderly population is the difference in risk rates for the development of tardive dyskinesia. When older patients are treated with conventional antipsychotic medications, they have a corrected annual risk rate for the development of TD that approaches 30% (Jeste, Lacro, Palmer, et al., 1999). After 3 years of treatment, the risk rate approaches the lifetime risk for development of TD in patients with up to 35 years of treatment, about 60% (Jeste et al., 1998). In contrast, the risk rates for the development of TD in older patients with newer antipsychotic medications are about 3% per year for newly initiated treatment (Jeste, Lacro, Bailey, et al., 1999). This risk rate is very low on a cross-sectional basis and may be consistent with the rate of spontaneous dyskinesias reported in patients with schizophrenia.

Newer medications have an increased likelihood of causing weight gain compared to older medications (Beasley et al., 1997). This weight gain also appears to be more substantial with olanzapine and clozapine than with the other newer medications, despite the fact that greater weight gains when treated with these medications were correlated with greater beneficial effects (Czobor et al., 2002). Although this is often a potentially significant problem in younger patients, it is not clear if weight gain would be a similar problem in older patients where being underweight is more common than being overweight. The one study that can directly address this issue reported that patients treated with olanzapine gained slightly more weight over an eight-week period than patients treated with risperidone (Jeste, Barak, et al., 2003). Much more evidence will be required to draw firm conclusions about the importance of this side effect in older patients.

A potentially more salient problem is the induction of diabetes. Several of the newer antipsychotics have been reported to be associated with increased risk of type 2 diabetes (Haupt & Newcomer, 2001; Newcomer et al., 2002). Because this condition has more medical morbidity and risk for mortality in older than in younger patients, significant research on this topic in older patients will be required. Unfortunately, this appears to be a side effect that, if linked causally to newer antipsychotic medications, might be as negative as the effects of older medications such as tardive dyskinesia.

CONCLUSION

Newer antipsychotic medications have multiple benefits for patients with schizophrenia, and these benefits would appear to be even more substantial in older patients. Although there are clear suggestions of clinical and cognitive benefits relative to older medications, which could result in changes in functional outcome for older patients, the biggest potential benefit is in the domain of side effects. The fact that risk for EPS is reduced leads to reduced need to "treat" this side effect with medications that impair memory. In addition, the fact that the risk for TD is so markedly low is enough reason to suggest that no older patient with psychosis should ever be treated with conventional antipsychotic medications. At the same time, substantial research is needed to fully determine the benefits of treatment with newer medications for older patients with schizophrenia. More than other aspects of the illness, treatment in older patients has not received as much attention as it has with younger patients.

11

BEHAVIORIAL TREATMENTS FOR SCHIZOPHRENIA

Behavioral–psychological treatment for schizophrenia has been implemented for more than 100 years. Although current psychological treatment interventions do not typically focus on individual psychotherapy, particularly dynamically oriented therapies, the implementation of various behavioral interventions remains a cornerstone of the treatment of schizophrenia. These interventions fall into three broad domains: cognitive–behavioral interventions designed to reduce the severity of positive symptoms; skills training aimed at social, independent living and self-care domains; and cognitive remediation as a treatment strategy. Although each of these has been studied in detail in younger patients, there are two completed studies that have focused on older patients and one large-scale treatment intervention that is in the works. Because many of these interventions may eventually be applied to this population, the details of each domain of treatment is reviewed briefly. In addition, because functional expectations are quite different with older individuals, the applicability of previous interventions to older patients is examined. Although there is little research to date with older patients, the promise of these interventions in younger patients will certainly lead to their being attempted in older patients in the near future.

COGNITIVE–BEHAVIORAL THERAPY

This therapeutic intervention was developed to provide a psychological intervention to supplement or supersede pharmacological treatments with psychotic symptoms. Based on the fact that, in particular, hallucinations are perceptual experiences that have no real-world basis, this intervention attempts to train patients to more carefully evaluate their experiences before reaching the conclusion that hallucinations are truly "real." Similarly, delusional beliefs are evaluated and the schizophrenic patient is encouraged to reevaluate the decision-making process that leads to the development of these beliefs.

These approaches are potentially useful in a large number of patients with schizophrenia. In addition, the intervention itself is deliverable by trained paraprofessionals, which allows for a broader delivery of these services in environments where funding may be limited and a PhD-level psychologist may not be available to treat the patients. These treatments can be delivered in both individual and group formats, and manualized treatment interventions have been shown to be delivered with high fidelity.

Strengths of Cognitive–Behavioral Therapy

It has been reported that the severity of delusions and hallucinations is notably reduced in some patients with schizophrenia who receive this treatment (Alford & Beck, 1994). In addition, ratings of patients' awareness of illness are also improved. Patients who fail to respond to treatment with antipsychotic medications also may respond to cognitive–behavioral interventions. Many schizophrenic patients commit offenses on the basis of their hallucinations or delusions, so reduction of these symptoms is sure to reduce the likelihood of legal involvement and risk to others.

Weaknesses of Cognitive–Behavioral Therapy

Positive symptoms are not as strongly correlated with functional outcome as cognitive impairments. Thus, is it not clear whether functional changes could reasonably be expected following this treatment. Cognitive impairments on the part of patients receiving treatment may have the potential to reduce the likelihood of success in this type of intervention. Thus, many patients are likely to fail to benefit, particularly because patients with treatment-refractory psychotic symptoms have the most severe cognitive impairments. It is not yet clear the extent to which these interventions are limited by cognitive impairments, but this is an important topic to consider.

Applicability to Older Patients

This intervention strategy is likely to be broadly applicable to older patients with schizophrenia. Persistent psychotic symptoms are a feature of many older patients with schizophrenia. There are many patients who would seem likely to benefit. In addition, there are no age-related changes in the need for reduction of psychotic symptoms, in contrast to the typical age-related changes in expectations for aspects of functional outcome (e.g., employment and independent living).

SKILLS-TRAINING APPROACHES

Skills-training approaches use educational and practice-related interventions to allow the participant to increase his or her skills levels in several domains. These domains include social functions (conversational skills, assertion skills), self-care (cooking, cleaning, clothing maintenance), and independent living skills (e.g., household maintenance and bill paying). Contemporary training methods often involve realistically simulated work environments, patient-operated stores or restaurants, and video-taped feedback regarding social skills performance.

These interventions are aimed at disability reduction. As demonstrated before, functional deficits are a major source of disability in schizophrenia, and they are persistent into later life. Although there is some evidence that pharmacological cognitive enhancement occurs with treatment with newer antipsychotic medications, it is also likely that patients with schizophrenia, particularly older individuals, will not be able to spontaneously learn functional skills that have been absent from their repertoires for decades. Thus, focused interventions are likely to be important.

Strengths of Skills Training

Skills deficits are directly linked to disability in schizophrenia, and the more closely the skills-training approach simulates the task of focus, the more likely that success will result. Many different skills are required for functional success, and training in each of these domains is more likely to lead to success than any type of generic approach. Many current training environments simulate realistic work environments, and work placements have been shown to enhance patients' outcome, even in seemingly unrelated areas such as positive symptoms and hospital readmission. As noted earlier, spontaneous development of functional skills may be too much to expect after decades of deprivation.

Weaknesses of Skills Training

Skills-training approaches are intrinsically learning-based approaches. As a result, cognitive impairments, in domains of attention and episodic memory, have the potential to interfere with the rates of skills learning in these training programs. This has been demonstrated empirically, in that patients with more substantial deficits in vigilance are less likely to benefit from skills-training approaches (see Green, 1996, for a review). Similar to cognitive–behavioral interventions described earlier, cognitive limitations may need to be addressed before the approach can be successful.

Applicability to Older Patients

As we saw before, persistent functional deficits characterize many older patients with schizophrenia. Many patients have persistent social deficits and impairments in self-care. Independent-living impairments have increased importance in aging populations, because changes in independent living skills are a common consequence of aging in healthy populations. Employment issues change with aging, because it is not expected in Western culture that older individuals seek and maintain full-time competitive employment. Although there are some minor changes in expectations, improving functional status is still important for older patients with schizophrenia.

COGNITIVE REMEDIATION

This intervention directly attacks the problem of cognitive impairment in schizophrenia by attempting to improve cognitive functioning (Wykes & van der Gaag, 2001). Multiple different techniques have been used, based on concepts initially developed from rehabilitation of head-trauma patients. Patients are provided training on a variety of cognitive skills, including attention, memory, and conceptual functioning. This training is often presented on a fairly repetitive basis and is often presented via computerized programs.

Strengths of Cognitive Remediation

The principal strength of this approach is that it directly attacks a major problem in schizophrenia. Other approaches that require intact cognitive functioning often find that cognitive impairments serve as a rate limiter. In contrast, the direct remediation of cognitive impairments can proceed even in patients with severe impairments, through adjustment of the initial difficulty of the training. In addition, by targeting critical areas of cognitive deficits, the deficits most strongly related to functional outcome can be worked on. This approach can combined with other interventions, such as skills training, to simultaneously target multiple problem areas. A recent meta-analytical review of the effectiveness of cognitive remediation has suggested that, overall, cognitive remediation is effective in patients with schizophrenia (Krabbendam & Aleman, 2003).

Limitations of Cognitive Remediation

The principal limitation of the approach is that there has remained little evidence of generalizability of the treatment to other cognitive functions. For example, memory training does not lead to increases in problem-solving performance (Medalia, Revheim, & Casey, 2001). In addition, the statistically significant effects during training often do not lead to increases in performance in real-world cognitive tests or in functional status domains (Medalia, Dorn, & Watras-Gans, 2000). Some evidence (Harvey, Moriarty, Serper, et al., 2000) has suggested that patients receiving treatment with newer antipsychotic medications are more likely to improve when exposed to cognitive remediation or provided with extensive practice in performing attentional tests.

Relevance to Older Patients With Schizophrenia

Cognitive impairments are persistent in older patients with schizophrenia, possibly even more persistent than psychotic and negative symptoms (Jeste, Twamley, et al., 2003). Cognitive impairments are the primary determinant of functional impairments in older patients, just like in younger ones. As a result, any interventions that reduce these impairments are potentially important. Finally, because some cognitive benefit from treatment with newer antipsychotic medications has been reported (Harvey et al., 2003), combined treatments with newer antipsychotic medications or other cognitive-enhancing medications and cognitive remediation seems most promising. In fact, several published reports suggest that treatment with newer antipsychotic medications leads to more improvement for younger patients involved in cognitive remediation interventions (Mortimer, 2001; Naber, 2000).

Behavioral Interventions in Older Patients With Schizophrenia

There is no area of research on schizophrenia in late life in which there is a greater lack of data than in the domains of behavioral interventions. There are only three studies that have attempted to address this issue, all with limited samples. McQuaid et al. (2000) developed the first training program directly aimed at older patients with schizophrenia. In this program they used a combination of two of the techniques described earlier: cognitive–behavioral therapy (CBT) and skills training. The CBT was aimed at reducing some of the negative beliefs present in this population that interfere with participation in treatment and provided the patients with assistance in symptom self-management. Skills training provided repetitive practice in the areas of social and language skills. Role-plays, structured feedback, and homework assignments were provided to the participants in the program. Although the sample size of the study ($n = 9$) was too small for formal statistical analyses, case reports presented by the authors suggested that some of the patients received significant benefit from their participation. When the results of a randomized clinical trial, also with a small sample size, were reported (Granholm, McQuaid, McClure, Pedrelli, & Jeste, 2002), these results were confirmed. This is clearly an area in which additional research is required.

Functional deficits are clearly persistent into later life. Treatments for schizophrenia may be more effective at reducing functional limitations if they are *aimed* directly at functional limitations. It is not at all clear that cognitive enhancement alone would improve the execution of adaptive skills without some assistance provided to the patient regarding the nature of the skills, the environmental triggers for skills execution, and the need for spontaneous execution of skills.

A structured program for training older patients in the performance of functional skills has recently been developed. This program, referred to as Functional Adaptation Skills Training (FAST), was developed by Patterson and colleagues at the University of California, San Diego (UCSD Performance-Based Skills Assessment; Patterson et al., 2003). This program focused directly on six different areas of life functioning, including medication management, social skills, communication skills, organization and planning, and financial management. The program includes 24 twice-weekly sessions for 120 minutes each, led by a master's- to doctoral-level therapist. In the pilot study, 16 patients who were residents in board and care facilities received the pilot intervention and were compared to 16 patients who received treatment as usual. Patients who received the treatment were found to have statistically significant and relatively substantial improvements in a performance-based measure of functional skills, the UPSA (Patterson, Goldman, et al., 2001). Improvements in functional skills performance was stable three months after the termination of the intervention, suggesting that there was reasonable persistence of these gains over an intermediate term follow-up. There were no differences in scores on measures of psychopathology, including both psychotic and general symptoms measured by the Positive and Negative Syndromes Scale (PANSS; Kay, 1991).

These findings indicate that there is substantial promise for reducing functional impairments that is not dependent on the reduction of other symptoms of the illness. Although there is no evidence in this study regarding changes in functional skills performance in the outside environment, this appears to be a first step in the direction of improvement of functional skills deficits in older patients with schizophrenia.

SPECIAL CONSIDERATIONS WITH OLDER PATIENTS

There are multiple considerations that are unique to older patients with schizophrenia when behavioral interventions are considered. These include special needs of older patients and modifications in expectations for outcome based on those generated in younger patients. Clearly, certain expectations need to be modified, and these modifications may be more important the older the patients who are treated.

Special Needs

With aging, medical burden increases. As with individuals without any lifetime history of psychopathology, older patients with schizophrenia need to be able to interact effectively with medical professionals and to be able to manage the increasing number of treatments that they require for their physical illnesses. Thus, medication management training for older patients with schizophrenia will need to be more broadly focused than simply on adherence with psychiatric medications. Studies such as FAST have attempted to address this issue. Interacting with health care professionals in an assertive manner may be required to enhance physical well-being as well, given the fact that many patients with schizophrenia may not have a primary care physician who sees them regularly and manages their overall medical care. Being able to monitor one's own physical condition, report potential symptoms, and to persist in seeking appropriate treatment are important skills in elderly individuals in general. For people with schizophrenia, handicapped by a lifetime of social skills impairments, this is a particularly important challenge and is a more important area than it is for younger patients.

An additional issue associated with successfully adapting to older age is the need to overcome that "ageist" bias, one that would suggest that older patients with schizophrenia have little potential for improvement in their clinical and functional status. This bias may be reflected in the fact that newer medication treatments are offered to older patients at lower rates than younger patients, despite the evidence presented earlier that these treatments have at least as great a benefit to older patients as younger ones.

Quality of life is often reduced in some older individuals. Although schizophrenia patients, by virtue of being much less likely than the general population to be married and to have children, are less likely to be affected by the death of a spouse, there are many aspects of quality of life that are adversely affected in aging patients with schizophrenia. Many institutionalized patients are moved from residential facilities where they have lived for decades and sent to nursing home care. As noted in previous chapters, there appears to be adverse influences of these transfers. Moving to nursing home care often leads to reductions in the opportunities for adaptive functions, and quality of life in older patients may depend on their ability to perform some of their own self-care activities and to have certain opportunities for social activities as well.

Special Circumstances

Work and independent living expectations change with age in healthy individuals. These changes occur in elderly patients with schizophrenia but have somewhat different parameters. Older patients with schizophrenia are often housed in residential settings that are different from those for younger patients. Many of these patients are residents of nursing home care or other supported residences and have limited opportunities to perform certain adaptive skills. For instance, shopping and cooking may not be potential areas for skills performance, and focusing on skills training in these domains may not be productive.

Furthermore, social and sexual activities also have adjusted expectations in older individuals. It may be that the ability to participate meaningfully in structured and supervised social activities may be a more practical goal than focusing on social skills in dating contexts. It will be important to focus on enhancement of activities that are practical to perform, without an exclusive reliance on the same areas of adaptive skills that are important in younger patients, such as focusing on obtaining employment and living as independently as possible.

Employment is also an area in which modifications of expectations are potentially important. Full-time work may not be a reasonable goal, and a certain proportion of older patients with schizophrenia have never worked in their lives. It is unlikely that these patients will benefit from interventions aimed at anything more than casual part-time employment. In addition, there are notable disincentives for employment, such as reduction in social security benefits. Despite the clear benefits of employment for younger patients, skills training in older patients may be more productively aimed at social and self-care skills.

CONCLUSION

Treating older patients with schizophrenia is the area of greatest inattention in the entire research literature. There are no empirically derived treatment algorithms for older patients, either for purely pharmacological or behavioral interventions. Only one research group has attempted skills-based interventions with older patients with schizophrenia.

As described in the next chapter, development of better behavioral instruments is a situation that requires attention. As much as the lack of attention is paid to adequate housing for older patients, the nearly complete lack of attention to developing empirically validated treatments for older patients with schizophrenia is quite troubling. This situation is made even worse because older patients with schizophrenia respond as well to newer treatments for the illness as younger patients. Because their pattern of treatment response is so good, such treatment should inspire considerable optimism. It is my concern that older patients with schizophrenia have not received state-of-the-art treatments with the same frequency as younger patients because of ageist bias and a general bias against individuals who have lived a life of complete disability. This issue of lower standards for older patients is addressed in much more detail in the next chapter.

12

LATE-LIFE SCHIZOPHRENIA IN THE NEW MILLENNIUM

As seen in the rest of this book, schizophrenia persists into later life in most cases. The knowledge that we have about schizophrenia in late life is only in the development stage, and there are many gaps in what we know. At the same time, older patients with schizophrenia still have treatment, personal, and social needs, many of which are not being met. As previously noted by Jeste (e.g., Jeste, 2000; Jeste, Alexopoulous, et al., 1999), there is a developing crisis in the treatment of older patients with schizophrenia. Partly based on inaccurate and outdated ideas carried forward from the time when there was no empirical information available about older patients with schizophrenia, treatments have not been developed at a pace that keeps up with the number of older patients with schizophrenia. There are several issues, raised throughout the book, that will be major matters of concern in the near future.

The purpose of this final chapter is to examine some of the critical issues regarding the characteristics and treatment of older individuals with schizophrenia, making some recommendations for future research, clinical efforts, and public policy. Some of these recommendations are within the reach of clinicians who work with this population, whereas others are related to research directions that could be initiated. Finally, public policy issues will require the attention of all of the various stakeholders in the mental health research and services areas, including advocacy groups whose focus has not been on aging as much as other issues in schizophrenia. This chapter seeks to offer advice in the area of advocacy for older patients.

DETERMINING WHERE THESE PATIENTS WILL LIVE AND WHO WILL PAY THE BILL

There are many patients with a lifelong history of schizophrenia who reside in nursing home care; many others reside in board and care homes that are little different from nursing homes. Although there may be hundreds of thousands of such patients (although determining the numbers is controversial), the level of care that they receive is likely to be substandard. Many older individuals with schizophrenia have intermediate levels of disability and may not require nursing home care, but they have few alternatives. A large number of these older patients with schizophrenia have never worked and have no personal or familial financial resources available. They cannot find an apartment and go to live in it even if they could manage the activities of daily living that are required. Their age and associated physical limitations suggests that they are not best housed in group residences with younger patients with schizophrenia. Such living situations would lead to increased risk for victimization and injury for the elderly patients. In addition, group-home staff members are not necessarily prepared to assist in the management of medications for physical illnesses or to perform medical monitoring of older individuals.

One possibility for the housing of these older patients could be development of specialized geriatric residences. Such residences could be purely residential and nontherapeutic in their orientation for many patients. Much like the supported living opportunities offered to individuals who have carefully saved over their lifetimes to be able to afford some help with their self-maintenance, these residential facilities could provide no frills group care to a number of older patients with schizophrenia. Although medical specialization on site may not be required, staff members at such specialized group residences would need to be familiar with aging and willing to monitor nonpsychiatric medications. In addition, such a staff would have to be willing to ensure that these older individuals attended programming aimed at their lifelong psychiatric conditions and complied with medication and behavioral treatments offered to them.

Although such residences appear costly, they are unlikely to have a greater total cost than alternative residential placements. Failure to ensure the safety of older patients and failure to monitor their medical conditions is likely to be associated with increased financial and personal costs. A residence such as this is quite unlikely to cost more per day than nursing home care and is likely to be considerably more cost-effective overall.

One of the problems with such a plan is the question of payment responsibility. Many state psychiatric-service delivery systems have been doing their best to eliminate their long-time responsibility for the care of chronically ill patients. Older psychiatric patients, because of their long-term financial dependence on others, have even more disadvantages than younger ones when they are discharged from inpatient care. Some older patients with schizophrenia do not have Medicare or Social Security income, because they never worked enough (or at all) to qualify and were never awarded a disability. As a result, public assistance income may be the only source of payment, with these funds notably inadequate to cover the cost of housing. Previously, government agencies have had a difficult time understanding the concept of total cost for psychiatric conditions, choosing to focus entirely on reducing the direct cost of treatment by moving patients into lower levels of care. At the same time, leaving older patients on their own to find their own way will likely result in overall increased costs associated with medical comorbidity and mortality, not to mention inflated short-term costs associated with use of expensive services such as emergency rooms for routine medical and psychiatric care.

A BETTER STANDARD OF MEDICAL CARE FOR OLDER PATIENTS WITH SCHIZOPHRENIA

Medical care for outpatients with schizophrenia is often marked by the presence of indicators of poor quality of care (Druss et al., 2001). Because many of these indicators have essentially no unit or delivery cost (e.g., aspirin), the only explanation is that concern about the quality of care that is delivered is lacking. For patients who live in nursing home care, there is considerable information available to suggest that their functional status deteriorates quite rapidly after referral from state psychiatric hospitals to nursing home care (Harvey et al., 1999). In contrast, patients who reside in state psychiatric facilities, where their care is much more aggressively monitored, appear to have a relatively reduced incidence of new major medical problems (Friedman et al., 2002).

There are several ways to rectify the problem of substantial medical care. First is getting medical providers to recognize the problem. Second is monitoring of quality of care for patients with schizophrenia. If providers are aware of what the quality standards are and that they are monitored, then they are much more likely to perform adequately. Third is the more judicious use of nursing homes as a referral source for patients with schizophrenia. Although some nursing homes specialize in the care of older individuals with psychiatric conditions, most do not. Unfortunately, the homes that are most likely to be willing to take older psychiatric patients as direct referrals from state psychiatric centers may be variable in their quality. These long-stay patients are not model residents and, as a result, homes with a greater proportion of open beds are more willing to take these referrals, which may be an indication of reduced overall quality of the facility.

The fourth way to reduce the problem of low-quality care and poor health outcomes has to do with funding. Preventative care is much more important with older individuals, regardless of their lifetime history, than younger ones. Current Medicaid policies do not adequately cover preventative care. The cost of preventative health visits is negligible compared to the cost of care for preventable medical outcomes (e.g., stroke because of untreated hypertension). Patients with schizophrenia in later life will continue to experience low-quality medical care until funding is available to cover the cost of quality care.

A HIGHER STANDARD OF MENTAL HEALTH CARE FOR OLDER PATIENTS WITH SCHIZOPHRENIA

Some older patients with schizophrenia have been exposed to older treatments for the illness, including possibly excessive use of electroconvulsive therapy and the use of frontal lobotomy to treat schizophrenia. They then lived through the time period of treatment with conventional antipsychotic medications. The consequence has been that they have a 60% or greater chance of experiencing tardive dyskinesia. Newer medications do not carry this same level of risk. It is hard to understand, therefore, why older patients with schizophrenia are still generally less likely to be treated with newer medications than younger patients. There may be several reasons for this.

1. *Therapeutic nihilism:* There is an idea that patients who have had a lifetime of poor outcome, chronic symptoms, and generally poor treatment response may lead clinicians to the idea that there is nothing that can be done. Yet all of these earlier treatment failures were based on treatments with older medications. Because these older treatments are known to be less effective than newer treatments, failure to respond to older treatments does not predict failure to respond to newer treatments. As described previously (Harvey et al., 2003; Jeste, Barak, et al., 2003), newer medications actually are associated

with greater response for older patients than the older treatments. Thus, it is not at all true that these older patients cannot be treated effectively.

2. *Ageist bias:* It may be believed that treating older patients is intrinsically "not worth it." Many previous conceptions of the course of schizophrenia focused on the inevitability of various poor outcomes in old age. As a result, resources may not be allocated for treating elderly patients. This would appear to be especially true for medication treatment of schizophrenia, in which the treatment is not a cure in any sense of the term.

3. *Financial bias:* Many older patients with schizophrenia have never worked and never paid taxes. Because of their lifelong disability, they have never "contributed to society." One of the results is a reluctance on the part of some providers to request that more expensive (on a unit-cost basis) newer medications are offered to older patients with schizophrenia. It is clear that newer medications, despite a high initial acquisition cost, have a reduced total cost (Rosenheck et al., 1999) compared with older medications, which can result in side effects that are much more medically challenging and potentially life-threatening to older individuals. In addition, Medicare insurance does not cover prescriptions, so older patients with schizophrenia, who are likely to be at the bottom of the list of low-income seniors, do not have insurance coverage for medication and thus might not be able to pay for some medications even if they were prescribed to them.

4. *Absence of a constituency:* There are few people advocating for older patients with schizophrenia. Although organizations such as the National Association for the Mentally Ill (NAMI) lobbies regularly for improved treatment of patients with schizophrenia, their principal focus is on younger patients and family issues associated with being a caregiver. Older patients with schizophrenia are less likely to be cared for by a relative than younger patients. Thus, older patients with schizophrenia are underrepresented, even for an illness that is underrepresented in general.

In summary, older patients with schizophrenia receive mental health care that does not include the most recently developed treatments. Recent evidence has suggested that pharmacological (Harvey et al., 2003; Jeste, Barak, et al., 2003) and behavioral (Patterson et al., 2003) treatments are, in fact, as effective for older patients with a long history of illness as they are for younger patients. This information needs to be transmitted to practitioners and used to ensure that newer medications are used for older patients and that they also receive referrals for behavioral interventions as well. These behavioral treatments and medications are not cures for the illness, but they represent a major step forward in critical domains that are particularly relevant to older patients with schizophrenia.

MORE RESEARCH ON BEHAVIORAL INTERVENTIONS FOR OLDER PATIENTS WITH SCHIZOPHRENIA

As noted in the previous chapter, there is no area in late-life schizophrenia with less research than on behavioral interventions. This is a particularly important area, because skills-training programs have the potential to directly address lifelong deficits in older patients. Generic skills-training programs may not be applicable to older populations, because of their typical focus on work skills. Because older patients are retirement age, even if they have never been employed, more age-appropriate programs should be considered. This is an area in which there is potential for implementing behavioral interventions. As described in the previous chapter, several behavioral interventions have been piloted in older patients, but larger scale implementation is clearly required.

It is well known that severely and persistently ill individuals are an underserved population, from the perspective of services provided by psychologists. This situation is exacerbated for older patients, where only two previous interventions have been documented. Even these interventions were essentially pilot studies, as described in the last chapter, and there is little evidence that similar interventions are being developed.

These behavioral interventions could address two critical needs: skills deficits and cognitive impairments. Both of these domains are critical and generally lacking in previous attention. Skills deficits that are relevant in late life fall into several critical domains.

Medication Management

More than just psychotropic medications require management. Older patients with schizophrenia need to manage multiple medications for physical illnesses. These skills are deficient in younger patients and are potentially even more important in older patients than in younger ones.

Social Skills

Older patients with schizophrenia have social needs, just like younger patients. Their lifelong deficits in social skills, often combined with relatively isolated lifestyles, are clearly persistent into later life. These deficits are also correlated with reductions in quality of life. Social needs are clearly different, and dating skills are probably less important than a focus on the ability to communicate and have basic social interactions.

Self-Care Skills

Associated with aging and expected changes in health status are increased self-care needs. Feeding, dressing, and dietary management are important domains in which clear deficits have been identified but no interventions have been attempted. This is clearly a priority, and specialized interventions could have marked benefit.

Impulse Control

Some older patients with schizophrenia are shown to have notable deficits in impulse control (Bowie et al., 2001). There are several potential adverse implications of these deficits, including the possibility of self-injury as well as the high risk of injuring others. Impulse control interventions have been applied to younger patients with schizophrenia, but these interventions, although clearly necessary, have not even been piloted in older populations.

Cognitive-remediation interventions have been developed for younger patients with schizophrenia, as described in the previous chapter. Cognitive deficits are clearly notable in older patients with schizophrenia and have the same functional importance as in younger patients. There is no reason to expect that these interventions would not have the same effects as in younger patients, in that pharmacological interventions designed to enhance cognition have the same or greater effects as in younger patients (Harvey et al., 2003). In addition, the combination of state of the art pharmacological interventions and cognitive-remediation interventions have been shown to have beneficial effects in younger patients (Harvey, Moriarty, Serper, et al., 2000). This same combination therapy should be tried with older patients with schizophrenia.

In summary, notable areas of cognitive and skills deficit have been identified in older patients with schizophrenia, but there is no evidence in the literature of evidence-based treatments being applied to these patients. This is an area in which psychological interventions have been developed and need to be adapted for use in older patients with schizophrenia.

ADDITIONAL IMPORTANT ISSUES

There are additional societal issues associated with aging and schizophrenia. These include more general issues of health care reimbursement and funding of the care of older patients, as well as societal attitudes toward mental illness and aging in general.

Funding

Older patients with schizophrenia often have Medicare insurance. This is one form of insurance coverage in which psychological and psychiatric services are reasonably well reimbursed. Yet whenever there is an attempt to cut federal budgets, Medicare is often at the forefront of cuts. This insurance also does not cover medication, as noted earlier, and although many patients also have other coverage such as Medicaid, some older patients have no way to purchase any medications. As noted in several places earlier in the book, the total cost of treatment of schizophrenia increases markedly in patients who do not receive state of the art care. It is also clear that lobbying efforts are directly linked with funding for research and treatment of neuropsychiatric conditions. It is incumbent on the mental health profession to keep policy makers aware that no money is saved by cutting mental health treatment costs, particularly for older patients with schizophrenia.

Attitudes Toward Mental Illness

Patients with schizophrenia typically have no history of employment, stable residence, or other attributes that would lead them to be characterized as contributing to society. The stigma associated with schizophrenia in younger patients is likely to be compounded for older ones. It is difficult for the general population to understand and accept that these individuals do not necessarily have a volitional component to their lifetime history of functional and financial dependence. In times when attitudes about public assistance and entitlements are in question, as they are now, there is often little sympathy for individuals with a history of disability.

Attitudes About Aging

Although there has been a long-term and cross-cultural appreciation for elderly individuals, particularly in terms of respect that they deserve and the wisdom they can offer, there have been some changes in these attitudes over the years. Regular governmental discussions about borrowing from money allocated to social security to balance current budgets also suggests that the financial well-being of elderly individuals is open to compromise in the political arena. In general, the attitude that older individuals should step aside and consider the needs of younger people is often expressed. Elderly people as a group could be characterized as better organized than patients with schizophrenia. U.S. organizations such as the American Association of Retired People (AARP) have extensive lobbying efforts to ensure that older individuals are well represented and well informed. Yet the AARP Web site has no substantial mention of serious mental illness. A search of this Web site with the key word schizophrenia leads to only two irrelevant hits, whereas depression leads to 95. It is not likely that many individuals with serious mental illness have joined this organization, and as a result, the AARP lobbying and informational efforts that are so beneficial to elderly individuals in general are not reaching people with schizophrenia in later life.

CONCLUSION

Older individuals with schizophrenia have been through a lot in their lifetimes. Many spent decades in chronic psychiatric hospitals, housed in large wards with many other seriously disturbed patients. Others have experienced significant psychiatric symptoms for many years. They have lived through the period of treatments with high levels of adverse effects, including insulin coma, frontal lobotomy, and older antipsychotic medications that cause long-term neurological side effects. They have been the subjects of countless (well-meaning) social experiments, such as deinstitutionalization and "community care." They have been the target of multiple generations of politicians whose goal was to get state mental health systems as disengaged as possible from the treatment of individuals with severe mental illnesses such as schizophrenia. They represent the poorest segment of society, and are less likely to live independently than any other adult segment of society. Many have been sent to low-quality community residences because that care is cheaper than the psychiatric hospital they came from, despite the fact that it has been known for 20 years that patients deteriorate when sent to nursing home care. Little effort has been spent in developing behavioral treatments for them, and until 10 years ago they have largely been ignored by mental health researchers. It was thought that they had no more symptoms, and they were characterized as "burned-out" by mental health authorities.

As noted in this chapter, there are a number of things that can be done for these older people with schizophrenia, and they deserve the attention. Schizophrenia is a serious illness that requires serious attention and a determined effort on the part of mental health researchers and clinicians to improve the situation of those suffering from the illness. Schizophrenia in later life will continue to be prevalent until a cure or effective preventive intervention for schizophrenia is discovered. Attention to the problems of patients with schizophrenia in late life is a first step. Bringing their care to the level of that provided to younger patients is another. Developing treatments that are particularly beneficial to these patients is yet another important step. When we take these first steps, we will start down the path toward addressing the needs of older schizophrenic patients.

REFERENCES

Addington, J. (2000). Cognitive functioning and negative symptoms in schizophrenia. In T. Sharma & P. D. Harvey (Eds.), *Cognition in schizophrenia* (pp. 193–209). Oxford, England: Oxford University Press.

Addington, J., Addington, D., & Maticka-Tyndale, E. (1991). Cognitive functioning and positive and negative symptoms in schizophrenia. *Schizophrenia Research, 4,* 123–134.

Akbarian, S., Kim, J. J., Potkin, S. G., Hetrick, W. P., Bunney, W. E., Jr., & Jones, E. G. (1996). Maldistribution of interstitial neurons in prefrontal white matter of the brains of schizophrenic patients. *Archives of General Psychiatry, 53,* 425–436.

Albert, M. S., Jones, K., Savage, C. R., Berkman, L., Seeman, T., Blazer, D., et al. (1995). Predictors of cognitive change in older persons: MacArthur studies of successful aging. *Psychology and Aging, 10,* 578–589.

Albert, M. S., & Moss, M. B. (1988). *Geriatric neuropsychology.* New York: Guilford Press.

Albus, M., & Maier, W. (1995). Lack of gender differences in age at onset in familial schizophrenia. *Schizophrenia Research, 18,* 51–57.

Alford, B. A., & Beck, A. T. (1994). Cognitive therapy of delusional beliefs. *Behavior Research and Therapy, 32,* 369–380.

Almeida, O., Howard, R. J., Levy, R., & David, A. S. (1995). Psychotic states arising in late life: Psychopathology and nosology. *British Journal of Psychiatry, 166,* 205–214.

Almeida, O., Howard, R. J., Levy, R., David, A. S., Morris, R. G., & Sahakian, B. (1995). Clinical and cognitive diversity of psychotic states arising in late life. *Psychological Medicine, 25,* 699–714.

Almeida, O., Levy, R., Howard, R. J., & David, A. S. (1996). Insight and paranoid disorders in late life. *International Journal of Geriatric Psychiatry, 11,* 653–658.

Amador, X. F., Strauss, D. H., Yale, S. A., & Gorman, J. (1991). Awareness of illness in schizophrenia. *Schizophrenia Bulletin, 17,* 113–132.

American Psychiatric Association. (1980). *Diagnostic and statistical manual of mental disorders* (3rd ed.). Washington, DC: Author.

American Psychiatric Association. (1987). *Diagnostic and statistical manual of mental disorders* (3rd ed., rev.). Washington, DC: Author.

American Psychiatric Association. (1994). *Diagnostic and statistical manual of mental disorders* (4th ed.). Washington, DC: Author.

Andia, A. M., Zisook, S., Heaton, R. K., Hesselink, J., Jernigan, T., Kuck, J., et al. (1995). Gender differences in schizophrenia. *Journal of Nervous and Mental Disease, 183,* 522–528.

Andreasen, N. C. (1979). Thought, language, and communication disorders: II. Diagnostic significance. *Archives of General Psychiatry, 36,* 1325–1330.

Andreasen, N. C., Arndt, S., Allinger, R., Miller, D., & Flaum, M. (1995). Symptoms of schizophrenia: Methods, meanings, mechanisms. *Archives of General Psychiatry, 52,* 341–351.

Andreasen, N. C., & Grove, W. M. (1986). Thought, language, and communication in schizophrenia: Diagnosis and prognosis. *Schizophrenia Bulletin, 12,* 348–359.

Angermeyer, M. C., Goldstein, J. M., & Kuehn, L. (1989). Gender differences in schizophrenia: Rehospitalization and community survival. *Psychological Medicine, 19,* 365–382.

Arango, C., Barba, A. C., González-Salvador, T., & Ordóñez, A. C. (1999). Violence in inpatients with schizophrenia: A prospective study. *Schizophrenia Bulletin, 25,* 493–503.

Arndt, S., Allinger, R. J., & Andreasen, N. C. (1991). The distinction of positive and negative symptoms: A failure of a two-factor model. *British Journal of Psychiatry, 158,* 317–322.

Arnold, S. E., Gur, R. E., Shapiro, R. M., Fisher, K. R., Moberg, P. J., Gibney, M. R., et al. (1995). Prospective clinicopathological studies of schizophrenia: Accrual and assessment of patients. *American Journal of Psychiatry, 152,* 731–737.

Arnold, S. E., Trojanowski, J. Q., Gur, R. E., Blackwell, P., Han, L. Y., & Choi, C. (1998). Absence of neurodegeneration and neural injury in the cerebral cortex in a sample of elderly patients with schizophrenia. *Archives of General Psychiatry, 55,* 225–232.

Arriagada, P. V., Marzloff, K., & Hyman, B. T. (1992). Distribution of Alzheimer-type pathologic changes in nondemented elderly individuals matches the pattern in Alzheimer's disease. *Neurology, 42,* 1681–1688.

Ashman, T., Harvey, P. D., & Mohs, R. C. (1999). Cognition and aging. In W. R. Hazzard, J. P. Blass, W. H. Ettinger Jr., J. B. Halter, & J. G. Ouslander (Eds.), *Principles of geriatric medicine and gerontology* (pp. 1219–1228). New York: McGraw-Hill.

Aspinwall, L. G., & Staudinger, U. M. (2002). *A psychology of human strengths: Fundamental questions and future directions for a positive psychology.* Washington, DC: American Psychological Association.

Auslander, L. A, Lindamer, L. L., Delapena, J., Harless, K., Polichar, D., Patterson, T. L., et al. (2001). A comparison of community-dwelling older schizophrenia patients by residential status. *Acta Psychiatrica Scandanavia, 103,* 380–386.

Bartels, S. J., Mueser, K. T., & Miles, K. M. (1997a). Functional impairments in elderly patients with schizophrenia and major affective disorders living in the community: Social skills, living skills, and behavior problems. *Behavior Therapy 28,* 43–63.

Bartels, S. J., Mueser, K. T., & Miles, K. M. (1997b). A comparative study of elderly patients with schizophrenia and bipolar disorder in nursing homes and the community. *Schizophrenia Research, 27,* 181–190.

Baxter, D., & Appleby, L. (1999). Case register study of suicide risk in mental disorders. *British Journal of Psychiatry, 175,* 322–326.

Beasley, C. M., Jr., Hamilton, S. H., Crawford, A. M., Dellva, M. A., Tollefson, G. D., Tran, P. V., et al. (1997). Olanzapine versus haloperidol: Acute phase results of the international double-blind olanzapine trial. *European Neuropsychopharmacology, 7,* 125–137.

Bedard, M. A., Scherer, H., Delorimier, J., Stip, E., & Lalonde, P. (1996) Differential effects of D2 and D4 blocking neuroleptics on the procedural learning of schizophrenic patients. *Canadian Journal of Psychiatry, 41,* S21–S24.

Bedard, M. A., Scherer, H., Stip, E., Cohen, H., Rodriguez, J. P., & Richer, F. (2000). Procedural learning in schizophrenia: Further consideration on the deleterious effect of neuroleptics. *Brain and Cognition, 43,* 31–39.

Benson, D. F., Stuss, D. T., Naeser, M. A., Weir, K. A., Kaplan, E. F., & Levine, H. (1981). Long-term effects of prefrontal leucotomy. *Archives of Neurology, 38,* 165–169.

Berg, G., Edwards, D. F., Danzinger, W. L., & Berg, L. (1987). Longitudinal change in three brief assessments of SDAT. *Journal of American Geriatrics Society, 35,* 205–212.

Berenbaum, H., Oltmanns, T. F., & Gottesman, I. I. (1985). Formal thought disorder in schizophrenic patients and their twins. *Journal of Abnormal Psychology, 94,* 3–16.

Berman, I., Merson, A., Sison, C., Allan, E., Schaefer, C., Loberboym, M., et al. (1996). Regional cerebral blood flow changes associated with risperidone treatment in elderly schizophrenia patients: A pilot study. *Psychopharmacology Bulletin, 32,* 95–100.

Bilder, R. M., Goldman, R. S., Robinson, D., Reiter, G., Bell, L., Bates, J. A., et al. (2000). Neuropsychology of first-episode schizophrenia: Initial characterization and clinical correlates. *American Journal of Psychiatry, 157,* 549–559.

Bilder, R. M., Goldman, R. S., Volavka, J., Czobor, P., Hoptman, M., Sheitman, B., et al. (2002). Neurocognitive effects of clozapine, olanzapine, risperidone, and haloperidol in patients with chronic schizophrenia or schizoaffective disorder. *American Journal of Psychiatry, 159,* 1018–1028.

Bland, R., & Harrison, C. A. (1995). Investigating discharge destinations for schizophrenic patients. *Australian and New Zealand Journal of Psychiatry, 29,* 288–292.

Bleuler, E. (1911). *Dementia praecox; or the group of schizophrenias.* New York: International Universities Press.

Bleuler, M. (1978). *The schizophrenic disorders: Long-term patient and family studies.* New Haven, CT: Yale University Press.

Bleuler, M. (1979). On schizophrenic psychoses. *American Journal of Psychiatry, 136,* 1403–1409.

Bloom, J. D., Williams, M. H., Land, C., McFarland, B., & Reichlin, S. (1998). Changes in public psychiatric hospitalization in Oregon over the past two decades. *Psychiatric Services, 49,* 366–369.

Blum, C., & Harvey, P. D. (1997). Working memory in lobotomized patients [Abstract]. *Biological Psychiatry, 42*, 286.

Blyler, C. R., & Gold, J. M. (2000). Cognitive effects of typical antipsychotic medication treatment: Another look. In T. Sharma & P. D. Harvey (Eds.), *Cognition in schizophrenia* (pp. 241–265). Oxford, England: Oxford University Press.

Boone, K. B., Ghaffarian, S., Lesser, I. M., Hill-Gutierrez, E., & Berman, N. G. (1993). Wisconsin Card Sorting Test performance in healthy, older adults: Relationship to age, sex, education, and IQ. *Journal of Clinical Psychology, 4*, 54–60.

Bowie, C. R., Moriarty, P. J., Harvey, P. D., Parrella, M., White, L., & Davis, K. L. (2001). Verbal and physical aggression in elderly patients with schizophrenia. *Journal of Neuropsychiatry and Clinical Neurosciences, 13*, 357–366.

Breitner, J. C. S., & Anderson, D. N. (1994). The organic and psychological antecedents of delusional jealous in old age. *International Journal of Geriatric Psychiatry, 9*, 703–707.

Brekke, J. S., Kohrt, B., & Green, M. F. (2001). Neuropsychological functioning as a moderator of the relationship between psychosocial functioning and the subjective experience of self and life in schizophrenia. *Schizophrenia Bulletin, 27*, 697–708.

Bridge, T. P., Cannon, E. H., & Wyatt, R. J. (1978). Burned-out schizophrenia: Evidence for age effects on schizophrenic symptomatology. *Journal of Gerontology, 33*, 835–839.

Bridge, T. P., Kleinman, J. E., Karoum, F., & Wyatt, R. J. (1985). Postmortem central catecholamines and antemortem cognitive impairment in elderly schizophrenics and controls. *Neuropsychobiology*, 57–61.

Brown, S., Inskip, H., & Barraclough B. (2000). Causes of the excess mortality of schizophrenia. *British Journal of Psychiatry, 177*, 212–217.

Buchanan, R. W., Strauss, M. E., Kirkpatrick, B., Holstein, C., Breier, A., & Carpenter, W. T. (1994). Neuropsychological impairments in deficits vs. nondeficit forms of schizophrenia. *Archives of General Psychiatry, 51*, 804–811.

Burns, B. J., Wagner, H. R., Taube, J. E., Magaziner, J., Permutt, T., & Landerman, L. R. (1993). Mental health service use by the elderly in nursing homes. *American Journal of Public Health, 83*, 331–337.

Byne, W., Stamu, C., Harvey, P. D., White, L., Parrella, M., & Davis, K. L. (2000). Parkinsonism in elderly schizophrenic inpatients: Clinical and cognitive correlates. *International Journal of Geriatric Psychiatry, 15*, 7–15.

Byne, W., White, L., Parrella, M., Adams, R., Harvey, P. D., & Davis, K. L. (1998). Tardive dyskinesia in a chronically institutionalized population of elderly schizophrenic patients: Prevalence and association with cognitive impairment. *International Journal of Geriatric Psychiatry, 13*, 473–479.

Cahn-Weiner, D. A., Malloy, P. F., Boyle, P. A., Marran, M., & Salloway, S. (2000). Prediction of functional status from neuropsychological tests in community-dwelling elderly individuals. *Clinical Neuropsychologist, 14*, 187–195.

Caligiuri, M. P., Lacro, J. P., Rockwell, E., McAdams, L. A., & Jeste, D. V. (1997). Incidence and risk factors for severe tardive dyskinesia in older patients. *British Journal of Psychiatry, 171*, 148–153.

Callicott, J. H., Bertolino, A., Mattay, V. S., Langheim, F. J., Duyn, J., Coppola, R., et al. (2000). Physiological dysfunction of the dorsolateral prefrontal cortex in schizophrenia revisited. *Cerebral Cortex, 10*, 1078–1092.

Cannon, T. D., Rosso, I. M., Hollister, J. M., Bearden, C. E., Sanchez, L. E., & Hadley, T. (2000). A prospective cohort study of genetic and perinatal influences in the etiology of schizophrenia. *Schizophrenia Bulletin, 26*, 351–366.

Carpenter, W. T., Jr., & Gold, J. M. (2002). Another view of therapy for cognition in schizophrenia. *Biological Psychiatry, 51*, 969–971.

Carpenter, W. T., Jr., Heinrichs, D. W., & Wagman, A. M. (1988). Deficit and nondeficit forms of schizophrenia: The concept. *American Journal of Psychiatry, 145*, 578–583.

Castle, D. J., & Howard, R. (1992). What do we know about the etiology of late-onset schizophrenia? *European Psychiatry, 7*, 99–108.

Castle, D. J., & Murray, R. M. (1993). The epidemiology of late-onset schizophrenia. *Schizophrenia Bulletin, 19*, 691–700.

Castle, D. J., Wessely, S., Howard, R., & Murray, R. M. (1997). Schizophrenia with onset at the extremes of adult life. *International Journal of Geriatric Psychiatry, 12*, 712–717.

Castle, N. G., & Shea, D. G. (1997). Mental health services and the mortality of nursing home residents. *Journal of Aging and Health, 9*, 498–513.

Chanpattana, W., & Somchai Chakrabhand, M. L. (2001). Combined ECT and neuroleptic therapy in treatment-refractory schizophrenia: Prediction of outcome. *Psychiatry Research, 105*, 107–115.

Childers, S. E., & Harding, C. M. (1990). Gender, premorbid social functioning, and long-term outcome in DSM–III schizophrenia. *Schizophrenia Bulletin, 16*, 309–318.

Christensen, H., & Henderson, A. S. (1991). Is age kinder to the initially more able? A study of eminent scientists and academics. *Psychological Medicine, 21*, 935–946.

Christensen, R., & Blazer, D. (1984). Epidemiology of persecutory ideation in an elderly population in the community. *American Journal of Psychiatry, 141*, 1088–1091.

Ciompi, L. (1980). Catamnestic long-term study on the course of life and aging of schizophrenics. *Schizophrenia Bulletin, 6*, 606–618.

Cohen, C. I., & Talavera, N. (2001). Functional impairment in older schizophrenic persons. Toward a conceptual model. *American Journal of Geriatric Psychiatry, 8*, 237–244.

Cohen-Mansfield, J., Marx, M. S., Lipson, S., & Werner, P. (1999). Predictors of mortality in nursing home residents. *Journal of Clinical Epidemiology, 52*, 273–280.

Cohen-Mansfield, J., & Werner, P. (1998). Longitudinal changes in behavioral problems in old age: A study in an adult day care population. *Journal of Gerontology, Biological Sciences, and Medical Science, 53*, 65–71.

Crow, T. J., Done, D. J., & Sackler, A. (1995). Childhood precursors of psychosis as clues to its evolutionary origins. *European Archives of Psychiatry and Clinical Neuroscience, 245*, 61–69.

Crum, R. M., Anthony, J. C., Bassett, S. S., & Folstein, M. F. (1993). Population based norms for the Mini-Mental State Examination by age and education level. *Journal of the American Medical Association, 269*, 2386–2391.

Csernansky, J. G., Mahmoud, R., & Brenner, R. (2002). A comparison of risperidone and haloperidol for the prevention of relapse in patients with schizophrenia. *New England Journal of Medicine, 346*, 16–22.

Cuesta, M. J., & Peralta, V. (1993). Does formal thought disorder differ among patients with schizophrenic, schizophreniform, and manic schizoaffective disorders? *Schizophrenia Research, 10*, 151–158.

Cummings, J. L., & Benson, D. F. (1983). *Dementia: A clinical approach* (2nd ed.). Boston: Butterworth's-Heinemann.

Czobor, P., Volavka, J., Sheitman, B., Lindenmayer, J. P., Citrome, L., McEvoy, J., et al. (2002). Antipsychotic-induced weight gain and therapeutic response: A differential association. *Journal of Clinical Psychopharmacology, 22*, 244–251.

Davidson, M., Harvey, P. D., Powchick, P., Parrella, M., White, L., Knobler, H., et al. (1995). Severity of symptoms in chronically institutionalized geriatric schizophrenic patients. *American Journal of Psychiatry, 152*, 197–205.

Davidson, M., Harvey, P. D., Vervarcke, J., Gagiano, C. A., De Hooge, J. D., Bray, G., et al. (2000). A long-term multicenter, open-label study of risperidone in elderly patients with psychosis. *International Journal of Geriatric Psychiatry, 15*, 506–514.

Davidson, M., Harvey, P. D., Welsh, K., Powchik, P., Putnam, K. M., & Mohs, R. C. (1996). Cognitive impairment in old-age schizophrenia: A comparative study of schizophrenia and Alzheimer's disease. *American Journal of Psychiatry, 153*, 1274–1279.

Davidson, M., Kahn, R. S., Knott, P., Kaminsky, R., Cooper, M., DuMont, K., et al. (1991). Effects of neuroleptic treatment on symptoms of schizophrenia and plasma homovanillic acid concentrations. *Archives of General Psychiatry, 48*, 910–913.

Davidson, M., Reichenberg, A., Rabinowitz, J., Weiser, M., Kaplan, Z., & Mark, M. (1999). Behavioral and intellectual markers for schizophrenia in apparently healthy male adolescents. *American Journal of Psychiatry, 156*, 1328–1335.

Davis, K. L., Buchsbaum, M. S., Shihabuddin, L., Spiegel-Cohen, J., Metzger, M., Frecska, E., et al. (1998). Ventricular enlargement in poor outcome schizophrenia. *Biological Psychiatry, 43*, 783–793.

Delisi, L., Sakuma, M., Tew, W., Kushrer, M., Hoff, A., & Grimson, R. (1997). Schizophrenia as a chronic active brain process: A study of progressive brain structural change subsequent to the onset of psychosis. *Psychiatry Research Brain Imaging, 74,* 129–140.

D'Esposito, M., Zarahn, E., & Aguirre, G. K. (1999). Event-related functional MRI: Implications for cognitive psychology. *Psychological Bulletin, 125,* 155–164.

Dietz, P. E., & Rador, P. T. (1982). Battery incidents and batterers in a maximum security hospital. *Archives of General Psychiatry, 39,* 31–34.

Dijkstra, J. B., Van Boxtel, M. P., Houx, P. J., & Jolles, J. (1998). An operation under general anesthesia as a risk factor for age-related cognitive decline: Results from a large cross-sectional population study. *Journal of the American Geriatrics Association, 46,* 1258–1265.

Done, D. J., Crow, T. J., Johnstone, E. C., & Sacker, A. (1994). Childhood antecedents of schizophrenia and affective illness: Social adjustment at ages 7 and 11. *British Medical Journal, 309,* 699–703.

Donnelly, M., McGilloway, S., Mays, N., Perry, S., & Lavery, C. (1997). A 3- to 6-year follow-up of former long-stay psychiatric patients in Northern Ireland. *Social Psychiatry and Psychiatric Epidemiology, 32,* 451–458.

Doyle, M., Flanagan, S., Browne, S., Clarke, M., Lydon, D., Larkin, C., et al. (1999). Subjective and external assessments of quality of life in schizophrenia: Relationship to insight. *Acta Psychiatrica Scandinavia, 99,* 466–472.

Draelos, M. T., Jacobson, A. M., Weinger, K., Widom, B., Ryan, C. M., Finkelstein, D. M., et al. (1995). Cognitive function in patients with insulin-dependent diabetes mellitus during hyperglycemia and hypoglycemia. *American Journal of Medicine, 98,* 135–144.

Druss, B. G., Bradford, W. D., Rosenheck, R. A., Radford, M. J., & Krumholz, H. M. (2001). Quality of medical care and excess mortality in older patients with mental disorders. *Archives of General Psychiatry, 58,* 565–572.

Dwork, A. J., Susser, E. S., Keilp, J., Waniek, C., Liu, D., Kaufman, M., et al. (1998). Senile degeneration and cognitive impairment in chronic schizophrenia. *American Journal of Psychiatry, 155,* 1536–1543.

Estroff, S. E., Swanson, J. W., Lachicotte, W. S., Swartz, M., & Bolduc, M. (1998). Risk reconsidered: Targets of violence in the social networks of people with serious psychiatric disorders. *Social Psychiatry and Psychiatric Epidemiology, 33,* s95–s101.

Evans, D. A., Funkenstein, H. H., Albert, M. S., Scherr, P. A., Cook, N. R., Chown, M. J., et al. (1989). Prevalence of Alzheimer's disease in a community population of older persons. *Journal of the American Medical Association, 262,* 2551–2556.

Evans, J. D., Negron, A. E., Palmer, B. W., Paulsen, J. S., Heaton, R. K., & Jeste, D. V. (1999). Cognitive deficits and psychopathology in institutionalized versus community-dwelling elderly schizophrenia patients. *Journal of Geriatric Psychiatry and Neurology, 12,* 11–15.

Eyler-Zorrilla, L. T., Heaton, R. K., McAdams, L. A., Zisook, S., Harris, M. J., & Jeste, D. V. (2000). Cross-sectional study of older outpatients with schizophrenia and healthy comparison subjects: No differences in age-related cognitive decline. *American Journal of Psychiatry, 157,* 1324–1326.

Farde, L., Nordstrom, A.-L., Wiesel, F.-A., Pauli, S., Halldin, C., & Sedvall, G. (1992). Positron emission tomographic analysis of central D1 and D2 dopamine receptor occupancy in patients treated with classical neuroleptics and clozapine: Relation to extra-pyramidal side effects. *Archives of General Psychiatry, 49,* 538–544.

Fenton, W. S., & McGlashan, T. H. (1991). Natural history of schizophrenia subtypes, II: Positive and negative symptoms and long-term course. *Archives of General Psychiatry, 48,* 978–986.

Fenton, W. S., & McGlashan, T. H. (1994). Antecedents, symptoms progression, and long-term outcome of the deficit syndrome in schizophrenia. *Archives of General Psychiatry, 151,* 351–356.

Fink, M. (2001). Convulsive therapy: A review of the first 55 years. *Journal of Affective Disorders, 53,* 1–15.

Fleishman, M. (1997). The changing role of the psychiatrist in board-and-care homes. *Psychiatric Services, 48,* 510–513.

Folstein, M. F., Folstein, S. E., & McHugh, P. R. (1975). Mini-Mental State: A practical method for grading the cognitive state of patients for the clinician. *Journal of Psychiatric Research, 12,* 189–198.

Foong, J., Maier, M., Barker, G. J., Brocklehurst, S., Miller, D. H., & Ron, M. A. (2000). In vivo investigation of white matter pathology in schizophrenia with magnetization transfer imaging. *Journal of Neurology Neurosurgery and Psychiatry, 68,* 70–74.

Freedman, M. (1990). Object alternation and orbitofrontal system dysfunction in Alzheimer's and Parkinson's disease. *Brain and Cognition, 14,* 134–143.

Friedman, J., Harvey, P. D., Coleman, T., Moriarty, P. J., Bowie, C., Parrella, M., et al. (2001). A six year follow-up study of cognitive and functional status across the life-span in schizophrenia: A comparison with Alzheimer's disease and healthy subjects. *American Journal of Psychiatry, 158,* 1441–1448.

Friedman, J. I., Harvey, P. D., McGurk, S. R., White, L., Parrella, M., Raykov, T., et al. (2002). Correlates of change in functional status of institutionalized geriatric schizophrenic patients: Focus on medical co-morbidity. *American Journal of Psychiatry, 159,* 1388–1394.

Fucetola, R., Seidman, L. J., Kremen, W. S., Faraone, S. V., Goldstein, J. M., & Tsuang, M. T. (2000). Age and neuropsychologic function in schizophrenia: A decline in executive abilities beyond that observed in healthy volunteers. *Biological Psychiatry, 48,* 137–146.

Fux, M., Weiss, M., & Elhadad, D. (1995). Aggressive behavior as a cause of psychiatric admission: A comparison between schizophrenic and affective disorder patients. *Medicine and Law, 14,* 293–300.

Gold, J. M., Carpenter, C., Randolph, C., Goldberg, T. E., & Weinberger, D. R. (1997). Auditory working memory and the Wisconsin Card Sorting Test in schizophrenia. *Archives of General Psychiatry, 54,* 159–165.

Goldman, H. H., Feder, J., & Scanlon, W. (1986). Chronic mental patients in nursing homes: Reexamining data from the National Nursing Home Survey. *Hospital and Community Psychiatry, 37,* 269–272.

Goldman, L. S. (1999). Medical illness in patients with schizophrenia. *Journal of Clinical Psychiatry, 60*(Suppl. 21), 10–15.

Goldstein, J. M. (1988). Gender differences in the course of schizophrenia. *American Journal of Psychiatry, 145,* 684–689.

Goldstein, J. M., Tsuang, M. T., & Faraone, S. V. (1989). Gender and schizophrenia: Implications for understanding the heterogeneity of the illness. *Psychiatry Research, 28,* 243–253.

Gourovitch, M. L., Goldberg, T. E., & Weinberger, D. R. (1996). Verbal fluency deficits in patients with schizophrenia: Semantic fluency is differentially impaired as compared to phonological fluency. *Neuropsychology, 6,* 573–577.

Graham, C., Arthur, A., & Howard, R. (2002). The social functioning of older adults with schizophrenia. *Aging and Mental Health, 6,* 149–152.

Granholm, E., McQuaid, J. R., McClure, F. S., Pedrelli, P., & Jeste, D. V. (2002). A randomized controlled pilot study of cognitive behavioral social skills training for older patients with schizophrenia. *Schizophrenia Research, 53,* 167–169.

Granholm, E., Morris, S., Asarnow, R. F., Chock, D., & Jeste, D. V. (2000). Accelerated age-related decline in processing resources in schizophrenia: Evidence from pupillary responses recorded during the span of apprehension task. *Journal of the International Neuropsychological Society, 6,* 30–43.

Green, M. F. (1996). What are the functional consequences of neurocognitive deficits in schizophrenia? *American Journal of Psychiatry, 153,* 321–330.

Green, M. F., Kern, R. S., Braff, D. L., & Mintz, J. (2000). Neurocognitive deficits and functional outcome in schizophrenia: Are we measuring the "right stuff?" *Schizophrenia Bulletin, 26,* 119–136.

Green, M. F., Marder, S. R., Glynn, S. M., McGurk, S. R., Wirshing, W. C., Wirshing, D. A., et al. (2002). The neurocognitive effects of low-dose haloperidol: A two-year comparison with risperidone. *Biological Psychiatry, 51,* 972–978.

Greene, V. L., & Ondrich, J. I. (1990). Risk factors for nursing home admissions and exits: A discrete-time hazard function approach. *Journal of Gerontology, 45,* S250–S258.

Greenfield, T. K., McNiel, D. E., & Binder, R. L. (1989). Violent behavior and length of psychiatric hospitalization. *Hospital and Community Psychiatry, 40,* 809–814.

Gur, R. E., Petty, R. G., Turetsky, B. I., & Gur, R. C. (1996). Schizophrenia throughout life: Sex differences in severity and profile of symptoms. *Schizophrenia Research, 21,* 1–10.

Hafner, H., Riecher, A., Maurer, K., Loffler, W., Munk-Jorgensen, P., & Stromgren, E. (1989). How does gender influence age at first hospitalization for schizophrenia? A transnational case register study. *Psychological Medicine, 19,* 903–918.

Hakak, Y., Walker, J. R., Li, C., Wong, W. H., Davis, K. L., Buxbaum, J. D., et al. (2002). Genome wide expression analysis reveals dysregulation of myelination-related genes in chronic schizophrenia. *Proceedings of the National Academy of Science, 99,* 4746–4751.

Hamilton, M. (1960). A rating scale for depression. *Journal of Neurology, Neurosurgurgery, and Psychiatry, 23,* 56–62.

Hannerz, H., Borga, P., & Borritz, M. (2001). Life expectancies for individuals with psychiatric diagnoses. *Public Health, 115,* 328–337.

Harding, C. M., Brooks, G. W., Ashikaga, T., Strauss, J. S., & Breier, A. (1987a). The Vermont longitudinal study of persons with severe mental illness: I. Methodology, study sample, and overall current status 32 years later. *American Journal of Psychiatry, 144,* 718–726.

Harding, C. M., Brooks, G. W., Ashikaga, T., Strauss, J. S., & Breier, A. (1987b). The Vermont longitudinal study of persons with severe mental illness: II. Long term outcome of subjects who retrospectively met DSM–III criteria for schizophrenia. *American Journal of Psychiatry, 144,* 727–735.

Harris, M. J., Heaton, R. K., Schalz, A., Bailey, A., & Patterson, T. L. (1997). Neuroleptic dose reduction in older psychotic patients. *Schizophrenia Research, 27,* 241–248.

Harris, M. J., & Jeste, D. V. (1988). Late-onset schizophrenia: An overview. *Schizophrenia Bulletin, 14,* 39–55.

Harris, M. J., Jeste, D. V., Krull, A., Montague, J., & Heaton, R. (1991). Deficit syndrome in older schizophrenic patients. *Psychiatry Research, 39,* 285–292.

Hartman, M., Bolton, E., & Fehnel, S. E. (2001). Accounting for age differences on the Wisconsin Card Sorting Test: Decreased working memory, not inflexibility. *Psychology and Aging, 16,* 385–399.

Harvey, P. D. (1983). Speech competence in manic and schizophrenic psychoses: The association between clinically rated thought disorder and cohesion and reference performance. *Journal of Abnormal Psychology, 92,* 368–377.

Harvey, P. D., Bertisch, H., Friedman, J. I., Marcus, S., Parrella, M., White, L., et al. (2003). The course of functional decline in geriatric patients with schizophrenia: Cognitive functional and clinical symptoms as determinants of change. *American Journal of Geriatric Psychiatry, 11,* 610–619.

Harvey, P. D., & Davidson, M. (2002). Schizophrenia: Course over the lifetime. In K. L. Davis, D. Charney, J. Coyle, & C. Nemeroff (Eds.), *Neuropsychopharmacology: Fifth generation of progress* (pp. 641–656). Philadelphia: Lippincott.

Harvey, P. D., Davidson, M., Mueser, K. T., Parrella, M., White, L., & Powchick, P. (1997). The Social Adaptive Functioning Evaluation (SAFE): An assessment measure for geriatric psychiatric patients. *Schizophrenia Bulletin, 23,* 131–146.

Harvey, P. D., Docherty, N., Serper, M. R., & Rasmussen, M. (1990). Cognitive deficits and thought disorder: II. An eight-month follow-up study. *Schizophrenia Bulletin, 16,* 147–156.

Harvey, P. D., Howanitz, E., Parrella, M., White, L., Davidson, M., Mohs, R. C., et al. (1998). Symptoms, cognitive functioning, and adaptive skills in geriatric patients with lifelong schizophrenia: A comparison across treatment sites. *American Journal of Psychiatry, 155,* 1080–1086.

Harvey, P. D., Jacobsen, H., Mancini, D., Parrella, M., White, L., Haroutunian, V., & Davis, K. L. (2000). Clinical, cognitive and functional characteristics of long-stay patients with schizophrenia: A comparison of VA and state hospital patients. *Schizophrenia Research, 43,* 3–9.

Harvey, P. D., & Keefe, R. S. E. (2001). Interpreting studies of cognitive change in schizophrenia with novel antipsychotic treatment. *American Journal of Psychiatry, 158,* 176–184.

Harvey, P. D., Leff, J., Trieman, N., Anderson, J., & Davidson, M. (1997). Cognitive impairment and adaptive deficit in geriatric chronic schizophrenic patients: A cross national study in New York and London. *International Journal of Geriatric Psychiatry, 12,* 1001–1007.

Harvey, P. D., Lenzenweger, M. F., Keefe, R. S. E., Pogge, D. L., Serper, M. R., & Mohs, R. C. (1992). Empirical evaluation of the factorial structure of clinical symptoms in schizophrenia: Formal thought disorder. *Psychiatry Research, 44,* 141–151.

Harvey, P. D., Lombardi, J., Leibman, M., Parrella, W., White, L., Mohs, R. C., et al. (1996). Performance of chronic schizophrenic patients on cognitive neuropsychological measures sensitive to dementia. *International Journal of Geriatric Psychiatry, 11,* 621–627.

Harvey, P. D., Lombardi, J., Leibman, M., Parrella, M., White, L., Powchik, P., et al. (1997a). Age-related differences in formal thought disorder in chronically hospitalized patients with schizophrenia: A cross-sectional study across nine decades. *American Journal of Psychiatry, 154,* 205–210.

Harvey, P. D., Lombardi, J., Leibman, M., Parrella, M., White, L., Powchik, P., et al. (1997b). Verbal fluency deficits in geriatric and nongeriatric chronic schizophrenia patients. *Journal of Neuropsychiatry and Clinical Neurosciences, 9,* 584–590.

Harvey, P. D., Lombardi, J., Leibman, M., White, L., Parrella, M., Powchik, P., et al. (1996). Cognitive impairment and negative symptoms in schizophrenia: A prospective study of their relationship. *Schizophrenia Research, 22,* 223–231.

Harvey, P. D., Mohs, R. C., & Davidson, M. (1993). Leukotomy and aging in chronic schizophrenia: A follow-up study 40 years after psychosurgery. *Schizophrenia Bulletin, 19,* 723–732.

Harvey, P. D., Moriarty, P. J., Bowie, C. R., Friedman, J. I., Parrella, M., White, L., et al. (2002). Cortical and subcortical cognitive deficits in schizophrenia: Convergence of classifications based on language and memory skill areas. *Journal of Clinical and Experimental Neuropsychology, 24,* 55–66.

Harvey, P. D., Moriarty, P. J., Friedman, J. I., Parrella, M., White, L., Mohs, R. C., et al. (2000). Differential preservation of cognitive functions in geriatric patients with lifelong chronic schizophrenia: Less impairment in reading scores compared to other skill areas. *Biological Psychiatry, 47,* 962–968.

Harvey, P. D., Moriarty, P. J., Serper, M. R., Schnur, E., & Lieber, D. (2000). Practice-related improvement in information processing with novel antipsychotic treatment. *Schizophrenia Research, 46,* 139–148.

Harvey, P. D., Napolitano, J., Mao, L., & Gharabawi, G. (2003). Comparative effects of risperidone and olanzapine on cognition in elderly patients with schizophrenia or schizoaffective disorder. *International Journal of Geriatric Psychiatry, 18,* 820–829.

Harvey, P. D., Parrella, M., White, L., Mohs, R. C., & Davis, K. L. (1999). Convergence of cognitive and functional decline in poor outcome schizophrenia. *Schizophrenia Research, 35,* 77–84.

Harvey, P. D., Serper, M. R., White, L., Parrella, M., McGurk, S. R., Moriarty, P. J., et al. (2001). Convergence between estimates of cognitive impairment obtained by neuropsychological testing and clinical ratings. *Comprehensive Psychiatry, 42,* 306–313.

Harvey, P. D., Silverman, J. M., Mohs, R. C., Parrella, M., White, L., Powchik, P., et al. (1999). Cognitive decline in late-life schizophrenia: A longitudinal study of geriatric chronically hospitalized patients. *Biological Psychiatry, 45,* 32–40.

Harvey, P. D., Sukhodolsky, D., Parrella, M., White, L., & Davidson, M. (1997). The association between adaptive and cognitive deficits in geriatric chronic schizophrenic patients. *Schizophrenia Research, 27,* 211–218.

Harvey, P. D., Walker, E., & Wielgus, M. S. (1986). *Psychological markers of vulnerability to schizophrenia. Progress in experimental personality research* (Vol. 14). New York: Academic Press.

Harvey, P. D., White, L., Parrella, M., Putnam, K. M., Kincaid, M. M., Powchik, P., et al. (1995). The longitudinal stability of cognitive impairment in schizophrenia: Mini-Mental State scores at one and two year follow-ups in geriatric inpatients. *British Journal of Psychiatry, 166,* 630–633.

Haupt, D. W., & Newcomer, J. W. (2001). Hyperglycemia and antipsychotic medications. *Journal of Clinical Psychiatry, 62*(Suppl. 27), 15–26.

Heaton, R. K., Chellune, C. J., Talley, J. L., Kay, G. G., & Curtiss, G. (1993). *Wisconsin Card Sorting Test Manual–Revised and expanded.* Odessa, FL: Psychological Assessment Resources.

Heaton, R. K., Gladsjo, J. A., Palmer, B. W., Kuck, J., Marcotte, T. D., & Jeste, D. V. (2001). Stability and course of neuropsychological deficits in schizophrenia. *Archives of General Psychiatry, 58,* 24–32.

Heaton, R. K., Grant, I. S., & Matthews, C. G. (1991). *Comprehensive norms for an expanded Halstead–Reitan battery: Demographic corrections, research findings, and clinical applications.* Odessa, FL: Psychological Assessment Resources.

Heaton, R. K., Paulsen, J. S., McAdams, L.-A., Kuck, J., Zisook, S., Braff, D., et al. (1994). Neuropsychological deficits in schizophrenics: Relationship to age, chronicity, and dementia. *Archives of General Psychiatry, 51,* 469–476.

Heaton, R. K., & Pendleton, M. G. (1981). Use of neuropsychological tests to predict patients everyday functioning. *Journal of Consulting and Clinical Psychology, 49,* 807–821.

Hegarty, J. D., Baldessarini, R. J., & Tohen, M. (1994). One hundred years of schizophrenia: A meta-analysis of the outcome literature. *American Journal of Psychiatry, 151,* 1409–1416.

Heinik, J. (1998). Effects of trihexyphenidyl on MMSE and CAMCOG scores of medicated elderly patients with schizophrenia. *International Psychogeriatrics, 10,* 103–108.

Heinrichs, D. W., Hanlon, T. E., & Carpenter, W. T., Jr. (1984). The Quality of Life Scale: An instrument for rating the schizophrenic deficit syndrome. *Schizophrenia Bulletin, 10,* 388–398.

Herbert, M. E., & Jacobson S. (1967). Late paraphrenia. *British Journal of Psychiatry, 113,* 461–469.

Higgins, J., Gore, R., Gutkind, D., Mednick, S. A., Parnas, J., Schulsinger, F., et al. (1997). Effects of child-rearing by schizophrenic mothers: A 25-year follow-up. *Acta Psychiatrica Scandanavia, 96,* 402–404.

Hiroeh, U., Appleby, L., Mortensen, P. B., & Dunn, G. (2001). Death by homicide, suicide, and other unnatural causes in people with mental illness: A population-based study. *Lancet, 358,* 2110–2112.

Ho, B.-C., Andreasen, N., & Flaum, M. (1997). Dependence on public financial support early in the course of schizophrenia. *Psychiatric Services, 48,* 948–950.

Ho, B.-C., Andreasen, N. C., Flaum, M., Nopoulous P., & Miller, D. (2000). Untreated initial psychosis: Its relation to quality of life and symptom remission in first-episode schizophrenia. *American Journal of Psychiatry, 157,* 808–815.

Hoff, A. L., Riordan, H., O'Donnell, D. W., & DeLisi, L. E. (1991). Cross-sectional and longitudinal neuropsychological test findings in first episode schizophrenic patients. *Schizophrenia Research, 5,* 197–198.

Holohean, E. J., Banks, S. M., & Maddy, B. A. (1993). Patient subgroups in state psychiatric hospitals and implications for administration. *Hospital and Community Psychiatry, 44,* 1002–1004.

Howard, R. J., Almeida, O., & Levy, R. (1994). Phenomenology, demography and diagnosis in late paraphrenia. *Psychological Medicine, 24,* 397–410.

Howard, R. J., Castle, D. J., Wessely, S., & Murray, R. M. (1993). A comparative study of 470 cases of late-onset and early-onset schizophrenia. *British Journal of Psychiatry, 163,* 352–357.

Howard, R. J., Graham, C., Sham, P., Dennehey, J., Castle, D. J., Levy, R., et al. (1997). A controlled family study of late-onset non-affective psychosis (late paraphrenia). *British Journal of Psychiatry, 170,* 511–514.

Huber, G., Gross, G., & Schuttler, R. (1975). A long-term follow-up study of schizophrenia: Psychiatric course of illness and prognosis. *Acta Psychiatrica Scandanavia, 52,* 49–57.

Huff, F. J., Growdon, J. H., Corkin, S., & Rosen, T. J. (1987). Age at onset and rate of progression of Alzheimer's disease. *Journal of the American Geriatrics Society, 35,* 27–30.

Hunt, G. E., Bergen, J., & Bashir, M. (2002). Medication compliance and comorbid substance abuse in schizophrenia: Impact on community survival 4 years after a relapse. *Schizophrenia Research, 54,* 253–264.

Huppert, J. D., Weiss, K. A., Lim, R., Pratt, S., & Smith, T. E. (2001). Quality of life in schizophrenia: Contributions of anxiety and depression. *Schizophrenia Research, 51,* 171–180.

Hyde, T. M., Ziegler, J. C., & Weinberger, D. R. (1992). Psychiatric disturbances in metachromatic leukodystrophy. Insights into the neurobiology of psychosis. *Archives of Neurology, 49,* 401–406.

Jacobsen, C. F. (1935). Studies of cerebral function in primates. *Comparative Psychology Monographs, 13,* 1–68.

Janowsky, J. S., & Thomas-Thrapp, L. J. (1993). Complex figure recall in the elderly: A deficit in memory or constructional strategy? *Journal of Clinical and Experimental Neuropsychology, 15,* 159–169.

Jeste, D. V. (2000). Geriatric psychiatry may be the mainstream psychiatry of the future. *American Journal of Psychiatry, 157,* 1912–1914.

Jeste, D. V., Alexopoulos, G. S., Bartels, S. J., Cummings, J. L., Gallo, J. J., Gottlieb, G. L., et al. (1999). Consensus statement: The upcoming crisis in geriatric mental health: Research agenda for the next two decades. *Archives of General Psychiatry, 56,* 654–658.

Jeste, D. V., Barak, Y., Madhusoodanan, S., Gorssman, F., & Gharabawi, G. (2003). International multi-site double blind trial of the atypical antipsychotics risperidone and olanzapine in 175 elderly patients with chronic schizophrenia. *International Journal of Geriatric Psychiatry, 11,* 638–647.

Jeste, D. V., Eastham, J. H., Lacro, J. P., Gierz, M., Field, M. G., & Harris, M. J. (1996). Management of late-life psychosis. *Journal of Clinical Psychiatry, 57*(Suppl. 3), 39–45.

Jeste, D. V., Harris, M. J., Krull, A., Kuck, J., McAdams, L. A., & Heaton, R. K. (1995). Clinical and neuropsychological characteristics of patients with late-onset schizophrenia. *American Journal of Psychiatry, 152,* 722–730.

Jeste, D. V., Lacro, J. P., Bailey, A., Rockwell, E., Harris, M. J., & Caligiuri, M. P. (1999). Lower incidence of tardive dyskinesia with risperidone compared with haloperidol in older patients. *Journal of the American Geriatrics Society, 47,* 716–719.

Jeste, D. V., Lacro, J. P., Palmer, B., Rockwell, E., Harris, M. J., & Caligiuri, M. P. (1999). Incidence of tardive dyskinesia in early stages of low-dose treatment with typical neuroleptics in older patients. *American Journal of Psychiatry, 156,* 309–311.

Jeste, D. V., Lohr, J. P., Palmer, B., Rockwell, E., Harris, M. J., & Caliguri, M. (1998). Adverse effects of long-term use of neuroleptics: Human and animal studies. *Journal of Psychiatric Research, 32,* 201–214.

Jeste, D. V., Twamley, E. W., Eyler Zorrilla, L. T., Golshan, S., Patterson, T. L., & Palmer, B.W. (2003). Aging and outcome in schizophrenia. *Acta Psychiatrica Scandinavia, 107,* 336–343.

Jones, P. B., Bebbington, P., Foerster, A., Lewis, S. W., Murray, R. M., Russell, A., et al. (1993). Premorbid social underachievement in schizophrenia. Results from the Camberwell Collaborative Psychosis Study. *British Journal of Psychiatry, 162,* 65–71.

Joukamaa, M., Heliovaara, M., Knekt, P., Aromaa, A., Raitasalo, R., & Lehtinen, V. (2001). Mental disorders and cause-specific mortality. *British Journal of Psychiatry, 179,* 498–502.

Kane, J., Honigfeld, G., Singer, J., & Meltzer, H. Y. (1988). Clozapine for the treatment-resistant schizophrenic: A double-blind comparison with chlorpromazine. *Archives of General Psychiatry, 45,* 789–796.

Kapur, S., & Remington, C. (2001). Dopamine D(2) receptors and their role in atypical antipsychotic action: Still necessary and may even be sufficient. *Biological Psychiatry, 50,* 873–883.

Karson, C. N., Bracha, H. S., Powell, A., & Adams, L. (1990). Dyskinetic movements, cognitive impairment, and negative symptoms in elderly neuropsychiatric patients. *American Journal of Psychiatry, 147,* 1646–1649.

Kasckow, J. W., Twamley, E., Mulchahey, J. J., Carroll, B., Sabai, M., Strakowski, S. M., et al. (2001). Health-related quality of well-being in chronically hospitalized patients with schizophrenia: Comparison with matched outpatients. *Psychiatry Research, 103,* 69–78.

Kaszniak, A. W., Poon, L. W., & Riege, W. L. (1986). Assessing memory deficits: An information-processing approach. In L. W. Poon, *Clinical memory assessment of older adults* (pp. 277–284). Washington, DC: American Psychological Association.

Katzman, R. (1976). The prevalence and malignancy of Alzheimer's disease: A major killer. *Archives of Neurology, 33,* 217–218.

Kay, S. R. (1991). *Positive and negative syndromes in schizophrenia.* New York: Brunner/Mazel.

Keefe, R. S. E., Mohs, R. C., Losonczy, M., Davidson, M., Silverman, J. M., & Kendler, K. S. (1987). Characteristics of very poor outcome schizophrenia. *American Journal of Psychiatry, 144,* 889–895.

Keefe, R. S. E., Perkins, S., Silva, S. M., & Lieberman, J. A. (1999). The effect of atypical antipsychotic drugs on neurocognitive impairment in schizophrenia: A review and meta-analysis. *Schizophrenia Bulletin, 25,* 201–222.

Khachaturian, Z. S. (1985). Diagnosis of Alzheimer's disease. *Archives of Neurology, 42,* 1097–1105.

Kiraly, S. J., Gibson, R. E., Ancill, R. J., & Holliday, S. G. (1998). Risperidone: Treatment response in adult and geriatric patients. *International Journal of Psychiatry and Medicine, 28,* 255–263.

Klapow, J. C., Evans, J., Patterson, T. L., Heaton, R. K., & Jeste, D. (1997). Direct assessment of functional status in older patients with schizophrenia. *American Journal of Psychiatry, 154*, 1022–1024.

Kojima, S., & Goldman-Rakic, P. S. (1982). Delay-related activity of prefrontal neurons in rhesus monkeys performing delayed response. *Brain Research, 23*, 43–49.

Koreen, A. R., Siris, S. G., Chakos, M., Alvir, J., Mayerhoff, D., & Lieberman, J. A. (1993). Depression in first episode schizophrenia. *American Journal of Psychiatry, 150*, 1643–1648.

Krabbendam, L., & Aleman, A. A. (2003). Cognitive rehabilitation in schizophrenia: A quantitative analysis of controlled studies. *Psychopharmacology, 169*, 376–382.

Kraepelin, E. (1919). *Dementia praecox and paraphrenia.* Edinburgh, Scotland: E. & S. Livingstone.

Krakowski, M. I., & Czobor, P. (1994). Clinical symptoms, neurological impairment, and prediction of violence in psychiatric inpatients. *Hospital and Community Psychiatry, 45*, 700–705.

Krakowski, M. I., Kunz, M., Czobor, P., & Volavka, J. (1993). Long-term high-dose neuroleptic treatment: Who gets it and why? *Hospital and Community Psychiatry, 44*, 640–644.

Krystal, J. H., Belger, A., Abi-Saab, W., Moghaddam, B., Charbey, D. S., & Anand, A. (2000). Glutamatergic contributions to cognitive dysfunctions in schizophrenia. In T. Sharma & P. Harvey (Eds.), *Cognition in schizophrenia* (pp. 126–156). Oxford, England: Oxford University Press.

Kurtz, M. M., Moberg, P. J., Mozley, L. H., Hickey, T., Arnold, S. E., Bilker, W. B., et al. (2001). Cognitive impairment and functional status in elderly institutionalized patients with schizophrenia. *International Journal of Geriatric Psychiatry, 16*, 631–638.

Landi, F., Onder, G., Cattel, C., Gambassi, G., Lattanzio, F., Cesari M., et al. (2001). Functional status and clinical correlates in cognitively impaired community-living older people. *Journal of Geriatric Psychiatry and Neurology, 14*, 21–27.

Langfelt, G. (1937). *The prognosis in schizophrenia and factors influencing the course of the disease.* Copenhagen: Munksgaard.

Larsen, T. K., McGlashan, T. H., Johannessen, J. O., & Vibe-Hansen, L. (1996). First-episode schizophrenia: II. Premorbid patterns by gender. *Schizophrenia Bulletin, 22*, 257–269.

Lawton, M. P., & Salthouse, T. A. (Eds.). (1998). *Essential papers on the psychology of aging.* New York: New York University Press.

Leff, J. P., Thornicroft, G., Coxhead, N., & Trieman, N. (1994). The TAPS Project. 22: A five-year follow-up of long stay psychiatric patients discharged to the community. *British Journal of Psychiatry, 165*(Suppl. 25), 13–17.

Lenze, E. J., Miller, M. D., Dew, M. A., Martire, L. M., Mulsant, B. H., Begley, A. E., et al. (2001). Subjective health measures and acute treatment outcomes in geriatric depression. *International Journal of Geriatric Psychiatry, 16,* 1149–1155.

Levy, R., & Goldman-Rakic, P. S. (2000). Segregation of working memory functions within the dorsolateral prefrontal cortex. *Experimental Brain Research, 133,* 23–32.

Lewine, R. R., Haden C., Caudle, H., & Shurett, R. (1997). Sex-onset effects on neuropsychological function in schizophrenia. *Schizophrenia Bulletin, 23,* 51–61.

Lezak, M. D. (1995). *Neuropsychological assessment* (3rd ed.). New York: Oxford University Press.

Liddle, P. F. (1987). The symptoms of chronic schizophrenia: A re-examination of the positive–negative dichotomy. *British Journal of Psychiatry, 151,* 145–151.

Lieberman, J. A. (1999). Is schizophrenia a neurodegenerative disorder? A clinical and neurobiological perspective. *Biological Psychiatry, 46,* 729–739.

Lim, K. O., Hedehus, M., Moseley, M., de Crespigny, A., Sullivan, E. V., & Pfefferbaum, A. (1999). Compromised white matter tract integrity in schizophrenia inferred from diffusion tensor imaging. *Archives of General Psychiatry, 56,* 367–374.

Lindamer, L. A., Lohr, J. B., Harris, M. J., & Jeste, D. V. (1997). Gender, estrogen, and schizophrenia. *Psychopharmacology Bulletin, 33,* 221–228.

Linn, M. W., Gurel, L., Williford, W. O., Overall, J., Gurland, B., Laughlin, P., et al. (1985). Nursing home care as an alternative to psychiatric hospitalization. A Veterans Administration cooperative study. *Archives of General Psychiatry, 42,* 544–551.

Lisanby, S. H., Maddox, J. H., Prudic, J., Devanand, D. P., & Sackeim, H. A. (2000). The effects of electroconvulsive therapy on memory of autobiographical and public events. *Archives of General Psychiatry, 57,* 581–590.

Llorente, M. D., Olsen, E. J., Leyva, O., Silverman, M. A., Lewis, J. E., & Rivero, J. (1998). Use of antipsychotic drugs in nursing homes: Current compliance with OBRA regulations. *Journal of the American Geriatric Society, 46,* 198–201.

Loewenstein, D. A., Amigo, E., Duara, R., Guterman, A., Hurwitz, D., Berkowitz, N., et al. (1989). A new scale for the assessment of functional status in Alzheimer's disease and related disorders. *Journal of Gerontology, 44,* 114–121.

Marder, S. R., & Meibach, R. C. (1994). Risperidone in the treatment of schizophrenia. *American Journal of Psychiatry, 151,* 825–835.

Marin, D. B., Green, C. R., Schmeidler, J., Harvey, P. D., Lawlor, B. A., Ryan, T. M., et al. (1997). Noncognitive disturbances in Alzheimer's disease: Frequency, longitudinal course, and relationship to cognitive symptoms. *Journal of American Geriatrics Society, 45,* 1331–1338.

Mathieson, K. M., Kronenfeld, J. J., & Keith, V. M. (2002). Maintaining functional independence in elderly adults: The roles of health status and financial resources in predicting home modifications and use of mobility equipment. *Gerontologist, 42*, 24–31.

Mattis, S. (1973). *The dementia rating scale.* Odessa, FL: Psychological Assessment Resources.

McAdams, L. A., Harris, M. J., Bailey, A., Fell, R., & Jeste, D. V. (1996). Validating specific psychopathology scales in older outpatients with schizophrenia. *Journal of Nervous and Mental Disease, 184*, 246–251.

McDowd, J. M. (1986). The effects of age and extended practice on divided attention performance. *Journal of Gerontology, 41*, 764–769.

McEvoy, C. L., & Holley, P. E. (1990). Aging and the stability of activation and sampling in cued recall. *Psychology and Aging, 5*, 589–596.

McQuaid, J. R., Granholm, E., McClure, F. S., Roepke, S., Pedrelli, P., Patterson, T. L., et al. (2000). Development of an integrated cognitive–behavioral and social skills training intervention for older patients with schizophrenia. *Journal of Psychotherapy Practice and Research, 9*, 149–156.

Mechanic, D., & McAlpine, D. D. (2000). Use of nursing homes in the care of persons with severe mental illness: 1985 to 1995. *Psychiatric Services 51*, 354–358.

Medalia, A., Dorn, H., & Watras-Gans, S. (2000). Treating problem-solving deficits on an acute care psychiatric inpatient unit. *Psychiatry Research, 97*, 79–88.

Medalia, A., Gold, J., & Merriam, A. (1988). The effects of antipsychotics on neuropsychological test results of schizophrenics. *Archives of Clinical Neuropsychology, 3*, 249–271.

Medalia, A., Revheim, N., & Casey, M. (2001). The remediation of problem-solving skills in schizophrenia. *Schizophrenia Bulletin, 27*, 259–267.

Meltzer, H. Y., Alphs, L., Green, A. I., Altamura, A. C., Anand, R., Bertoldi, A., et al. (2003). Clozapine treatment for suicidality in schizophrenia: International Suicide Prevention Trial (InterSePT). *Archives of General Psychiatry, 60*, 82–91.

Menninger, W. (1948). Facts and statistics of interest for psychiatry. *Bulletin of the Menninger Clinic, 12*, 1–25.

Mirsky, A. F., & Orzack, M. H. (1977). Final report on the psychosurgery pilot study [Unpaginated appendix]. In *Psychosurgery: Report and recommendations.* Washington, DC: U.S. Government Printing Office.

Mitchell, D. B. (1989). How many memory systems? Evidence from aging. *Journal of Experimental Psychology: Learning, Memory, and Cognition, 15*, 31–49.

Moniz, E. (1964). Essay on a surgical treatment for certain psychoses. *Journal of Neurosurgery, 21*, 1108–1114. (Original work published 1936)

Moriarty, P. J., Lieber, D., Bennett, A., White, L., Parella, M., Harvey, P. D., et al. (2001). Gender differences in poor outcome schizophrenia. *Schizophrenia Bulletin, 27*, 103–113.

Morris, J. C., Edland, S., Clark, C., Galasko, D., Koss, E., Mohs, R., et al. (1993). The Consortium to Establish a Registry for Alzheimer's Disease (CERAD):

Part IV. Rates of cognitive change in the longitudinal assessment of probable Alzheimer's disease. *Neurology, 43,* 2457–2465.

Mort, J. R., & Aparasu, R. R. (2002). Prescribing of psychotropics in the elderly: Why is it so often inappropriate. *CNS Drugs, 16,* 99–109.

Mortimer, A. M. (2001). First-line atypical antipsychotics for schizophrenia are appropriate with psychosocial interventions. *Psychiatric Bulletin, 25,* 287–288.

Mueser, K. T., Salyers, M. P., & Mueser, P. R. (2001). A prospective analysis of work in schizophrenia. *Schizophrenia Bulletin, 27,* 281–296.

Mueser, K. T., Yarnold, P. R., Rosenberg, S. D., Swett, C., Jr., Miles, K. M., & Hill, D. (2000). Substance use disorder in hospitalized severely mentally ill psychiatric patients: Prevalence, correlates, and subgroups. *Schizophrenia Bulletin, 26,* 179–192.

Munk-Jorgensen, P. (1999). Has deinstitutionalization gone too far? *European Archives of Psychiatry and Clinical Neurosciences, 249,* 136–143.

Naber, D. (2000). Long-term phase of schizophrenia: Impact of atypical agents. *International Clinical Psychopharmacology, 15*(Suppl. 4), S11–S14.

National Center for Health Statistics. (1995). *National nursing home survey.* Washington, DC: Author.

Nebes, R. D., & Brady, C. (1992). Generalized cognitive slowing and severity of dementia in Alzheimer's disease: Implications for the interpretation of response-time data. *Journal of Clinical and Experimental Neuropsychology 14,* 317–326.

Nebes, R. D., & Madden, D. J. (1988). Different patterns of cognitive slowing produced by Alzheimer's disease and normal aging. *Psychology and Aging, 3,* 102–104.

Nelson, H. E., & O'Connell, A. (1978). Dementia: Estimation of premorbid intelligence levels using new adult reading test. *Cortex, 14,* 234–244.

Newcomer, J. W., Haupt, D. W., Fucetola, R., Melson, A. K., Schweiger, J. A., Cooper, B. P., et al. (2002). Abnormalities in glucose regulation during antipsychotic treatment of schizophrenia. *Archives of General Psychiatry, 59,* 337–345.

Newman, S. C., & Bland, R. C. (1991). Mortality in a cohort of patients with schizophrenia: A record linkage study. *Canadian Journal of Psychiatry, 36,* 239–245.

Nicholas, M., Obler, L., Albert, M., & Goodglass, H. (1985). Lexical retrieval in healthy aging. *Cortex, 21,* 595–606.

O'Carroll, R. E., Baikie, E. M., & Whittick, J. E. (1987). Does the NART hold in dementia? *British Journal of Clinical Psychology, 26,* 315–316.

Oojordsmoen, J. (1988). Hypochondriacal psychoses: A long-term follow-up. *Acta Psychiatrica Scandanavia, 77,* 587–597.

Osby, U., Correia, N., Brandt, L., Ekbom, A., & Sparen P. (2000). Mortality and causes of death in schizophrenia in Stockholm County, Sweden. *Schizophrenia Research, 45,* 21–28.

Pakkenberg, B. (1989). What happens in the leucotomised brain? A postmortem morphological study of brains from schizophrenic patients. *Journal of Neurology, Neurosurgery, and Psychiatry, 52,* 156–161.

Palmer, B. W., & Heaton, R. K. (2000). Executive functioning in schizophrenia. In T. Sharma & P. D. Harvey (Eds.), *Cognition in schizophrenia* (pp. 51–72). Oxford, England: Oxford University Press.

Palmer, B. W., Heaton, R. K., & Jeste, D. V. (1999). Extrapyramidal symptoms and neuropsychological deficits in schizophrenia. *Biological Psychiatry, 45,* 791–794.

Palmer, B. W., Heaton, R. K., Paulsen, J. S., Kuck, J., Braff, D., Harris, M. J., et al. (1997). Is it possible to be schizophrenic and neuropsychologically normal? *Neuropsychology, 11,* 437–447.

Parasuraman, R., Nestor, P., & Greenwood, P. (1989). Sustained-attention capacity in young and older adults. *Psychology and Aging, 4,* 339–345.

Parkin, A. J., & Lawrence, A. (1994). A dissociation in the relation between memory tasks and frontal lobe tests in the normal elderly. *Neuropsychologia, 32,* 1523–1532.

Patterson, T. L., Goldman, S., McKibbin, C. L., Hughs, T., & Jeste, D. V. (2001). UCSD Performance-Based Skills Assessment: Development of a new measure of everyday functioning for severely mentally ill adults. *Schizophrenia Bulletin, 27,* 235–245.

Patterson, T. L., Kaplan, R. M., Grant, I., Semple, S. J., Moscona, S., Koch, W. L., et al. (1996). Quality of well-being in late-life psychosis. *Psychiatry Research, 63,* 169–181.

Patterson, T. L., McKibbin, C., Taylor, M., Goldman, S., Davila-Fraga, W., Bucardo, J., et al. (2003). Functional adaptation skills training (FAST): A pilot psychosocial intervention study in middle-aged and older patients with chronic psychiatric disorders. *American Journal of Geriatric Psychiatry, 11,* 17–23.

Patterson, T. L., Moscona, S., McKibbin, C. L., Davidson, K., & Jeste, D. V. (2001). Social skills performance assessment among older patients with schizophrenia. *Schizophrenia Research, 48,* 351–360.

Patterson, T. L., Shaw, W., Semple, S. J., Moscona, S., Harris, M. J., Kaplan, R. M., et al. (1997). Health related quality of life in older patients with schizophrenia and other psychoses: Relationships among psychosocial and psychiatric factors. *International Journal of Geriatric Psychiatry, 12,* 452–461.

Paulsen, J. S., Butters, N., Sadek, J. R., Johnson, S. A., Salmon, D. P., Swerdlow, N. R., et al. (1995). Distinct cognitive profiles of cortical and subcortical dementia in advanced illness. *Neurology, 45,* 951–956.

Paulsen, J. S., Heaton, R. K., Sadek, J. R., Perry, W., & Jeste, D. V. (1995). The nature of learning and memory impairments in schizophrenia. *Journal of the International Neuropsychological Society, 1,* 88–99.

Pearlson, G. D., Kreger, L., Rabins, P. V., Chase., G. A., Cohen, B., Wirth, J. B., et al. (1989). A chart review study of late-onset and early onset schizophrenia. *American Journal of Psychiatry, 146,* 1568–1574.

Peralta, V., Cuesta, M. J., & deLeon, J. (1992). Formal thought disorder in schizophrenia: A factor analytic study. *Comprehensive Psychiatry, 33,* 105–110.

Pogue-Geile, M. F., & Harrow M. (1985). Negative symptoms in schizophrenia: Their longitudinal course and prognostic importance. *Schizophrenia Bulletin, 11,* 427–439.

Post, F. (1966). *Persistent persecutory states of the elderly.* Oxford, England: Pergamon Press.

Powchik, P., Davidson, M., Haroutunian, V., Gabriel, S., Purohit, D., Perl, D., et al. (1998). Post-mortem studies in schizophrenia. *Schizophrenia Bulletin, 24,* 325–342.

Praeger, S., & Jeste, D. V. (1993). Sensory changes in late-life schizophrenia. *Schizophrenia Bulletin, 19,* 755–772.

Prohovnik, I., Dwork, A. J., Kaufman, M. A., & Willson, N. (1993). Alzheimer-type neuropathology in elderly schizophrenia. *Schizophrenia Bulletin, 19,* 805–816.

Purdon, S. E., Jones, B. D., Stip, E., Labelle, A., Addington, D., David, S. R., et al. (2000). Neuropsychological change in early phase schizophrenia during 12 months of treatment with olanzapine, risperidone, or haloperidol. The Canadian Collaborative Group for research in schizophrenia. *Archives of General Psychiatry, 57,* 249–258.

Purohit, D. P., Perl, D. P., Haroutunian, V., Powchik, P., Davidson, M., Losonczy, M., et al. (1998). Alzheimer's disease and related neurodegenerative diseases in elderly schizophrenia patients: A postmortem neuropathologic study of 100 cases. *Archives of General Psychiatry, 55,* 205–211.

Putnam, K. M., & Harvey, P. D. (1999). Memory performance in geriatric and nongeriatric chronic schizophrenic patients: A cross-sectional study. *Journal of the International Neuropsychological Society, 5,* 494–501.

Putnam, K. M., & Harvey, P. D. (2001). Cognitive impairment and enduring negative symptoms: A comparative study of geriatric and nongeriatric schizophrenic patients. *Schizophrenia Bulletin, 26,* 867–878.

Putnam, K. M., Harvey, P. D., Parrella, M., White, L., Kincaid, M., Powchik, P., et al. (1996). Symptom stability in geriatric chronic schizophrenic inpatients: A one-year follow-up study. *Biological Psychiatry, 39,* 359–377.

Quilter, R. E., Giambra, L. M., & Benson, P. E. (1983). Longitudinal age changes in vigilance over an eighteen year interval. *Journal of Gerontology, 38,* 51–54.

Quinn, J., Moran, M., Lane, A., Kinsella, A., & Waddington, J. L. (2000). Long-term adaptive life functioning in relation to initiation of treatment with antipsychotics over the lifetime trajectory of schizophrenia. *Biological Psychiatry, 48,* 163–166.

Quitkin, F., Rifkin, A., Kaplan, J. H., & Klein, D. F. (1975). Treatment of acute schizophrenia with ultra-high-dose fluphenazine: A failure at shortening time on a crisis-intervention unit. *Comprehensive Psychiatry, 16,* 279–283.

Rabins, P. V., Pauker, S., & Thomas, J. (1984). Can schizophrenia begin after age 44? *Comprehensive Psychiatry, 25,* 290–243.

Randolph, C., Braun, A. R., Goldberg, T. E., & Chase, T. N. (1993). Semantic fluency in Alzheimer's, Parkinson's, and Huntington's disease: Dissociation of storage and retrieval failures. *Neuropsychology, 1,* 82–88.

Rapoport, J. L., Giedd, J., Kumra, S., Jacobsen, L., Smith, A., Nelson, L. J., et al. (1997). Childhood onset schizophrenia: Progressive ventricular change during adolescence. *Archives of General Psychiatry, 54,* 897–903.

Raven, J. C. (1976). *The Raven coloured progressive matrices.* London: H. Lewis.

Rebok, G. W., & Folstein, M. F. (1993). Dementia. *Journal of Neuropsychiatry and Clinical Neuroscience, 5,* 265–276.

Reichler-Rosser, A. (1999). Late onset schizophrenia: The German concept and literature. In R. Howard, R. Rabins, & D. J. Castle (Eds.), *Late-onset schizophenia* (pp. 3–16). Petersfield, UK: Wrightson Medical.

Revicki, D. A., Genduso, L. A., Hamilton, S. H., Ganoczy, D., & Beasley, C. M., Jr. (1999). Olanzapine versus haloperidol in the treatment of schizophrenia and other psychotic disorders: Quality of life and clinical outcomes of a randomized clinical trial. *Quality of Life Research, 8,* 417–426.

Robinson, D., Werner, M. G., Alvir, J. M., Bilder, R., Goldman, R., Geisler, S., et al. (1999). Predictors of relapse following response from a first episode of schizophrenia or schizoaffective disorder. *Archives of General Psychiatry, 56,* 241–247.

Robinson, D. G., Werner, M. G., Alvir, J. M., Geisler, S., Koreen, A., Sheitman, B., et al. (1999). Predictors of treatment response from a first episode of schizophrenia or schizoaffective disorder. *American Journal of Psychiatry, 156,* 544–549.

Rockwell, E., Krull, A. J., Dimsdale, J., & Jeste, D. V. (1994). Late-onset psychosis with somatic delusions. *Psychosomatics, 35,* 66–72.

Rosen, W. G., Mohs, R. C., & Davis, K. (1984). A new rating scale for Alzheimer's disease. *American Journal of Psychiatry, 141,* 1356–1364.

Rosenhan, D. L. (1973). On being sane in insane places. *Science, 179,* 250–258.

Rosenheck, R., Cramer, J., Allan, E., Erdos, J., Frisman, L. K., Xu, W. C., et al. (1999). Cost-effectiveness of clozapine in patients with high and low levels of hospital use. Department of Veterans Affairs Cooperative Study Group on Clozapine in Refractory Schizophrenia. *Archives of General Psychiatry, 56,* 565–572.

Rowe, J. W., & Kahn, R. L. (1998). Successful aging. *Aging (Milano), 10,* 142–144.

Rund, B. R. (1998). A review of longitudinal studies of cognitive functions in schizophrenia patients. *Schizophrenia Bulletin, 24,* 425–435.

Salmon, D. P., Thal, L. J., Butters, N., & Heindel, W. C. (1990). Longitudinal evaluation of dementia of the Alzheimer type: A comparison of 3 standardized mental status examinations. *Neurology, 40,* 1225–1230.

Sands, J. R., & Harrow, M. (1999). Depression during the longitudinal course of schizophrenia. *Schizophrenia Bulletin, 25,* 57–71.

Sauer, H., Hornstein, C., Richter, P., Mortimer, A., & Hirsch, S. R. (1999). Symptom dimensions in old-age schizophrenics. Relationship to neuropsychological and motor abnormalities. *Schizophrenia Research, 39,* 31–38.

Saykin, A. J., Gur, R. C., Gur, R. E., Mozeley, D., Mozeley, L. H., & Resnick, S. M. (1991). Neuropsychological function in schizophrenia: Selective impairment in memory and learning. *Archives of General Psychiatry, 48,* 618–623.

Saykin, A. J., Shtasel, D. L., Gur, R. E., Kester, D. B., Mozley, L. H., Stafiniak, P., et al. (1994). Neuropsychological deficits in neuroleptic naive patients with first episode schizophrenia. *Archives of General Psychiatry, 51,* 124–131.

Schaie, K. W. (1989). Perceptual speed in adulthood: Cross-sectional and longitudinal studies. *Psychology and Aging, 4,* 443–453.

Schwartz, R. C., & Cohen, B. N. (2001). Psychosocial correlates of suicidal intent among patients with schizophrenia. *Comprehensive Psychiatry, 42,* 118–123.

Seeman, T. E., Berkman, L. F., Charpentier, P. A., Blazer, D. G., Albert, M. S., & Tinetti, M. E. (1995). Behavioral and psychosocial predictors of physical performance: MacArthur studies of successful aging. *Journal of Gerontological and Biological Sciences and Medical Science, 50,* 177–183.

Seidman, L. J., Kalinowski, A. G., Kremen, W. S., Faraone, S. V., Oscar-Berman, M., Ajilore, O., et al. (1995). Experimental and clinical neuropsychological measures of prefrontal dysfunction in schizophrenia. *Neuropsychology, 9,* 481–490.

Seidman, L. J., Pepple, J. R., & Faraone, S. V. (1993). Neuropsychological performance in chronic schizophrenia in response to neuroleptic dose reduction. *Biological Psychiatry, 33,* 575–584.

Selemon, L. D., & Goldman-Rakic, P. S. (1998). The reduced neuropil hypothesis: A circuit-based model of schizophrenia. *Biological Psychiatry, 45,* 17–25.

Seno, H., Shibata, M., Fujimoto, A., Koga, K., Kanno, H., & Ishino, H. (1998). Evaluation of Mini Mental State Examination and Brief Psychiatric Rating Scale on aged schizophrenic patients. *Psychiatry and Clinical Neuroscience, 52,* 567–570.

Shea, D. G., Streit, A., & Smyer, M. A. (1994). Determinants of the use of specialist mental health services by nursing home residents. *Health Services Research, 29,* 169–185.

Sherrell, K., Anderson, R., & Buchwalter, K. (1998). Invisible residents: The chronically mentally ill elderly in nursing homes. *Archives of Psychiatric Nursing, 12,* 131–139.

Simpson, G. M., & Lindenmayer, J. P. (1997). Extrapyramidal symptoms in patients treated with risperidone. *Journal of Clinical Psychopharmacology, 17,* 194–201.

Shorter, E. (1997). *A history of psychiatry.* New York: John Wiley.

Siris, S. G. (2001). Suicide in schizophrenia. *Journal of Psychopharmacology, 15,* 127–135.

Siris, S. G., Harmon, G. K., & Endicott, J. (1981). Postpsychotic symptoms in hospitalized schizophrenic patients. *Archives of General Psychiatry, 38,* 1122–1123.

Somberg, B. L., & Salthouse, T. A. (1982). Divided attention abilities in young and old adults. *Journal of Experimental Psychology: Human Perception and Performance, 8,* 651–663.

Sommer, B. R., White, L., Parrella, M., Harvey, P. D., Knobler, H. Y., Powchik, P., et al. (1998). Naturalistic study of antipsychotic medication prescribed to elderly patients with schizophrenia. *Journal of Practical Psychiatry and Behavioral Health, 6,* 379–381.

Soyka, M. (2000). Substance misuse, psychiatric disorder and violent and disturbed behaviour. *British Journal of Psychiatry, 176,* 345–350.

Spohn, H. E., & Strauss, M. E. (1989). Relation of neuroleptic and anticholinergic medication to cognitive functions in schizophrenia. *Journal of Abnormal Psychology, 98,* 478–486.

Spreen, O., & Strauss, E. (1998). *A compendium of neuropsychological tests and norms* (2nd ed.). New York: Oxford.

Squires, L. R., & Zola-Morgan, S. (1996). Structure and function of declarative and nondeclarative memory systems. *Proceedings of the National Academy of Sciences, 93,* 13515–13522.

Steinert, T., Wiebe, C., & Gebhardt, R. P. (1999). Aggressive behavior against self and others among first-admission patients with schizophrenia. *Psychiatric Services, 50,* 85–90.

Steinhausen, H. C., Meier, M., & Angst, J. (1998). The Zurich long-term outcome study of child and adolescent psychiatric disorders in males. *Psychological Medicine, 28,* 375–383.

Strauss, J. S., Carpenter, W. T., & Bartko, J. J. (1974). Speculations on the processes that underlie schizophrenic symptoms and signs. *Schizophrenia Bulletin, 1,* 61–75.

Strauss, M. E., Reynolds, K. S., Jayaram, G., & Tune, L. E. (1990). Effects of anticholinergic medication on memory in schizophrenia. *Schizophrenia Research, 3,* 127–129.

Stuss, D. T., & Benson, D. F. (1986). *The frontal lobes.* New York: Raven Press.

Sunderland, T., Tariot, P. N., Cohen, R. M., Weingartner, H., Mueller, E. A., III, & Murphy, D. L. (1987). Anticholinergic sensitivity in patients with dementia of the Alzheimer type and age-matched controls: A dose response study. *Archives of General Psychiatry, 44,* 418–426.

Swanson, J. W., Holzer, C. E., III, Ganju, V. K., & Jono, R. T. (1990). Violence and psychiatric disorder in the community: Evidence from the Epidemiologic Catchment Area surveys. *Hospital and Community Psychiatry, 41,* 761–770.

Teri, L., Rabins, P., Whitehouse, P., Berg, L., Riesberg, B., Sunderland, T., et al. (1992). Management of behavior disturbance in Alzheimer's disease: Current knowledge and future directions. *Alzheimer's Disease and Associated Diseases*, 77–88.

Terry, R., & Katzman, R. (1992). Alzheimer's disease and cognitive loss. In R. Katzman & J. W. Rowe (Eds.), *Principles of geriatric neurology* (pp. 207–265). Philadelphia: F. A. Davis.

Teuber, H. L., Corkin, S., & Twitchell, T. (1997). A study of cingulotomy in man [Unpaginated appendix]. In *Report and recommendations*. Washington, DC: U.S. Government Printing Office.

Tien, A. Y. (1991). Distribution of hallucinations in the population. *Social Psychiatry and Psychiatric Epidemiology, 26*, 287–292.

Timko, C., Nguyen, A. T., Williford, W. O., & Moos, R. H. (1993). Quality of care and outcomes of chronic mentally ill patients in hospitals and nursing homes. *Hospital and Community Psychiatry, 44*, 241–246.

Tracy, J. I., McCrory, A. C., Josiassen, R. C., & Monaco, C. A. (1996). A comparison of reading and demographic based estimates of premorbid intelligence in schizophrenia. *Schizophrenia Research, 22*, 103–109.

Trieman, N., & Leff, J. (1996). Difficult to place patients in a psychiatric hospital closure programme: The TAPs project 24. *Psychological Medicine, 26*, 765–774.

Trieman, N., Hughes, J., & Leff, J. (1998). The TAPS Project 42: The last to leave hospital—A profile of residual long-stay populations and plans for their resettlement. *Acta Psychiatrica Scandanavia, 98*, 354–359.

Trieman, N., Wills, W., & Leff, J. (1996). TAPS project 28: Does reprovision benefit elderly long-stay mental patients? *Schizophrenia Research, 21*, 199–206.

Tulving, E. (1983). *Elements of episodic memory*. New York: Academic Press.

Tune, L. E. (2000). Serum anticholinergic activity levels and delirium in the elderly. *Seminars in Clinical Neuropsychiatry, 5*, 149–153.

Tune, L. E. (2001). Anticholinergic effects of medication in elderly patients. *Journal of Clinical Psychiatry, 62*(Suppl. 21), 11–14.

Valenstein, E. S. (1986). *Great and desperate cures: The rise and decline of psychosurgery and other radical treatments for mental illness*. New York: Basic Books.

Van Dijk, D., Jansen, E. W., Hijman, R., Nierich, A. P., Diephuis, J. C., Moons, K. G., et al. (2002). Cognitive outcome after off-pump and on-pump coronary artery bypass graft surgery: A randomized trial. *Journal of the American Medical Association, 287*, 1405–1412.

Velligan, D. I., Mahurin, R. K., Diamond, P. L., Hazleton, B. C., Eckert, S. L., & Miller, A. L. (1997). The functional significance of symptomatology and cognitive function in schizophrenia. *Schizophrenia Research, 25*, 21–31.

Waddington, J. L. (1995). Psychopathological and cognitive correlates of tardive dyskinesia in schizophrenia and other disorders treated with Neuroleptic drugs. *Advances in Neurology, 65*, 211–229.

Waddington, J. L., & Youssef, H. A. (1996). Cognitive dysfunction in chronic schizophrenia followed prospectively over 10 years and its longitudinal relationship to the emergency of tardive dyskinesia. *Psychological Medicine, 26,* 681–688.

Wagman, A. M. I., Heinrichs, D. W., & Carpenter, W. T. (1987). Deficit and nondeficit forms of schizophrenia: Neuropsychological evaluation. *Psychiatry Research, 22,* 319–330.

Wechsler, D. (1998). *The Wechsler Adult Intelligence scales* (3rd ed.). San Antonio, TX: Psychological Corporation.

Weickert, T. W., Goldberg, T. E., Gold, J. M., Bigelow, L. B., Egan, M. F., & Weinberger, D. R. (2000) Cognitive impairments in patients with schizophrenia displaying preserved and compromised intellect. *Archives of General Psychiatry, 57,* 907–913.

Weingartner, H. R., Eckart, M., Grafman, J., Molchan, S., Putnam, K., Rawlings, R., & Sunderland, T. (1993). The effects of repetition on memory performance in cognitively impaired patients. *Neuropsychology, 1,* 385–395.

Welsh, K. A., Butters, N., Hughes, J., Mohs, R. C., & Heyman, A. (1991). Detection of abnormal memory decline in mild cases of Alzheimer's disease using CERAD neuropsychological measures. *Archives of Neurology, 48,* 278–281.

Welsh, K. A., Butters, N., Hughes, J., Mohs, R. C., & Heyman, A. (1992). Detection and staging of dementia in Alzheimer's disease: Use of the neuropsychological measures developed for the Consortium to Establish a Registry for Alzheimer's Disease (CERAD). *Archives of Neurology, 49,* 448–452.

White, L., Harvey, P. D., Lindenmeyer, J.-P., & Opler, L. (1997). Empirical assessment of the factorial structure of clinical symptoms in schizophrenia: A multisite, multi-model evaluation of the factorial structure of the Positive and Negative Syndrome Scale (PANSS): The PANSS Study group. *Psychopathology, 30,* 263–274.

White, L., Harvey, P. D., Parrella, M., Sevy, S., Knobler, H., Powchik, P., et al. (1994). Empirical assessment of the factorial structure of clinical symptoms in schizophrenia: Symptom structure in geriatric and nongeriatric samples. *New Trends in Experimental and Clinical Psychiatry, 10,* 75–83.

White, L., Parrella, M., McCrystal-Simon, J., Harvey, P. D., Masiar, S., & Davidson, M. (1997). Characteristics of elderly psychiatric patients retained in a state hospital during downsizing: A prospective study with replication. *International Journal of Geriatric Psychiatry, 12,* 474–480.

Wickens, C. D., Braune, R., & Stokes, A. (1987). Age differences in the speed and capacity of information processing: 1. A dual-task approach. *Psychology and Aging, 2,* 70–78.

Widom, B., & Simonson, D. C. (1990). Glycemic control and neuropsychologic function during hypoglycemia in patients with insulin-dependent diabetes mellitus. *Annals of Internal Medicine, 112,* 904–912.

Wilkinson, G. S. (1993). *The Wide Range Achievement Test* (3rd ed.). Wilmington, DE: Jastak Associates.

World Health Organization. (1972). *The international pilot study of schizophrenia.* Geneva, Switzerland: Author.

World Health Organization. (1997). *International classification of diseases* (10th ed.). Geneva, Switzerland: Author.

Wyatt, R. J. (1991). Neuroleptics and the natural course of schizophrenia. *Schizophrenia Bulletin, 17,* 325–351.

Wykes, T., & van der Gaag, M. (2001). Is it time to develop a new cognitive therapy for psychosis—Cognitive remediation therapy (CRT)? *Clinical Psychology Review, 21,* 1227–1256.

Young, D. A., Davila, R., & Scher, H. (1993). Unawareness of illness and neuropsychological performance in schizophrenia. *Schizophrenia Research, 10,* 117–124.

Zakaznis, K. K., & Heinrichs, R. W. (1999). Schizophrenia and the frontal brain: A quantitative review. *Journal of the International Neuropsychological Society, 5,* 556–566.

Zec, R. F. (1993). Neuropsychological functioning in Alzheimer's disease. In R. W. Parks, R. F. Zec, & R. S. Wilson (Eds.), *Neuropsychology of Alzheimer's disease and related disorders* (pp. 3–80). New York: Oxford.

Zisook, S., McAdams, L. A., Kuck, J., Harris, M. J., Bailey, A., Patterson, T. L., et al. (1999). Depressive symptoms in schizophrenia. *American Journal of Psychiatry, 156,* 1736–1743.

Zubin, J., & Spring, B. (1977). Vulnerability—A new view of schizophrenia. *Journal of Abnormal Psychology, 86,* 103–126.

INDEX

ABOUT THE AUTHOR

Philip D. Harvey, PhD, is professor of psychiatry at Mt. Sinai School of Medicine and chief psychologist at Mt. Sinai Hospital. He received his PhD in clinical psychology from the State University of New York at Stony Brook in 1982. He is the author of more than 200 scientific articles and 300 abstracts, and he has written more than 25 book chapters. He has also written three books and edited four more. In addition, he has given more than 1,000 presentations at scientific conferences and medical education events.

His research has focused on cognition in schizophrenia, and he has written extensively on aging in schizophrenia, functional impairments in the illness, and the cognitive effects of typical and atypical antipsychotics. He has also studied the effects of cognitive enhancing agents in various conditions, including schizophrenia and traumatic brain injury. He directs a large and successful biennial conference on cognition that is an official satellite of the International Congress on Schizophrenia Research.